National Forest

Scenic Byways II

By BEVERLY MAGLEY

FALCON PRESS®

Helena, Montana

ACKNOWLEDGMENTS

I wish to thank the many people with the Forest Service who spent hours giving me valuable and insightful information about the scenic byways. This book reflects the dedication and genuine interest of Forest Service rangers and employees who shared their knowledge so willingly.

Sincere thanks to the staff at Falcon Press for their support, particularly Mac Bates and Shannon Indreland for constant, positive encouragement and input.—Beverly Magley

Front cover photo

The reds, yellows, and purples of Cedar Breaks National Monument, along Utah's Cedar Breaks Scenic Byway, are the result of oxidation of minerals like iron and manganese. Photo by Larry Ulrich.

Back cover photos

The Blue Ridge Mountains dazzle highway travelers on the Highland Scenic Tour in Virginia each fall. Photo by Larry Ulrich.

Fishing is just one type of outdoor recreation visitors to Idaho's Teton Scenic Byway will find. Photo by Larry Ulrich

Inside photos

All photos in inside color section by Larry Ulrich.

Library of Congress Number 91-77726
ISBN 1-56044-112-7

 Printed on Recycled Paper

In loving memory of Virginia Walton

CONTENTS

The Scenic Byways
Far West

Rocky Mountains

East

South

PARTNERS IN SCENIC BYWAYS

The National Forest Scenic Byways program has benefitted from a unique partnership with the Forest Education Foundation. This partnership represents a new era of cooperation between government and the private sector to promote recreation on public lands.

The Forest Education Foundation is a nonprofit educational foundation chartered to raise funds through public donations and commercial sector grants. Funds are disbursed through program grants to support worthy projects, primarily in the area of recreation on public lands.

The Foundation manages partnerships between the USDA Forest Service and private sector firms such as Plymouth and Cruise America, supports national promotion of the scenic byways through programs, and provides funds for byways signage, turnouts, and site improvements in the forest. The Foundation exhibit promoting National Forest Scenic Byways visitation travels the length and breadth of America each year. The Foundation also funded production of the scenic byways brochure for the USDA Forest Service.

The Forest Education Foundation and the USDA Forest Service demonstrate how working together can enhance the recreational opportunities for all Americans.

For information about the Forest Education Foundation, contact the Forest Education Foundation, P.O. Box 25469, Anaheim, CA 92825-5469, (714) 634-1050.

THE SCENIC BYWAYS SERIES

Scenic driving is the most popular form of outdoor recreation on our national forests. In response to this enjoyable pastime, the Forest Service established the national forest scenic byways program in May 1988. Altogether, there are 100 designated national forest scenic byways in the United States.

Scenic Byways II is the second of a series of scenic driving guides that describes America's most beautiful roads. This volume covers forty-eight drives in twenty-two states. Volume I in the series, *Scenic Byways,* describes the other fifty routes in twenty-six states.

The third book in the series, *Back Country Byways,* covers thirty-eight unpaved roads designated by the Bureau of Land Management. These roads traverse 1,900 miles through eleven western states.

In addition to byway descriptions, each guide contains maps, photographs, and essential travel information. The books include historic sites, travel season, geology, and outdoor recreation opportunities.

See the back page for more information on how to order this series of guidebooks.

INTRODUCTION

Scenic driving is the most popular form of outdoor recreation on our national forests. In response to this enjoyable pastime, the Forest Service established the national forest scenic byways program in May, 1988. Altogether, there are one hundred designated national forest scenic byways in the United States. Volume 1 of *National Forest Scenic Byways* describes the first fifty designated byways. This volume covers the remaining scenic byways.

Each byway was selected by national forest employees, who have an insider's knowledge of their forest. Their choices are wonderful. These spectacular routes take visitors alongside trout-filled sparkling streams, through diverse hardwood forests, over 12,000-foot mountain passes, and to high alpine meadows, peaceful lakes, far-ranging vista points, and much more.

The byways in this book cover 2,489 miles in twenty-two states. Altogether, the national forest scenic byways travel 5,157 miles in thirty-three states. These are some of the most beautiful and interesting places in the nation. Each byway is described in detail in either Volume I or Volume II of *National Forest Scenic Byways*.

Americans often think of national parks when planning a vacation, but national forests are the foremost providers of outdoor recreation in the country. Americans visit national forests twice as often as they visit national parks. One reason is that national forests are usually more accessible. There are 156 national forests in forty-four states, covering a total of 8.5 percent of the United States. Most Americans live within a day's drive of one or more national forests.

National forests have much to offer. About half of the nation's big game animals reside on national forests, along with a wide variety of other animals and plants, including rare and endangered species. These lands also contain 329 wilderness areas, 99,468 miles of trails, more than 6,000 campgrounds and picnic areas, over 1,100 boating sites, and 307 winter sports areas.

In addition to traveling through magnificent countryside, national forest scenic byways provide access to varied recreational activities. Visitors can simply enjoy the scenery from the car, or get out and meander along interpretive nature walks, picnic at a scenic overlook, boat on the many lakes and rivers, camp in secluded sites, or hike into wilderness areas for days or weeks.

Byway travel is also educational. Through brochures, interpretive displays, visitor centers, and their own experiences, byway travelers learn about natural history, human history, archaeology, geology, and national forest management, to name just a few subjects.

The byways are as varied as the landscape. Peter Norbeck winds seventy miles through the Black Hills of South Dakota, pigtailing through the Needles area. Seward Highway travels 127 miles through Alaska, past whales in the sound and glaciers on the mountains. North Shore Drive follows fifty-eight miles along the beautiful shore of Lake Superior. Kings Canyon meanders fifty miles through groves of giant sequoia trees in California.

This scenic byways program is also exciting as a way people and businesses can form productive partnerships with the Forest Service. Various community organizations, volunteers, and national and local businesses are helping with the byways program. Their efforts in the next few years will make your trip more pleasurable and enlightening, when such facilities as interpretive signs, paved overlooks, and hiking trails are installed. In this way, the scenic byways program not only invites us to visit the national forests, it provides opportunities to get involved in conservation.

Whether you seek solitude or active participation, enjoy the national forest scenic byways.

The Rio Fernando de Taos, along the Enchanted Circle, is stocked with rainbow trout. Carson National Forest photo.

HOW TO USE THIS BOOK

National Forest Scenic Byways II describes forty-eight scenic byways across the United States with maps, photos, and informative text. *National Forest Scenic Byways* featured the first fifty-two designated byways. Between the two volumes, the country's 100 designated national forest scenic byways are covered.

Each byway description features a travel map that shows the byway, campgrounds, special features such as visitor centers and recreation areas, connecting roads, and nearby towns. Each map also displays a mileage scale and a state map that shows the general location of the byway. All byways are marked on the United States map on pages xii and xiii.

Each text description is divided into ten categories. Most are self-explanatory, but the following information may help you get the most from each description.

General description provides a quick summary of the length, location, and scenic features of the byway.

Special attractions are prominent and interesting activities and natural features found on the byway. Additional attractions are included in the description. Some activities, such as fishing and hunting, require permits or licenses which must be obtained locally.

Location gives the name of the national forest, and the general area of the state in which the byway is located. It also describes exactly where the scenic byway designation begins and ends. The road numbers are normally found on a state highway map and are posted along the route. Occasionally, the scenic byways are on back roads that are not numbered on the state highway maps. In that case, the map of the byway includes primary routes from a nearby city or primary highway.

Byway route numbers are the specific highway numbers on which the scenic byway travels, such as U.S. Hwy 12, or Arkansas Route 23, or Forest Road 1243.

Travel season notes if the byway is open year-round or closed seasonally. Many byways are closed to automobiles in winter, due to snow cover, but are delightful for snowshoeing, cross-country skiing, and snowmobiling. Opening and closing dates are approximate and subject to regional weather variations. Always check for local conditions.

Camping on the national forests can be a rich and varied experience. Services basic to all developed national forest campgrounds along the byway are listed in this category. Individual national forest campground names and their additional services or features are noted in the **Description**. Many campgrounds charge a fee, noted at the campground entrance. National forest campgrounds generally provide the basics: toilets, picnic tables, and fire grates. Drinking water and garbage pickup are found at some, and electrical, water, and sewer hookups are rare.

Primitive dispersed camping is permitted on all national forests, subject to local and special restrictions. Check with the individual national forest for details.

Selected campsites may be reserved on some national forests, through the MISTIX computerized reservation system. Call 1-800- 283-CAMP for campsite availability information. A fee is charged for the service.

Privately owned campgrounds, usually with full hookups, showers, and other amenities, are often located near the byways. Check with the local Chambers of Commerce for details.

Services lists communities with at least a restaurant, groceries, lodging, phone, and gasoline. When a community has each of the services, but perhaps only one motel, and a small cafe, it is noted as having services with limited availability.

Nearby attractions are major features or activities found within about fifty miles of the byway. Many of these make an interesting sidetrip and can be combined with byway travel.

For more information lists the names, addresses, and phone numbers of the national forest(s) for each scenic byway. The supervisor's office is first, followed by ranger districts. Travelers may wish to contact the district rangers for detailed area maps and information on specific subjects.

The maps in this book cover each byway thoroughly. However, if you plan to take side trips or explore the area further, a Forest Service map is invaluable and can be obtained at all national forest offices for a small fee.

Description provides detailed traveler information, along with interesting regional history, geology, and natural history. Attractions are presented in the order a traveler encounters them when driving the route in the described direction. If you travel the route from the opposite direction, simply refer to the end of the byway descriptions first.

Byron Glacier dominates Portage Valley along the Seward Highway. Chugach National Forest photo.

SCENIC BYWAY SIGNS

Look for these distinctive road signs along every national forest scenic byway. Each byway will be marked with the basic scenic byway sign, shown below, and some of these signs will carry a plate with the name of that byway. The smaller "blaze" sign will appear as a reminder sign along the route. The signs are in color—purple mountains, dark green trees and lettering, and pale, bluish-green foreground.

LOCATIONS OF THE SCENIC BYWAYS

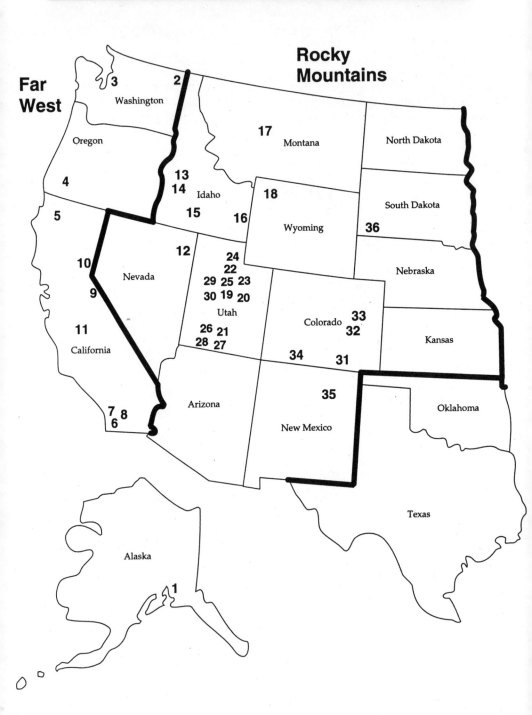

East

South

Maine
Vermont
New Hampshire
Mass.
Conn. R.I.
New York
New Jersey
Pennsylvania
Maryland
West Virginia
Virginia
North Carolina
South Carolina
Ohio
Indiana
Kentucky
Tennessee
Georgia
Alabama
Mississippi
Louisiana
Florida
Arkansas
Missouri
Iowa
Illinois
Wisconsin
Michigan
Minnesota

38 37
39
40
41
44
43
42
46
48
45 47

MAP LEGEND

Byway		Interstate	
Interstate and Four-lane Highway		U. S. Highway State or Other	
All Other roads		Principal Road	375
Points of Interest	6	Forest Road	0000
Bridge		Pass or Saddle	
Hiking Trail		Mountain	
Overlook		River, Creek, Drainage	
Ranger Station		Falls	
Ski Area		Lakes	
Picnic Area		Meadow or Swamp	
Campground		Springs	
Building		Byway Location Map and Mile Scale	
National Forest Boundary			
Wilderness Boundary			
State Boundary			
Recreation Areas			
State Parks			

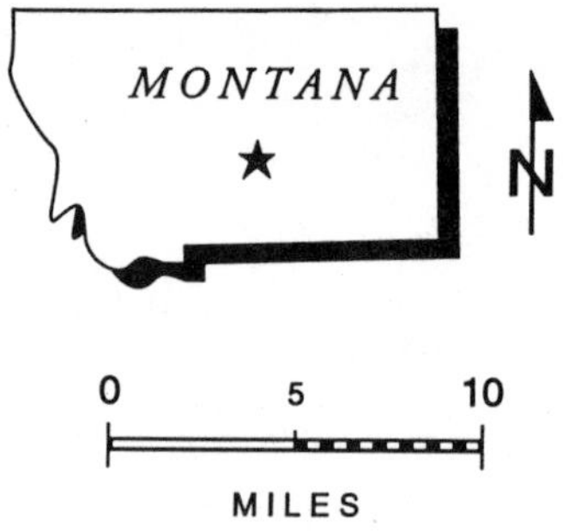

MONTANA

N

0   5   10

MILES

General description: A 127-mile highway through a spectacular region of glaciers, bays, mountains, and lakes.

Special attractions: Abundant wildlife, Chugach State Park, downhill skiing, glaciers, wildflowers, fishing, and camping.

Location: South-central Alaska on the Chugach National Forest. The byway travels between Anchorage and Seward.

Byway route numbers: Alaska State Highway 1 and Alaska State Highway 9.

Travel season: Year-round.

Camping: Nine national forest campgrounds within five miles of the byway, with picnic tables, fire rings, toilets, and drinking water. One state park campground, with picnic tables, firepits, toilets, and drinking water.

Services: All traveler services in Anchorage. All services, with limited availability, in Girdwood Junction, Girdwood, Summit Lake Resort, Moose Pass, and Seward.

Nearby attractions: Kenai Fjords National Park, Kenai National Wildlife Refuge.

For more information: Chugach National Forest, 201 E. 9th Avenue Suite 206, Anchorage, AK 99501, (907) 271-2500. Glacier Ranger District, P.O. Box 129, Girdwood, AK 99587, (907) 783-3242. Seward Ranger District, P.O. Box 390, Seward, AK 99664, (907) 224-3374.

Description: The Seward Highway runs through a spectacular array of scenic attractions between Anchorage and Seward. The two-lane highway is paved and has frequent turnouts. Traffic is moderate most summer days, but weekends can be very busy. Winter traffic is light.

Expect summer daytime temperatures in the forties to sixties. Winters average between the mid-teens to the mid-thirties. Scattered rain and snow showers occur throughout the year. Watch for slippery roads, especially between October and April.

The highway is breathtaking driven in either direction. The byway begins in Anchorage at Potter Point State Game Refuge, a marsh refuge for thousands of nesting waterfowl such as arctic terns, pintail ducks, greenwinged teals, and Canada geese. A short boardwalk, or a longer hiking trail, enable you to get a closer look at the wildlife.

The byway and railroad travel along the edge of Turnagain Arm, named for Captain James Cook's maneuver when he sailed up the arm in search of a through passage in 1778. Turnagain Arm is an extension of Cook Inlet, part of the Pacific Ocean.

Chugach State Park borders the east side of the highway. Visit the railroad museum and Potter Section House, where the visitor center has good displays, maps, and information.

McHugh Peak reaches 4,298 feet elevation. Brightly clad rock climbers, bicyclists, and windsurfers can often be spotted near the highway. The picnic area provides access to the Turnagain Arm Trail, which parallels the highway for about ten miles. Berry pickers will delight in the abundant currants, blueberries, and watermelon berries growing along the creek.

A mile farther, look for whales and Dall sheep through the telescope at Beluga Point, then drive on to numerous other vista points. Each offers a slightly different perspective on this beautiful region. Waterfalls splash down the mountains, bluebells brighten the fields, and beluga and orca whales feed on the salmon and hooligan in the ocean. You may see Dall sheep on the cliffs above the highway.

Indian Creek and Bird Creek are popular with anglers. Both have pink salmon, sea-run Dolly Vardens, and some coho salmon and rainbow trout. Bird Creek state campground has nineteen sites in the trees on a bluff above Turnagain Arm. You can bicycle or hike on the paved trails. Avoid the mudflats and sandy areas at low tide—the quicksand is treacherous, and the "bore tides" are fast rolling walls of water up to six feet high.

The byway now enters an avalanche-prone area and the road becomes narrow and winding. Most residents of Girdwood left its original location after the 1964 earthquake, and moved up the road. A side trip up the Alyeska (al-ee-ES-ka) Road leads to the historic Crow Creek gold mine, which is open for tours, as well as the resort community of Girdwood, Alyeska downhill ski area and good hiking routes.

Back on the byway, the route enters the Chugach National Forest. Twentymile River wetlands support a wide variety of flora and fauna. An elevated platform provides scenic views of the valley and wildlife. The river is known for hooligan fishing in May, and pink, red, and silver salmon, and Dolly Varden, in summertime. Look northeast up the river valley to see Twentymile Glacier, source of the river.

Most of Portage was destroyed in the 1964 earthquake, which caused some sections of land to drop several feet and brought a tidal wave. You can see spruce skeletons in a sunken forest, killed by salt water on their roots. Take a side trip here to Alaska's most popular tourist attraction: Portage Glacier and the Begich, Boggs Visitor Center. En route, two national forest campgrounds provide seventy sites. Williwaw Creek has an easy self-guided nature trail, and an observation platform for watching spawning red and dog salmon.

The visitor center has interpretive displays about glaciers, and natural history films. Naturalist-led and self-guided hikes are very informative, and the views are breathtaking. The icebergs floating in Portage Lake calved off Portage Glacier. The glacier is located on the far end of the lake and is visible on clear days. A lodge offers lunches and a gift shop. Lake cruises to the face of Portage Glacier are available.

The byway loops around Turnagain Arm, providing views of Skookum and Twentymile glaciers. Wildflower enthusiasts will find mountain meadows of violets, paintbrush, lupine, geranium, fireweed, and mountain heliotrope, surrounded by stands of spruce, birch, and cottonwood.

Snowmobilers frequent the area northwest of the highway at Turnagain Pass, and cross-country skiers enjoy the southeast side. Snow can accumulate over twelve feet deep here. Nearby, Bertha Creek Campground has twelve sites in the trees along the creek, just off the highway. Johnson Pass Trail is an easy hike or mountain bicycle ride which follows part of the old Iditarod route. You can follow it twenty-three miles, find some fine fishing in several lakes along the way, and end up back on the highway at Upper Trail Lake.

Granite Creek Campground marks the halfway point on the scenic byway. There are nineteen sites well off the highway along the creek, which has

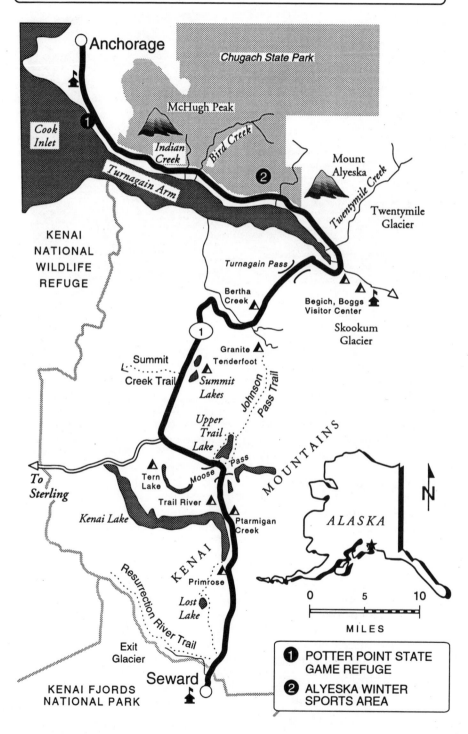

Anchorage

Chugach State Park

McHugh Peak

Cook Inlet

Indian Creek

Bird Creek

Mount Alyeska

Twentymile Creek

Twentymile Glacier

Turnagain Arm

KENAI NATIONAL WILDLIFE REFUGE

Turnagain Pass

Bertha Creek

Begich, Boggs Visitor Center

Skookum Glacier

Granite

Tenderfoot

Summit Creek Trail

Summit Lakes

Johnson Pass Trail

Upper Trail Lake

To Sterling

Tern Lake

Moose Pass

Trail River

Kenai Lake

Ptarmigan Creek

K E N A I   M O U N T A I N S

ALASKA

Resurrection River Trail

Primrose

Lost Lake

Exit Glacier

Seward

KENAI FJORDS NATIONAL PARK

N

0   5   10

MILES

1 POTTER POINT STATE GAME REFUGE

2 ALYESKA WINTER SPORTS AREA

3

Visitors can picnic next to a glacier in the Portage Valley, accessible from the Seward Highway. Chugach National Forest photo

small Dolly Varden. The highway then follows East Fork Creek. Bear left at the Hope Highway junction to stay on the Seward Highway, and follow Canyon Creek upstream to picturesque Upper and Lower Summit lakes. Tenderfoot Campground, on Upper Summit Lake, provides twenty-eight sites. A boat launch is available at the resort.

The Kenai Peninsula was once underwater, and the bedrock is derived from ancient sea sediments. Interbedded layers of slate and graywacke (a sandstone) compose the bedrock. Glaciation and uplift caused extensive shifting, faulting, and fracturing. The veins of white you see are quartz intrusions, which sometimes contain gold.

The byway continues straight ahead on Alaska State Highway 9 to Seward. (A side trip on the Sterling Highway leads to Cooper Landing, Soldotna, Homer, and great fishing opportunities.) Just west of the junction, Tern Lake Campground has twenty-five sites, a canoe launch, and good bird watching opportunities.

The byway travels through the Kenai Mountains, and waterfalls or icefalls decorate the slopes. Johnson Creek Trail, Carter-Crescent Trail, a bicycle route along Trail Lake, a fish hatchery display, a boat launch, and a big water wheel entice visitors to stop in the Moose Pass area.

Trail River Campground has sixty-four sites in the woods on the lake and river. Look for delicious cranberries and blueberries in August. Nearby, Ptarmigan Creek Campground has sixteen sites in the woods. Hike the Ptarmigan Creek Trail 3.5 miles to Ptarmigan Lake. You may be lucky enough to see Dall sheep, mountain goats, moose, or bears.

The highway runs alongside a portion of twenty-four mile long, aquamarine

Kenai Lake. At the south end of the lake, Primrose Campground has ten sites, and a beautiful trail through the forest to Lost Lake.

Look for moose in the ponds and meadows. Anglers find plenty of fishing opportunities in Grayling, Golden Fin, and Grouse lakes. Just before you reach Seward, take a side trip west on Exit Glacier Road to see the glacier and the Harding Icefield. A half-mile trail brings you to the base of the Exit Glacier, or a strenuous, 3.5 mile trail gets you to the icefield. On summer weekends, park ranger-naturalists lead hikes to the icefields, and give evening campfire programs.

The scenic byway ends in Seward, which offers traveler services and nice views of Resurrection Bay and surrounding mountains. A ranger station provides national forest information, maps, and permits. Don't miss visiting nearby Kenai Fjords National Park. □

2 SHERMAN PASS SCENIC BYWAY
Colville National Forest   *Washington*

General description: A thirty-five mile highway over the highest maintained mountain pass in Washington.

Special attractions: Camping, hiking, history, wildlife, winter recreation.

Location: Northeast Washington on the Colville National Forest. The byway travels Highway 20 from Republic to the junction of Highways 20 and 395 near Franklin D. Roosevelt Lake on the Columbia River.

Byway route number: Washington State Highway 20.

Travel season: Year-round.

Camping: Two national forest campgrounds, with picnic tables, fire grates, toilets, and drinking water.

Services: Traveler services in Republic and Kettle Falls, with limited availability.

Nearby attractions: Coulee Dam National Recreation Area, downhill ski areas, Curlew Lake State Park.

For more information: Colville National Forest, 695 South Main - Federal Building, Colville, WA 99114, (509) 684-4557. Kettle Falls Ranger District, 255 West 11th, Kettle Falls, WA 99141, (509) 738-6111. Republic Ranger District, 180 North Jefferson, P.O. Box 468, Republic, WA 99166, (509) 775-3305.

Description: Sherman Pass Scenic Byway travels through the forested Kettle River Range, crossing 5,575-foot Sherman Pass. The two-lane highway is paved and has frequent turnouts. Traffic is quite heavy and moves along at about fifty-five mph. This is a popular bicycling road.

Summer daytime temperatures generally range from the upper forties to the mid-seventies. Spring and fall dip down to the thirties, forties, and fifties, with lots of rain in springtime. Winter hovers around freezing. Snow on the pass generally sticks by the middle of October and covers the ground until late April.

The byway is scenic driven in either direction, but you may want to plan your drive to minimize sun glare. In the morning, drive east to west; afternoons drive west to east.

Sherman Pass Scenic Byway crosses the forested Kettle River Range. Colville National Forest photo.

When driving west to east, the byway begins near Republic. This small community was established in 1895 as Eureka, a gold mining boom town. Just north of town, Curlew Lake offers opportunities for water sports and recreation. Drive a few miles from Republic to the intersection of Highways 21 and 20. Follow Washington State Highway 20 east along O'Brien Creek, where open grassy hillsides mix with stands of ponderosa pine, Douglas-fir, and larch. Ninebark and oceanspray grow on the hot south-facing slopes.

The highway travels the same route used for centuries by the San Poil Indian tribe when they went to fish in the Columbia River near Kettle Falls. This same trail may have been used by ancient peoples 9,000 years ago. Turn-of-the-century miners expanded the trail into a wagon freight road, and roadhouses accommodated travelers. Mining faded out and logging took over. In the 1930s the Civilian Conservation Corps worked on roads, built lookouts and campgrounds, and logged. The paved Sherman Pass Highway was completed in 1954 and named for General William T. Sherman, who led an army expedition through the area in the mid-1800s.

Eight miles east of Republic, the byway enters the Colville National Forest.

Wildlife in the national forest includes mule deer, white-tailed deer, black bears, coyotes, squirrels, and chipmunks. Look for signs of more reclusive residents like mountain lions, bobcats, lynx, and pine martens. Bird watchers can find great variety, from northern three-toed woodpeckers to great horned owls to mountain bluebirds.

Snow Peak is a dominant feature to the south of the road as the byway climbs gradually up the pass. An information kiosk at the top of the pass explains what you see along the byway and teaches about the Native American heritage of this region. An easy quarter-mile trail leads through lodgepole pine, subalpine fir, and Douglas-fir to a good viewpoint. Look east to see CC Mountain, Mac Mountain, and King Mountain.

You can hike a portion of the Kettle Crest National Recreation Trail from the top of the pass. Walk north for fine views of high peaks and wildflower meadows. The trail is moderate and wanders in and out of timber and open hillsides. A spur trail climbs to a great viewpoint on Columbia Mountain. Several trails intersect the Kettle Crest National Recreation Trail and you can make a nice loop trip north on Kettle Crest, then east to Forest Road 2030 just below the pass.

You could also hike south on the Kettle Crest Trail. In less than a mile you'll be in the 1988 White Mountain burn area. It's interesting to see the mosaic of burned and unburned forest, and wildflowers such as fireweed and lupine fill the meadows. The trail climbs about a thousand feet onto the shoulder of Mount Sherman to provide extensive views of cliffs, mountains, and the Columbia River drainage to the east.

The byway descends from Sherman Pass, at 5,575 feet the highest maintained mountain pass in Washington. Sherman Overlook lies east of the pass. Interpretive signs identify surrounding peaks and teach about the fires. At this elevation you'll find lodgepole pine, subalpine fir, and larch. In autumn the larch turn golden in a beautiful, showy display.

Sherman Pass Campground has nine sites in the trees near the overlook. Stretch your legs on a very short interpretive trail around the campground.

A side trip north on Forest Road 2030 brings you to several trailheads for good hikes that connect to the Kettle Crest Trail. The road provides views of the base of the Kettle Crest.

The byway descends, and you'll catch glimpses of Paradise Peak and Scalawag Ridge to the south. The forest is fairly dense through here. The mountain slopes are quite dry, but the wetter drainages and forest understory host alder, cottonwoods, aspens, willows, serviceberries, oceanspray, snowberries, and huckleberries. Wildflower enthusiasts can look for arrowleaf balsamroot, yarrow, Oregon grape, and scarlet gilia on the dry hillsides. Orchids, lilies, and twinflowers hide in the shade of the forest.

A side trip east along Sherman Creek is very interesting. Along the creek you'll find grand fir, cedar, and spruce. A half-mile interpretive trail explains early logging history and the devastating 1929 Dollar Mountain fire. Anglers can try for native rainbow trout, as well as introduced brook trout.

A side trip south on Bangs Mountain Auto Tour gets you up pretty high on the flank of Bangs Mountain. The route allows you to see a lot of this glaciated region. The vista point provides views north and south along the Columbia, and east over Kettle Falls into Idaho.

Canyon Creek Campground has twelve sites on the creek. Nearby, East Portal Interpretive Site teaches about logging in the 1920s. The picnic area has barrier-

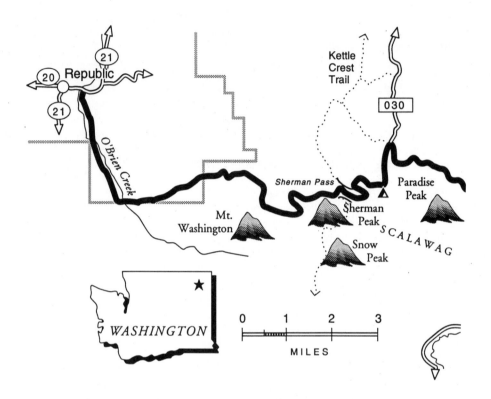

free facilities, and Trail 93 follows the creek between the campground and East Portal.

The byway enters Sherman Creek Wildlife Recreation Area, which provides good habitat for deer and wild turkeys. A side trip north on Forest Road 020 leads to Trout Lake Campground's four sites. The road is not recommended for towed or very large vehicles. Trout Lake has good fishing for rainbow trout, and you can hike up Hoodoo Canyon into a beautiful and remote area. The trail follows a series of benches along the canyon wall, and looks down into the canyon and over to Emerald Lake.

The byway travels north along the Columbia and ends at the junction of Highways 20 and 395. Nearby, St. Paul's Mission is one of the oldest church buildings in Washington. This Jesuit mission was built on a bluff overlooking the thirty-three-foot cascading Kettle Falls, next to an Indian summer fishing camp. Up to a thousand Indians from many tribes met here every year to fish the salmon run. Evidence of fishing camps here extend back at least 9,000 years. The falls is now submerged beneath the reservoir.

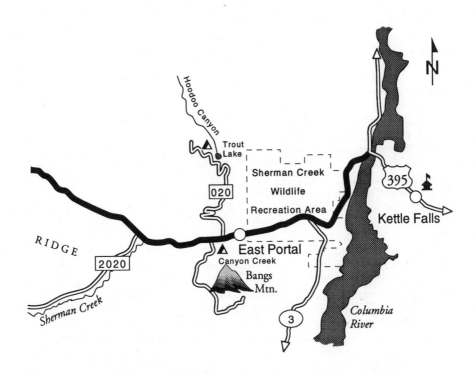

The Kettle Falls Ranger Station has national forest information and maps. The town has several interesting historic features.

Lake Roosevelt offers opportunities to swim, fish, boat, camp, picnic, and watch wildlife. More than thirty species of game fish live in the waters. □

General description: A fifty-mile drive through a lush forest, along rivers and over a low mountain pass.

Special attractions: Glacier Peak, Henry M. Jackson, and Boulder River wilderness areas; historic mining districts; fishing; hiking; extensive views; lush vegetation; camping.

Location: Northwest Washington on the Mt. Baker- Snoqualmie National Forest. The byway travels east on State Highway 92 between Granite Falls and Barlow Pass and north on Forest Road 20 to Darrington.

Byway route numbers: Washington State Highway 92 and Forest Road 20.

Travel season: Year-round from Granite Falls east to Deer Creek, and from Darrington southwest to Bedal. The middle section closed by winter snows from about mid-December until the end of May.

Camping: Seven national forest campgrounds, with picnic tables, fire grates, and toilets. Verlot, Turlo, and Gold Basin have drinking water.

Services: Traveler services in Darrington and Granite Falls, with limited availability. Phone, gas, and food near Verlot.

Nearby attractions: Pacific Crest National Scenic Trail, North Cascades National Park, Puget Sound, Seattle attractions, Wild & Scenic Skagit River.

For more information: Mt. Baker-Snoqualmie National Forest, 21905 64th Avenue West, Mountlake Terrace, WA 98043, (206) 775-9702. Darrington Ranger District, Darrington, WA 98241, (206) 436-1155.

Description: Mountain Loop Highway follows a horseshoe-shaped loop along several rivers and over a mountain pass. The route is a paved two-lane highway between Granite Falls and Barlow Pass; it becomes a one-lane gravel road between Barlow Pass and the confluence of the Sauk and White Chuck rivers and is again a two-lane paved surface from the confluence to Darrington.

Traffic is fairly heavy throughout the summer and during the fall hunting season. Undeveloped winter recreation opportunities generate moderate traffic. Please keep your headlights on when driving the one-lane, gravel section of byway. Use the pullouts when you meet an oncoming vehicle, and keep your speed very low.

Summer temperatures range from the fifties to the eighties. Spring and fall are generally between the forties and sixties. Most precipitation falls as sleet or snow in winter months, when temperatures dip into the twenties and thirties. The South Fork Stillaguamish River Valley is generally the coldest and wettest valley in the Cascades, so bring good foul weather gear. The area receives 120 to 200 inches of precipitation a year.

The byway is scenic driven in either direction. Beginning at Granite Falls, the route travels through scattered private developments and second- or third-growth forests of the Cascade foothills.

Stop at the Verlot Public Service Center in summer, located in the wide river valley just as you enter the national forest. You can obtain byway information, maps, permits, and peruse the informative, changing interpretive displays. Set in the trees along the South Fork Stillaguamish River, Verlot Campground provides twenty-six sites, and Turlo Campground has nineteen sites. Both campgrounds have drinking water available. A self-guided interpretive trail wanders through the area, informing walkers about the railroad which served logging and gold mining activities in the 1920s, plus the vegetation and history along the way.

A side trip southwest on Forest Road 42 brings you above timberline to the Mount Pilchuck trail, a popular destination. Located at the extreme western edge of the Cascades, the lookout on Pilchuck provides views of the surrounding state park and of Puget Sound and Seattle. On a clear day you can see over forty miles west to the Olympic Mountains. The three-mile trail gains 2,200 feet and is considered strenuous.

A trailhead right on the byway leads walkers south up a pretty creek 2.7 miles to Lake Twenty-two, a Research Natural Area. A mile farther east, Gold Basin Campground provides ninety-four sites on the forested river terrace. Drinking water and a grassy play area are available. Naturalist programs are presented during summer weekends. Nearby, the Gold Basin Mill Pond has a 1.25-mile, barrier-free trail that interprets the fish and wildlife habitat of a former mill pond.

Boardman Creek Campground has eighteen sites along the river, and good fishing access. Fishing in the Stillaguamish River is popular, but be prepared to release most of your catch immediately. The waters are closed to salmon fishing and open for trout, but fish grow slowly in the cold water so many are not large enough to keep. Still, it's fun to catch and release.

A barrier-free self-guided interpretive trail at Youth-On-Age leads along the river and points out the youth-on-age plant, an interesting forb that has young leaves and stems growing over older ones. Nearby, Red Bridge Campground has sixteen sites right on the river.

The byway continues its gentle climb through the dense forest. You'll see second- or third-growth western hemlock, Douglas-fir, western redcedar, black cottonwood, red alder, vine and bigleaf maple, and a few Sitka spruce. Marble Pass Viewpoint provides a view south across the valley to Marble Peak, Hall Peak, and other mountains. Gold mining was quite active around here at the turn-of-the-century. The steep, forested mountains in the Boulder River Wilderness are to the northwest.

A side trip north on Forest Road 4052 leads to a short, easy footpath along Deer Creek to Kelcema Lake. The lake sits near treeline, surrounded by steep, rocky slopes. Fishing is generally good, and winter recreationists enjoy the area on snowshoes or cross-country skis.

Stop at Big Four Ice Caves Trail and hike the gentle one-mile trail along the marsh, across the river, and up to the base of an ice field. Ice caves form each year from the melting ice, usually in late summer. The ice field and caves are interesting, and it's nice to get out of the dense forest and see the surrounding mountains. Don't walk into or on top of the caves—they are unstable.

A side trip north up Forest Road 4060 looks up the valley, and you can fish at Coal Lake. On the byway, a nice easy trail leads about two miles up Perry Creek through the dense forest to a waterfall. Look for some unusual ferns along the creek.

Typical flowers to look for in the shady forest include ground dogwood, trillium, and queens cup. In forest openings you'll find pearly everlastings, twinflowers, starflowers, violets, and foamflowers.

A side trip south on Forest Road 4065 provides a great view of the head-

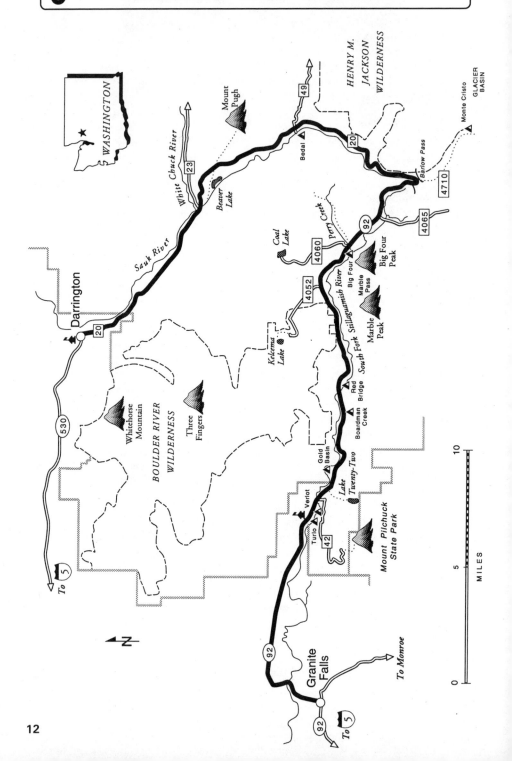

Visitors can take a short walk to these ice caves, located near the Mountain Loop Scenic Byway. Mount Baker-Snoqualmie National Forest photo.

waters of the South Fork Stillaguamish River. The river is fed by snowmelt from classic glacial cirques, and the vista is delightful.

The byway reaches an elevation of 2,361 feet at Barlow Pass. Many people like to hike or bicycle four miles south on the closed County Road 4710 into the old mine site at Monte Cristo. Interpretive signs there explain some of the history. There are some climbing routes on the rock faces off the road, and views south and southeast into the river valley. You may be lucky enough to see mountain goats on the rock outcrops. A trail, sometimes steep, leads about two miles up to Glacier Basin in the Henry M. Jackson Wilderness. It is definitely worth the effort to reach the basin, one of the most beautiful spots in the region.

The byway descends along the South Fork Sauk River on a narrow, one-lane gravel road. Monte Cristo Lakes are a wide spot in the river, and the willows and wetlands are interesting. There are primitive, dispersed campsites along the river. Anglers fish for rainbows, cutthroat, Dolly Varden, and whitefish. Most is catch and release, since the fish tend to be small.

Bedal Campground has eighteen sites right on the river in a stand of large, old-growth western hemlock, grand fir, western redcedar, and Douglas-fir. Look northeast to Mount Pugh and try to spot mountain goats perched on the rock outcrops. A side trip east on single-lane Forest Road 49 travels along the North Fork Sauk River and provides access to the Glacier Peak Wilderness. The road is best suited to high-clearance vehicles. About seven miles in, primitive Sloan Creek Campground is cradled in a narrow valley with the Glacier Peak Wilderness all around.

The lower mountain slopes around Bedal were logged in the 1920s and '30s, and now the forest is primarily hardwoods such as red alder, bigleaf maple, and black cottonwood. The byway provides occasional views of Mount Forgotten as it follows an upper terrace of the river. An easy three-mile footpath to Beaver Lake gets you down along the river and circles through a pretty beaver pond area. A couple of very large redcedar trees mark the upriver end of the trail.

The confluence of the Sauk and the White Chuck rivers marks the end of the one-lane gravel road, and the beginning of two-lane paved highway. This is a popular launch point for rafters and kayakers, and you'll catch occasional glimpses of them as the road descends. Clear Creek Campground offers ten sites on the river below the mouth of Clear Creek. Bald eagles can often be seen in winter, feeding on the dying salmon in the Sauk River.

The byway ends in the community of Darrington. You can obtain information, maps, and permits at the ranger station there. To make a complete loop, you can drive Highway 530 to Arlington, turn south on Highway 9, then east on Highway 92 back to Granite Falls. Another, more direct route back is via the Jordan Road (just east of Arlington), which runs south off Highway 530 just before the bridge crossing over the Stillaguamish River. Both routes are very scenic and travel through forest and farmlands.☐

Travelers along the Mountain Loop Highway will enjoy many rivers including the South Fork of the Stillaguamish River.

General description: A 172-mile route through rural, forested, and mountainous terrain on the west side of the Cascade Mountains.

Special attractions: Wild & Scenic Upper Rogue and North Umpqua rivers, Diamond Lake Recreation Area, Crater Lake National Park, four wilderness areas, geologic formations, spectacular vistas, fishing, hiking, camping, and winter sports.

Location: Southwest Oregon on the Rogue River and Umpqua national forests. The byway travels a horseshoe-shaped route between Roseburg and Diamond Lake on Highway 138; between Diamond Lake and Union Creek on Highway 230; between Union Creek and Shady Cove on Highway 62; and between Shady Cove and Gold Hill on Highway 234.

Byway route numbers: Oregon State Highways 138, 230, 62, and 234.

Travel season: Year-round.

Camping: Twenty-seven national forest campgrounds, with picnic tables, fire grates, and toilets. Some provide drinking water.

Services: Travelers services in nearby Roseburg, Medford, Ashland, and Grants Pass. Services on the byway, with very limited availability, in Gold Hill, Shady Cove, Prospect, Steamboat, Diamond Lake, and Union Creek.

Nearby attractions: Oregon Caves National Monument, downhill and cross-country ski areas.

For more information: Rogue River National Forest, 333 W. 8th Street, P.O. Box 520, Medford, OR 97501, (503) 776-3600. Prospect Ranger District, Prospect, OR 97536, (503) 560-3623. Umpqua National Forest, P.O. Box 1008, Roseburg, OR 97470, (503) 672-6601. North Umpqua Ranger District, Glide, OR 97443, (503) 496-3532. Summer only: Diamond Lake Information Center, Diamond Lake, Rural Station, Chemult, OR 97731, (503) 793-3310, or year-round: Diamond Lake Ranger District/Toketee Ranger Station, HC 60 Box 101, Idleyld Park, OR 97447, (503) 498-2531. Crater Lake National Park, Crater Lake, OR 97604, (503) 594-2211.

Description: The Rogue Umpqua Scenic Byway travels through the west side of the Cascades, a region of forests, volcanoes, and rushing streams. The two-lane highways are paved and being upgraded during the 1990s until the entire highway has wide shoulders and frequent turnouts. Traffic is generally moderate in summertime and light the remainder of the year. Watch out for logging trucks during the week.

Summer weather is generally dry, with daytime temperatures in the sixties to eighties. Spring and fall have occasional freezes, and daytime temperatures hover around fifty or sixty. Winter temperatures are usually well below freezing, and deep snow covers the ground between Toketee and Union Creek.

The byway is scenic driven in either direction. Beginning in Roseburg, travel east on Highway 138, through a rural landscape with farms and small communities. There is a county campground several miles north of the byway, at Whistler's Bend.

The confluence of the North Umpqua River and Little River is an impressive

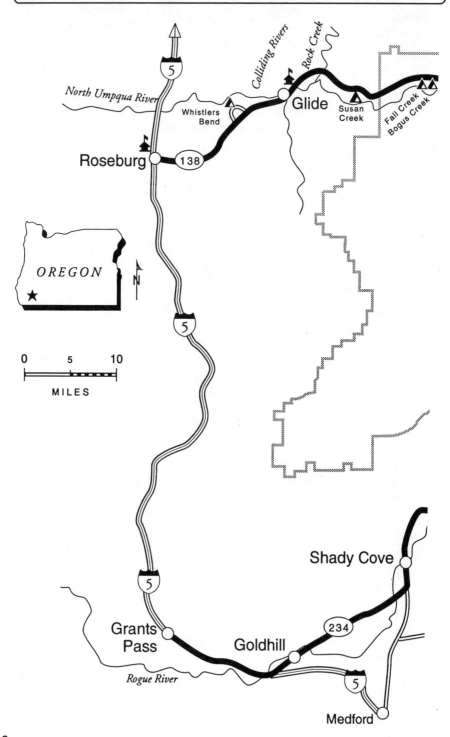

4 ROGUE UMPQUA SCENIC BYWAY

Colliding Rivers

Rock Creek

North Umpqua River

Whistlers Bend

Glide

Susan Creek

Fall Creek
Bogus Creek

Roseburg

138

OREGON

0   5   10

MILES

Shady Cove

Grants Pass

Goldhill

234

Rogue River

Medford

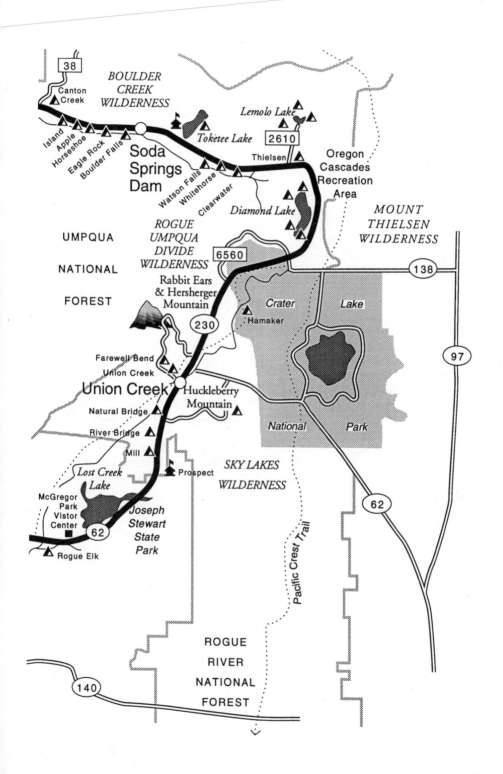

sight at Colliding Rivers. Nearby, the North Umpqua Ranger Station can provide information and maps. Farther east, there is a county picnic area and BLM information board along Rock Creek. The North Umpqua is a designated Wild & Scenic River between Rock Creek and Soda Springs Dam to the east. You'll likely see rafters and kayakers floating the white water.

The county picnic area is the first place to access a maintained portion of the North Umpqua Trail. This seventy-seven-mile trail parallels the North Umpqua River. You can hike east along the river for long or short segments. The trail is complete between the county picnic area and the Boulder Creek Wilderness near Eagle Rock Campground, and from Toketee Lake to Mount Thielsen. There are numerous access points to the trail from the Rogue-Umqua Scenic Byway. Maples and alders provide shade for hikers, and ferns and wildflowers abound. Be careful not to startle a shy rattlesnake.

The word Umpqua comes from the Umpqua Indians, who inhabited this region. They were hunter/gatherers and caught salmon with traps and spears. The North Umpqua River is known to be the best summer steelhead fishing on the West Coast. The height of the spawning run is August through September. Nearby lakes have rainbow, cutthroat, brook, and brown trout.

The byway travels east past Susan Creek Campground, a BLM site with thirty-three campsites in a stand of old-growth Douglas-fir. A few miles past the national forest boundary, stop at Fall Creek. There you can hike the easy one-mile National Scenic Trail along the stream through a very narrow crack in large rocks. Farther east, Bogus Creek Campground has fifteen sites in a stand of young Douglas-fir and good access to the river. The dominant tree species here in the western Cascades are Douglas-fir and western hemlock.

A side trip north on Forest Road 38 leads to Canton Creek Campground, with eight sites on Steamboat Creek.

On the byway, Island and Apple Creek campgrounds each provide seven sites along the river. Horseshoe Bend Campground is larger, with thirty-four sites nestled in a bend in the river. A few miles farther east, Eagle Rock has twenty-nine sites and Boulder Flat ten sites.

The Boulder Creek Wilderness lies adjacent to the north side of the byway. This wilderness protects a critical spawning stream for anadromous fish, as well as old-growth ponderosa pine and a variety of plants and interesting geologic formations. Look for the striking pillars of columnar basalt on Eagle Rock near Soda Springs Dam.

A massive ashfall covered this region when Mount Mazama erupted 6,800 years ago. That is evident today in the pumice banks along the route. Numerous basalt rock outcrops along the highway form interesting and recognizable shapes; look north of the highway to pick out Old Man Rock, Rattlesnake Rock, and Old Woman Rock.

Continue east on the highway to Toketee Junction, where a nearby .5-mile foot trail winds alongside the North Umpqua River cascades and ends at the picturesque waterfall. The Toketee Ranger Station is located at the south end of Toketee Lake. The lake offers opportunities for camping, boating, and fishing. Toketee Lake is one of a series of power-generating reservoirs that stretch from Lemolo Lake to Soda Springs.

Toketee Lake Campground provides thirty-three sites adjacent to the river. Fishing is good in the river, and there are some big brown trout in the lake.

The byway flattens out a bit and travels through vegetation typical of the high Cascades: true fir, mountain hemlock, and lodgepole. Watson Falls is the highest waterfall in southern Oregon—272 feet. A moderate .5-mile hike brings you to the base of the falls.

Whitehorse Falls is a tiny campground with eight sites along the Clearwater River. The picnic area has a wonderful view of the waterfall. Clearwater Falls Campground has nine sites along the river, and picnicking close to the falls.

A side trip north on Forest Road 2610 leads to Lemolo Lake, a pretty lake surrounded by mountains. Year-round recreation there includes a resort, camping, boating, fishing, hunting, hiking, cross-country skiing, and snow-mobiling. Poole Creek Campground provides forty sites. Bunker Hill has eight campsites and East Lemolo fifteen campsites. Fishing for elusive brown trout can be frustrating, but there are some trophy-size fish inhabiting the cold water at the bottom of the lake.

The byway turns south and heads along the west side of the 157,000-acre Oregon Cascades Recreation Area. Mount Thielsen, in the adjacent wilderness, is prominent in the background. A side trip to Diamond Lake leads to several campgrounds, hiking trails, lake recreation, and a resort. Diamond Lake lies in a basin formed by glaciation millions of years ago. You can get good information and see the interpretive displays at the information center, open in the summer.

Wildflowers are abundant and beautiful along this byway. Look for the showy colors of Indian paintbrush, lupine, fireweed, buttercup, and camas.

Diamond Lake Campground provides 240 sites, a dump station, boat ramps, and summer evening interpretive campfire programs. Broken Arrow Campground has 148 sites and a dump station. Thielsen View Campground has fifty-eight sites and a boat ramp. The South Shore Picnic Area provides picnic tables and five overnight sites for hikers and bicyclists only. South Shore also has a children's play area, a boat launch, and a bicycle trail. All of these campgrounds provide drinking water.

South of Diamond Lake, the byway leaves Highway 138 and turns southwest on Highway 230. However, a side trip south on 138 leads to Crater Lake National Park. This entrance is open spring to fall. The park is centered around extraordinary Crater Lake, formed more than 6,700 years ago when Mount Mazama erupted and collapsed. Ample opportunities exist to hike, camp, sightsee, and learn about the park and this region.

Back on the byway, follow Highway 230 through the lodgepole pine forest. The route exits the Umpqua National Forest and enters Rogue River National Forest. Crater Rim viewpoint provides a clear look southeast at the peaks and ridges above Crater Lake. From the viewpoint, you can hike about .25 mile out to the rim of Pumice Canyon and look down to the Wild and Scenic Rogue River. The trail continues along the top of the gorge, and hikers can walk for miles.

The byway descends through lava flows and forests. The rolling mountains of the Rogue-Umpqua Divide are prominent features, with glaciated Mount Bailey a centerpiece. About three miles south of Crater Rim, an easy trail takes off from the stock corral and goes to Beaver Meadow. There, a splendid beaver dam about eight feet high and twenty-five feet across has blocked the small stream and created a pond. You can also see the activities of other beaver families in the area.

The byway descends into a mixed conifer forest, and the trees get larger and larger as the elevation drops. White fir, mountain hemlock, Douglas-fir, and incense cedar are the dominant species.

The Rogue River cascades through this narrow gorge, seen from Rogue Gorge Overlook.
Rogue River National Forest photo.

Hamaker Campground has ten sites, drinking water, and good access for fishing. You can walk a portion of the Upper Rogue River National Recreation Trail, which extends over forty-five miles along the river. Nearby, Minnehaha Trail follows the creek. To get up into wildflower meadows, drive north on Forest Road 6560 to Hummingbird Meadows Trail, which leads through lovely fields of flowers such as violets, monkeyflowers, strawberries, lilies, and penstemon, and ultimately reaches the Rogue-Umpqua Wilderness.

The byway drops into the canyon and twists and winds along the Rogue River. Just beyond Highway Falls a big cut in the hillside shows where the 1964 floods blew out a piece of the canyon wall and caused a landslide which diverted the river.

The Rogue River has been subjected to numerous catastrophic events. When Mount Mazama blew up 6,800 years ago, lava filled the river canyon and the water had to erode a new channel. Today you can see the trees and logs from old logjams which were covered in lava and turned into charcoal. Look for them in the cutbanks along the river.

A side trip east on Forest Road 6530 brings you to a .5-mile-long trail leading down to a good view of National Creek Falls. The creek, which runs even in drought years, is fed by springs, and the lacy, wide cataract falls provides a cool respite from summer heat.

Continuing down the byway, you'll cross the Rogue River and climb to the other side. The trees form a tunnel-like corridor over the road, opening only once to provide a grand view of the unmistakeable Rabbit Ears, a massive volcanic plug. Most of the Cascades here are relatively new, geologically speaking, but the Rabbit Ears are a volcanic remnant predating even Mount Mazama. For a closer look, a side trip on Forest Roads 6510 and 6515 make a terrific loop through mountain meadows and a fir and hemlock forest, past the Rabbit Ears, and up to Hershberger Lookout. This lookout has been completely refurbished to its original 1925 condition and is on the National Register of Historic Lookouts. From the lookout you'll see Fish and Highrock mountains, Mount Bailey, and Mount Thielsen. On a clear day, look south to Mount McLoughlin and on to Mount Shasta in the distance.

The byway enters the Union Creek area, a hub of recreation. The forest now includes sugar pine, Douglas-fir, and ponderosa pine. Near the junction of Highways 230 and 62, Rogue Gorge Viewpoint overlooks the river cascading through a very narrow volcanic gorge. A short barrier-free interpretive loop trail leads to the river gorge, and you can continue hiking to Natural Bridge, past lava tubes and other volcanic formation.

Union Creek is a historic Civilian Conservation Corps work center. A walking tour provides an interesting glimpse into the past. Farewell Bend Campground has sixty-one sites in the trees along the river, drinking water, and a playground. Union Creek Campground provides eighty-five sites near Union Creek and the Rogue River. Evening naturalist programs are offered during the summer, and drinking water is available. There are easy hikes between the campgrounds and to the gorge on Rogue Gorge Trail, and fishing is good in the creek and the river. You can also hike about four miles to Union Falls, on the Union Falls Trail.

A side trip on Highway 62 east takes you to the west entrance of Crater Lake National Park. This entrance is open year round. Highway 62 also gains you access to Huckleberry Mountain, where huckleberries grow in abundance. The lookout at the top provides wonderful panoramic views. Look east over Rocktop Butte, Union Peak, and The Watchman. Behind them Mount Thielsen and Mount Bailey are easily recognized.

A few miles south on the byway, Natural Bridge has a barrier-free interpretive trail explaining why the river disappears and reappears. The campground has sixteen sites on the Rogue River.

About four miles off the byway, a side trip on Forest Road 68 leads to Abbott Creek Campground's twenty-three sites. Drinking water is available. This is a good place for families with children, since access to the river is generally quite safe here.

The byway continues south through an area of enormous trees, which form a canopy over the highway. Many reach well over 200-feet tall. Mammoth Pines Nature Trail wanders .25-mile through the mixed conifer forest. You'll learn the names and uses of more than a dozen trees and plants on this pleasant stroll.

Just off the byway, River Bridge Campground has six sites adjacent to the Rogue River. A few miles south, Mill Creek Campground provides eight sites along the creek.

The byway leaves the national forest at Prospect, where the ranger station has a large visitor center with books, information, maps, and interpretive displays. Just south of town, take a side trip to Mill Creek Falls. A short trail with two forks leads to this 172-foot waterfall, to another smaller falls, and to the Avenue of Giant Boulders.

The forest opens up more around Cascade Gorge, affording views of some open meadows and rock outcrops. Continuing south, Joseph Stewart State Park has 151 campsites, many with electrical hookups. Boating, swimming, water-skiing, and fishing for trout and bass are popular activities on Lost Creek Lake. There are three miles of paved hiking trails, as well as five miles of paved bicycle trails.

McGregor Park Visitor Center has displays about the lake and dam. Casey and Takelma provide picnic facilities, and Rogue Elk is a county campground. This stretch of river down to Shady Cove is very popular for family floating, in rafts, canoes, and even inner tubes.

Scattered private developments line the byway, and hardwoods such as madrone thrive. The byway leaves Highway 62 south of Shady Cove and turns west onto Highway 234, traveling through to its terminus at Gold Hill on Interstate 5. ☐

5 TRINITY HERITAGE SCENIC BYWAY
Shasta-Trinity National Forest   California

General description: A 111-mile route through forested mountains, along the Trinity River and Trinity Lake and through historic mining districts.

Special attractions: Wide-ranging vistas, historic towns and sites, Whiskeytown-Shasta Trinity National Recreation Area, water sports, house-boating, fishing, camping.

Location: Northwest California on the Shasta-Trinity National Forest. The byway travels Highway 3 north from Weaverville to the junction of Highway 3 and County Road 204 (Rush Creek Road); goes southeast on Rush Creek Road to Lewiston, then north and west along County Road 105 (Trinity Dam Boulevard) back to the junction of Highway 3; follows Highway 3 to Forest Road 17 (Parks Creek Road) fifteen miles north of Coffee Creek; and travels Parks Creek Road north to its intersection with Interstate 5 near Weed.

Byway route numbers: California State Highway 3, County Roads 204 and 105, and Forest Road 17.

Travel season: Year-round from Weaverville to the intersection of Highway 3 and Forest Road 17; Forest Road 17 closed by winter snows late November through the end of May.

Camping: Twelve national forest campgrounds, with picnic tables, fire grates, and toilets. Most campgrounds provide drinking water.

Services: All traveler services in Weaverville, Lewiston, Trinity Center, at Trinity Lake resorts, and Coffee Creek.

Nearby attractions: Lake Shasta Caverns; downhill skiing; Russian, Castle Crags, Marble Mountain, and Salmon-Trinity Alps wilderness areas; Castle Crags State Park.

For more information: Shasta-Trinity National Forests, 2400 Washington Avenue, Redding, CA 96001, (916) 246-5152. Weaverville Ranger District, P.O. Box 1190, Weaverville, CA 96093, (916) 623-2121. Mount Shasta Ranger District, 204 West Alma, Mount Shasta, CA 96067, (619) 926-4596.

5 TRINITY HERITAGE SCENIC BYWAY

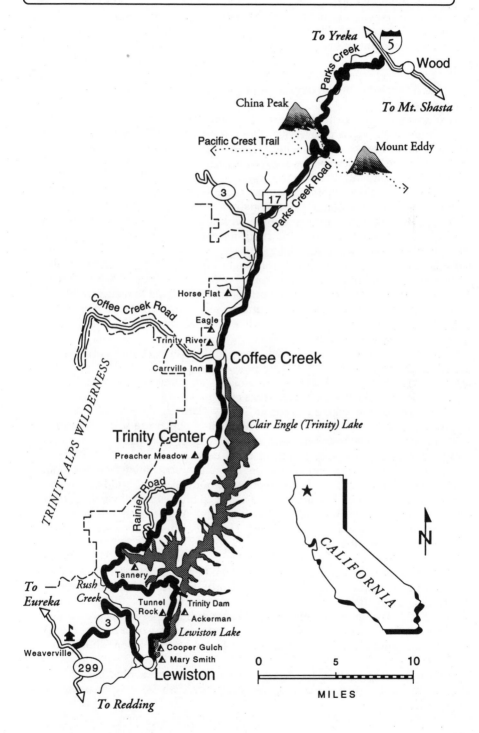

To Yreka

Parks Creek

5

Wood

To Mt. Shasta

China Peak

Pacific Crest Trail

Mount Eddy

3

17

Parks Creek Road

Coffee Creek Road

Horse Flat ▲

Eagle ▲

Trinity River ▲

Coffee Creek

Carrville Inn ■

Clair Engle (Trinity) Lake

TRINITY ALPS WILDERNESS

Trinity Center

Preacher Meadow ▲

Rainier Road

Tannery ▲

To Eureka

Rush Creek

Tunnel Rock ▲

Trinity Dam

▲ Ackerman

Lewiston Lake

3

Weaverville

299

▲ Cooper Gulch
▲ Mary Smith

Lewiston

To Redding

CALIFORNIA

★

N

0   5   10

MILES

Description: Trinity Heritage Scenic Byway traverses 111 miles of mountainous terrain, with beautiful views. Highways 3, 204, and 105 are paved two-lane roads. Forest Road 17 is a variable-lane, chip-seal surface. Portions of 17 are single lane and very narrow. Large recreational vehicles or towed units should exercise extreme caution on the northern section of this byway. Traffic on Highway 3 is moderately busy. Traffic is very light on Forest Road 17.

Summer temperatures average about eighty-five, and can reach over 100 degrees. Humidity is very low. Spring and fall temperatures are very moderate, in the fifties to eighties. Winters drop below freezing at night, and reach the forties and fifties during the day. Most of the year's sparse rain falls in winter and spring.

The byway is very scenic driven in either direction. When driving south to north, begin your tour in Weaverville. This historic gold rush town once boasted a population of 10,000, which included a Chinatown of over 3,000 inhabitants. Today, you can sample the past by walking through town. Many homes are over 100 years old and listed on the National Register of Historic Places. The Joss House is the oldest continually used Taoist temple on the West Coast, and individuals still use the building occasionally for worship. Now part of the state parks system, you may tour the temple with a guide. Jake Jackson Museum is an excellent small town museum, with indoor and outdoor exhibits on the history of northern California. Outdoor displays include a blacksmith's shop, old miner's cabin, and a stamp mill brought down from the mountains and reassembled at the museum. On certain holidays members of the historical society fire up the old steam engine and get the stamp mill breaking up rocks.

Weaverville also has an art gallery featuring many local artists. Weaver Bally, elevation 7,100 feet, dominates the skyline west of town. Bally is the Wintu Indian word for mountain.

Follow Highway 3 north out of town, through the evergreen forest of Douglas-fir, white fir, ponderosa pine, Jeffrey pine, sugar pine, incense cedar, and a mixture of hardwoods such as California black oak, Oregon white oak, bigleaf maple, and mountain dogwood. The peaks of Trinity Alps Wilderness are simply beautiful. The byway enters the Shasta-Trinity National Forest, and turns off Highway 3 to follow Rush Creek Road southeast. The entire scenic byway is well marked with the byway logo and arrows. Rush Creek is lined with willows and cottonwoods, and hosts plenty of mule deer.

Cross the one-lane bridge into Lewiston, a boom-and-bust town from the Gold Rush. The downtown of well-preserved, turn-of-the-century buildings, offers rustic restaurants and a historic hotel. There is a blue-ribbon, fly-fishing-only stretch of the Trinity River along the highway. Anglers fish primarily for steelhead. Nearby, the Trinity River Fish Hatchery offers self-guided tours of their fully-automated steelhead and salmon operations.

The byway travels north along the edge of Lewiston Lake. Mary Smith Campground provides drinking water, eighteen tent sites in the trees along the lake, and good fishing access. A few miles north, Cooper Gulch Campground has nine sites on the lake.

Lewiston Lake has an excellent cold water trout fishery. Eastern brook, rainbow, and brown trout inhabit the lake, and you can watch osprey diving for fish year round. Look for bald eagles perched in large snags or fishing along the shores.

Other fish-eating birds of the byway region include great blue herons and kingfishers. Bird watchers can look for songbirds such as western tanagers, towhees, and robins. Chickadees, nuthatches, hummingbirds, western wood pewees, juncos, red-winged blackbirds, Steller and scrub jays, and a variety of woodpeckers are also easy to spot.

Continuing north on the byway, Lewiston Lake is cradled by forested hills. A small resort and marina provide boat rentals and some services. Pine Cove Boat Ramp has barrier-free fishing piers, a picnic area, and restrooms. Tunnel Rock Campground has six sites tucked in the trees and is a favorite for anglers. Nearby, Ackerman Campground is situated on the river at the north end of the lake. Facilities include sixty-six campsites, drinking water, a trailer dump station, and flush toilets.

A scar on the western hillside above the highway shows where the world's longest conveyor belt once brought clay fill for Trinity Dam. The dam is a half-mile wide at the top, and 465 feet high. Water from Trinity and other manmade lakes of California's Central Valley Project generate power, and outflows eventually irrigate farmland in California's Central Valley.

The huge face of Trinity Dam is clearly visible from the byway. To the west, the granite peaks of the 513,000-acre Trinity Alps Wilderness rise above forested slopes.

Trinity Vista provides barrier-free viewing of Trinity Lake. On a clear day you can see the tip of Mount Shasta peeking over the ridge. Continue west for ten miles on Highway 105, and rejoin Highway 3 north. The byway climbs over Montgomery Ridge and drops into the Slate Creek drainage, which is resplendent with dogwood blossoms in springtime and brilliant red foliage in autumn.

Tannery Campground provides drinking water and eighty-three sites on the lake in the shade of evergreens. Campers can swim at the beach, launch their boats at the ramp, then park right near the campground when the lake level is high enough. Summer weekend naturalist programs are presented in the amphitheater.

You can picnic, swim, camp, boat, water-ski, and fish in Clair Engle (Trinity) Lake, the third-largest lake in California. In addition to the ever-popular rainbow and brown trout, Trinity Lake also has land-locked Kokanee salmon which turn brilliant red in the fall; cat fish; and large- and smallmouth bass. The nine-pound-one-ounce smallmouth bass caught here in 1976 is the California record.

Several resorts and marinas provide basic traveler services and houseboat rentals. Osprey Information Center has a self-service information kiosk.

A side trip off Highway 3 follows the gravel-surfaced Rainier Road north. You'll drive through various kinds of timber management—clearcuts, selective cuts, replanted areas, and a few untouched stands of old-growth timber. Look for the Samdam Tree—one of the largest sugar pines ever found in northern California. Another side trip turns south at Guy Covington Drive and goes 1.5 miles to the more than one-hundred-year-old Bowerman Barn.

The byway route stays on Highway 3 north, which winds up and down over ridges and across creek drainages. Preacher Meadow Campground has forty-five sites in a dense stand of timber, and drinking water.

Two miles north, stop at the Scott Museum in Trinity Center. Trinity Center has been moved twice—once to make way for the gold dredges and later to escape inundation by water. Most of the original town buildings are under the lake now, but a few were saved. The old 100F Odd Fellows Lodge is a popular building for photographers and artists.

The byway travels along the lakeshore, past acres and acres of old mine

A view of Trinity Lake National Recreation Area from the Trinity Alps Wilderness. Shasta-Trinity National Forest photo.

tailings. Huge floating dredges worked the area for gold. An interpretive sign at North Shore Vista explains the process. About a mile beyond the north end of the lake, the byway diverges briefly from Highway 3 and travels by the historic Carrville Inn. Herbert Hoover stayed there before he was elected president.

Coffee Creek is another Gold Rush town, and provides basic traveler services. A side trip west along Coffee Creek is beautiful. You can actually drive into the Trinity Alps Wilderness. The gravel road follows a tumbling stream for about twenty-one miles. Several guest ranches are located along the route. There are numerous trailheads into the wilderness area. Try the North Fork Coffee Creek Trail. This moderate, four-mile route takes you up to Hodges Cabin. The 1920s cabin is really a two-story house built of vertical logs. It's staffed from mid-June through August, and hosts will give you a tour through the house and buildings. You have to wade a creek to reach the house, so don't try this hike during high runoff (usually in May and June).

Traveling north on the byway, you are following a centuries-old Indian trail, later built into the old Portland-Sacramento Stagecoach Route. The highway follows the Trinity River, and the terrain opens up a bit at the head of the lake. Meadows are full of wildflowers such as Indian paintbrush, fireweed, yarrow, and lupines. Look for tiger lilies, columbines, monkeyflowers, and pitcher plants in the wetter streamside areas, and bleeding hearts and mountain violets in the shade of the forest.

Trinity River Campground has seven sites, and drinking water. Several other campgrounds are in this vicinity, just off the byway. Eagle Creek Campground has drinking water, and seventeen sites right on the river near the mouth of Eagle Creek. Horse Flat provides sixteen sites along Eagle Creek. There is some good fishing in the creek for brookies and rainbow. Stretch your legs on a nice easy hike along Eagle Creek. You can walk several miles into the Trinity Alps Wilderness, and find wonderful solitude and pretty views.

At the base of Scott Mountain the byway leaves Highway 3 and travels northeast on Forest Road 17 (Parks Creek Road), a variable-lane gravel road paralleling the Trinity River. The route twists and turns, climbing gradually up the drainage. Watch for deer and black bear on the road, as well as fallen rocks and big logging trucks. Fairly recent gold mining through here consisted of digging up the soil with backhoes and bulldozers, and you can see the sad evidence of this mining method.

The byway continues its climb, now on the shoulder of 9,025-foot Mount Eddy. Lakes and springs on this mountain combine with streams to form the Trinity, Shasta, and Sacramento rivers.

The byway reaches its highest point at 6,880 feet on the divide between the Trinity River and Shasta River drainages. Park your car and walk a portion of the Pacific Crest Trail, which travels 2,600 miles from Mexico to Canada. Walk north about three miles around the back side of China Peak, to a beautiful view of alpine lakes and broad vistas.

Along the byway, Mount Shasta dominates the eastern horizon. Shasta is the world's second-largest stratovolcano still classified as active. You'll continue north through rocky outcrops, meadows, and forest, with far-ranging views out over the Shasta Valley and north. The byway ends at Interstate 5 near Weed. □

6 SUNRISE NATIONAL SCENIC BYWAY
Cleveland National Forest   California

General description: A twenty-four mile route through desert mountains, with panoramic views across the Anza-Borrego Desert.

Special attractions: Anza-Borrego Desert State Park, Laguna Mountain Recreation Area, Cuyamaca Rancho State Park, bicycling, bird watching, Mount Laguna Observatory, broad vistas, hiking, camping, wildflowers.

Location: Southwest California on the Cleveland National Forest. The byway travels County Road S1, the Sunrise Highway, between Laguna Junction and the national forest boundary eleven miles south of Julian.

Byway route number: San Diego County Road S1.

Travel season: Year-round, with occasional, temporary closures in winter for snow removal.

Camping: Two national forest campgrounds, with picnic tables, fire grates, toilets, and drinking water.

Services: Traveler services in Pine Valley and Mount Laguna, available on a limited basis. All services in nearby San Diego.

Nearby attractions: Salton Sea, San Diego city attractions.

For more information: Cleveland National Forest, 10845 Rancho Bernardo Road, Rancho Bernardo, CA 92127-2107, (619) 673-6180. Descanso Ranger District, 3348 Alpine Blvd., Alpine, CA 91901, (619) 445-6235.

Description: The Sunrise National Scenic Byway travels through the Laguna Mountain Recreation Area, providing views of mountains, forests, and chaparral. The two-lane road is paved and has wide shoulders and scenic turnouts. Traffic is moderately busy.

Summer temperatures range from the seventies to the nineties. Spring and fall days are usually in the sixties and seventies and drop to the thirties and forties at night. In autumn, hot gale-force Santa Ana winds can blow. Winter days are usually above freezing, and nights may drop into the twenties. February and March are the rainiest times.

The byway is very scenic driven from either direction. From south to north, begin a mile east of the small community of Pine Valley, driving north on County Road S1. The byway climbs through chaparral into the timber. There are Coulter and Jeffrey pines, pinyon, California black oak, and canyon live oak. In spring the mountains are bright with blossoming lupine, mountain lilac, and scarlet penstemon.

Meadows Information Station is located at the entrance to Laguna Mountain Recreation Area. Bulletin boards display maps, regulations, and general information.

Fire danger in this region is extremely high. Check the regulations before cooking—stoves are subject to specific year-round restrictions.

Take a side trip west on Forest Road 15S10, to Wooded Hill Nature Trail. This gentle path climbs only about 250 feet elevation in about 1.5 miles, leading to one of the highest points along the byway—6,123 feet. On a clear day you might see as far as Point Loma in San Diego. There are lots of wildflowers in spring, and you may see chipper little ground squirrels. Watch for shy rattlesnakes—they don't like to be surprised. You can pick up a trail brochure at the Laguna Visitor Center.

The Sunrise Scenic Byway climbs up into cool mountain forests. Cleveland National Forest photo.

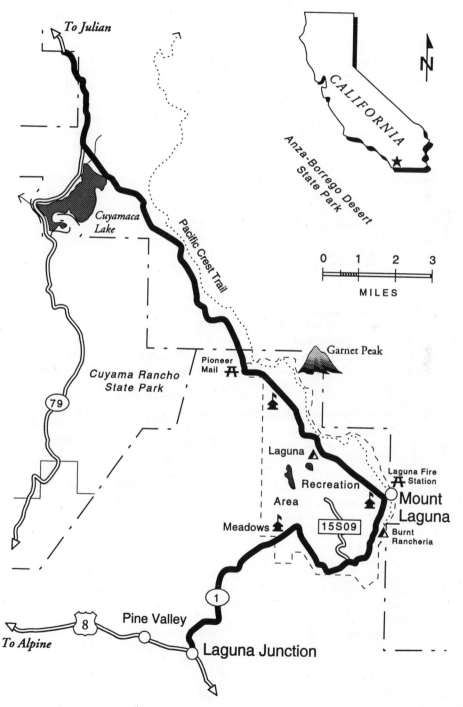

Wildlife abounds in this arid region. Look for large animals like mule deer, coyotes, and gray foxes. You may be lucky enough to spot a mountain lion or bobcat. Less shy are raccoons, badgers, ringtail cats, and a variety of shrews, mice, and squirrels. Best times to see wildlife are the cooler mornings and evenings. Many desert inhabitants are nocturnal, so you may hear rather than see them.

Burnt Rancheria Campground provides 108 sites in the shady pines and oaks. The Desert View Nature Trail leads about a mile to a very good view of the desert. You can see the Salton Sea, and Anza-Borrego State Park.

Another hiking option is the Pacific Crest National Scenic Trail from Burnt Rancheria Campground to Pioneer Mail Picnic Area. This route supplies beautiful views out over the desert as it winds five miles through the forest. For a shorter hike, you can get on and off at various points along the byway.

The Visitor Center in Mount Laguna has wildlife exhibits and lots of area information and books. Children love to see the rattlesnake display. Check the information board to learn about summer-weekend guided nature walks and environmental activities. The Visitor Center is open on summer weekends. Travelers find food, phone, lodging, and post office in this small community. Nearby, there are opportunities to picnic and hike.

On summer weekends, join a naturalist for the guided Star Party at the San Diego Observatory. Pick up a free ticket to this fun event at the Visitor Center or ranger station.

Near the Visitor Center, Kwaaymii Nature Trail meanders just over a mile through the oaks and pines. You can see where Indians used to grind their pinyon nuts.

If the Visitor Center is closed, the Laguna Fire Station is open June to October and has general information, brochures, and backcountry camping permits.

Three miles north of Mount Laguna, a side trip west brings you to Laguna Campground. The campground provides 104 sites in the pines and oaks. You can hike the 1.3-mile Lightning Ridge Trail from the campground amphitheater to a little knoll with a great view. On a clear day you may see out to Point Loma.

Little Laguna Lake usually dries out in the summer and the wildflower show is splendid. Showy blossoms of checkerbloom, buttercup, tidytips, yarrow, and goldenrod brighten the area.

The byway continues north, still at about 6,000 feet elevation. Vegetation is primarily Jeffrey pine and black oak, ceanothus, and mountain mahogany.

Garnet Information Center provides another information kiosk. The byway leaves the national forest near Pioneer Mail Picnic Area and travels next to Cuyamaca Rancho State Park. The park is known for great hiking and maintains 110 miles of footpaths. The trails are moderately strenuous, and elevations range from 4,000 to 6,500 feet. Slopes are covered with big Jeffrey pines, sugar pines, Coulter pines, incense cedars, black oak, and live oak. It's a good place to bird watch and look for wildlife; there are mule deer, mountain lions, bobcats, gray fox, coyotes, racoons, rabbits, squirrels, and rattlesnakes.

The byway ends at the north end of Cuyamaca Lake, a private lake offering boating, fishing, camping, and a restaurant.

You can make a nice loop trip back to the beginning of the byway by following California State Highway 79 south to Los Terrenitos, located on Interstate 8. Follow the interstate approximately eight miles east to return to the beginning of the byway.☐

General description: A sixty-four mile route from the city through the desert foothills and into the mountains.

Special attractions: Wide-ranging vistas, downhill and cross-country skiing, hiking, camping, unique geology, historic sites.

Location: Southwest California on the Angeles National Forest. The byway travels Highway 2 between La Canada and Mountain Top Junction.

Byway route number: California State Highway 2.

Travel season: Much of the byway is open year round. One section, from Islip Saddle east to the ski areas near Wrightwood, is closed by winter snows, usually from late December through early April.

Camping: Eleven national forest campgrounds on or near the byway, with picnic tables, fire grates, and toilets. Some supply drinking water.

Services: Traveler services in La Canada and Wrightwood.

Nearby attractions: Rim of the World National Forest Scenic Byway, Los Angeles city attractions, state beaches, Santa Catalina Island, state parks.

For more information: Angeles National Forest, 701 North Santa Anita Avenue, Arcadia, CA 91006, (818) 574-5200. Arroyo Seco Ranger District, Oak Grove Park, Flintridge, CA 91011, (818) 790-1151. Valyermo Ranger District, P.O. Box 15, Valyermo, CA 93563, (805) 944-2187.

Description: Angeles Crest Scenic Byway's motto is "urban places to mountain spaces." This byway, also a designated state scenic route, gets you out of the smog and up into areas that have some elbow room. The two-lane highway is paved, with frequent scenic turnouts. Traffic is moderately busy through the week, and busy on weekends.

The Angeles Crest Scenic Byway travels from about 1,200 feet elevation up to nearly 8,000 feet. Temperatures can vary dramatically from the low, western end to the higher elevations. Summer daytime temperatures at lower elevations are often in the nineties, while up high the temperatures are a cooler seventy or eighty. Spring and fall range from the seventies and eighties down low to the fifties and sixties up high. Above 6,000 feet (around Chilao), temperatures usually drop below freezing and snow covers the ground from late November through late March. Be prepared for hazardous road conditions all winter. Use snow tires or carry chains, and bring warm clothing.

The byway is beautiful driven in either direction. When driving west to east, start at the Oak Grove Ranger Station, to obtain maps, national forest information, permits, brochures, and other useful materials.

The byway begins at the junction of Highways 118 and 2, and follows Highway 2. The vegetation here is chaparral—primarily chemise, manzanita, ceanothus, sagebrush, yucca, and toyonberry. You can hike on footpaths paralleling the entire byway, and there are frequent access points along the highway for shorter walks. A number of walk-in-only picnic areas and campgrounds are located on the foot trails.

The highway climbs steadily to about 4,000 feet elevation. Clear Creek Ranger Station has brochures for the nearby Mount Lowe Railroad Self-Guiding

Angeles Crest Scenic Byway provides many far-ranging vistas, including this panorama along the Blue Ridge. Roy Murphy photo.

Trail. This walking tour of the historic railroad route is fun. Drive south on the Mount Wilson Road (Forest Road 2N52) to the locked gate, and the beginning of the tour. You can walk up to four miles to Inspiration Point, learning about the Mountain Trolley Line and seeing places like Devil's Slide and Horseshoe Curve. The view from Inspiration Point is extensive, and on a clear day you might see Santa Catalina Island, sixty miles away.

For a shorter walk next to the byway, stroll the mile-long self-guiding nature walk from Switzer's Picnic Area.

Farther east along the byway, a side trip south on Forest Road 2N52 leads to world-famous Mount Wilson Observatory. You can tour this interesting facility on weekends. A few more miles east on the byway leads to a side trip north, on Upper Big Tujunga Road (Forest Road 3N19). Here you'll find pretty streamside areas for picnics and walks, and good fishing for rainbow trout.

The byway continues to climb as you travel along, and in spring the roadside meadows are full of wildflowers such as sticky monkeyflower, vinca, Indian paintbrush, and morning glories. Blossoms on the California buckeye tree are splendid.

The huge, rugged canyons of the San Gabriel Wilderness are adjacent to the scenic byway. The wilderness protects more than 36,000 acres of dense chaparral, forested slopes, and mountain peaks. Elevations in the wilderness range from 1,600 to 8,200 feet. The tree-covered summit of Mount Mooney rises just east of the byway.

A good family hike leads three miles round-trip, from Charlton Flat up a ravine to a restored Forest Service fire lookout atop Vetter Mountain. You'll have a panoramic view and see into Devil's Canyon, over to the Twin Peaks, and all around the surrounding San Gabriel Mountains. An easier hike from Charlton Flat goes to Devil's Peak, offering excellent views down into the wilderness. This trail goes through a grove of Coulter pines, which have the largest cones of any pine tree. Some Coulter pinecones grow to the size of a volleyball and weigh up to fifteen pounds!

The San Gabriel Mountain Range is the only range in California on a transverse, or east-west axis. All the other ranges trend north-south. The San Andreas Fault forms the northern boundary of the mountains—this is a region of active earthquakes and movement. The San Gabriels are growing at the rate of about a half-inch every ten years, which in geologic terms is very fast. The range has both volcanic and sedimentary rocks.

A scenic turnout at milepost 50 provides a good view of the San Gabriel Wilderness, and an interpretive sign tells about the area. At this elevation, you're now out of the chaparral and into a forest of Jeffrey, ponderosa, and Coulter pines.

Chilao Campground lies at 5,200 elevation, and provides drinking water and ninety sites in a grassy meadow with panoramic views of the valley and peaks. Naturalist-led Saturday evening programs are offered in the amphitheater all summer. Topics include forest management, wildlife, astronomy, and geology.

Chilao Visitor Information Center is located about twenty-seven miles from the western terminus of the byway. Stop in to view the displays on natural and cultural history. There are books for sale, and pamphlets and other national forest information are available. You can participate in ranger-led nature walks or stroll one of the three self-guided loops. Two of the loops are barrier-free.

Wildlife on the Angeles National Forest includes mule deer, black bears, mountain lions, bighorn sheep, bobcats, mice, gophers, cottontail rabbits, racoons, opossums, skunks, gray foxes, and coyotes. Some of the interesting reptiles are king snakes, garter snakes, gopher snakes, ringneck snakes, and whip snakes. The Pacific rattlesnakes and mojave green rattlesnakes are the only poisonous snakes on the national forest. Children will delight in discovering newts, treefrogs, toads, and salamanders.

Bird watchers find abundant and delightful viewing opportunities. Look for flickers, woodpeckers, jays, wrens, finches, towhees, great horned owls, crows, ravens, killdeer, red-tailed hawks, kestrels, quail, mourning doves, hummingbirds, shrikes, and swifts. Bald eagles migrate through the area.

The Pacific Crest National Scenic Trail crosses the byway several times. The major trailhead is near Three Points. You can hike a portion of this 2,500-mile trail that goes from Mexico to Canada. Walking north on the trail gets you out into the high elevation brushland. Vegetation includes whitethorn, mountain mahogany, scrub oak, and chemise. Chemise has abundant seeds and provides food for quail and doves. You can also hike southeast on the trail. The climb up the ridge is somewhat steep, but the views are extensive.

Buckhorn Campground has thirty-nine sites set in a canyon of tall cedars and mixed conifers. The stream is lined with common and rare ferns. You could hike the 4.4-mile loop that climbs Mount Waterman and descends along Buckhorn Creek. Take time to admire the roses and lemon lilies.

Mount Waterman and Kratka Ridge ski areas offer downhill skiing in winter. Vistas along here are tremendous. You can see north into the desert or south to Los Angeles, and sometimes out to Santa Catalina Island in the Pacific

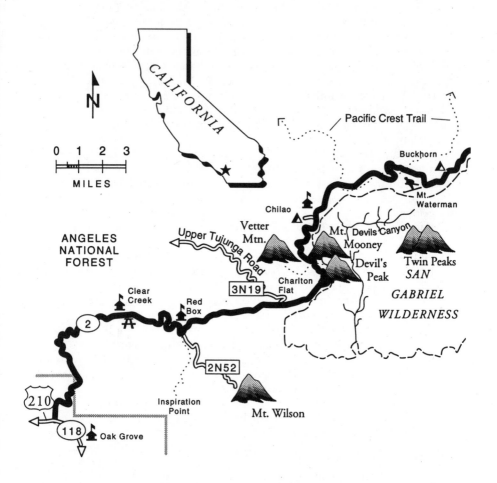

Ocean. There are several picnic areas along the road that offer great views.

Look for bighorn sheep on the slopes between Mount Waterman and Islip Saddle. Nelson bighorn sheep are now a thriving species and have been taken off the 'sensitive species' list. There are about 750 bighorn sheep on the Angeles National Forest.

Islip Saddle is the point at which snowplows stop removing snow. In winter you can put on cross-country skis and ski along the snow-packed road.

The byway climbs to Dawson Saddle, then begins a gradual descent. Sheep Mountain Wilderness lies south of the highway, protecting about 44,000 acres. Elevations in the wilderness range from about 2,400 feet to 10,060-foot Mount Baldy. Prominent peaks include Throop, Burnham, and Baden Powell. Mount

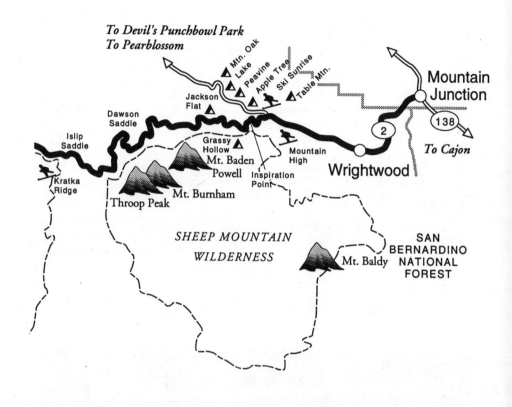

To Devil's Punchbowl Park
To Pearblossom

Mtn. Oak
Lake
Peavine
Apple Tree
Ski Sunrise
Table Mtn.

Jackson
Flat

Dawson
Saddle

Islip
Saddle

Grassy
Hollow
Mt. Baden
Powell
Inspiration
Point

Mountain
High

Wrightwood

Mountain
Junction

2

138

To Cajon

Kratka
Ridge

Throop Peak   Mt. Burnham

SHEEP MOUNTAIN

WILDERNESS

Mt. Baldy

SAN
BERNARDINO
NATIONAL
FOREST

Baden Powell is named for the founder of the Boy Scouts.

Wildflowers in the meadows at this elevation include yellow mustard, scarlet penstemon, purple beardstongue, California poppy, and yellow lupine. Mountain biking is popular on non-wilderness trails and roads all along the byway.

Grassy Hollow Campground has fifteen sites nestled among big ponderosa pines. The highway travels along the top of Blue Ridge, providing extensive views north and south. At Inspiration Point you can see the Punchbowl Fault, cutting right through the mountains, and look north into the high desert. A few miles east, stop at Big Pines Visitor Information Center to learn more about the San Andreas Fault. The fault is over a thousand miles long and runs right through the Big Pines Area. Displays teach you about such interesting things as fault flour, slickensides, and fault gouges. You can see evidence of the fault by looking at the very different rocks to the north and south. The south slopes are composed of shales and siltstones, while the north slopes are weathered and decomposed granites. Both types of rocks are about 500 million years old. For a leisurely view of the fault area, take a stroll on the short Lightning Ridge Nature Trail. There is also a self-guided automobile Earthquake Fault Tour.

There are two downhill ski areas near Big Pines. Both Mountain High and Holiday Hill ski areas offer day and night skiing. Ski Sunrise has daytime skiing. In summer, you can camp at one of five campgrounds located within a few miles of the byway in this area. Table Mountain Campground has 115 campsites, an amphitheater for naturalist-led evening programs, and a self-guided nature trail through the forest. Tree species here include Jeffrey, ponderosa, and sugar pine; white fir; incense cedar; and California black and canyon live oak.

The other four campgrounds are smaller. Apple Tree Campground has eight sites, Peavine has four, Lake has eight, and Mountain Oak provides seventeen. You can swim, picnic, and fish for trout in Jackson Lake. If you continue west on the Big Pines Road, Devil's Punchbowl County Park has hiking trails and a very good interpretive center with exhibits on the local flora, fauna, and geology.

The byway continues east through Wrightwood and ends at Mountain Top Junction, at the intersection of Highways 2 and 138. You can see more evidence of the active geology of this region in the giant Heath Canyon mudflow scar on the southern ridge above Wrightwood. □

8 RIM OF THE WORLD
San Bernardino National Forest   California

General description: A 107-mile route along the crest of the beautiful San Bernardino Mountains.

Special attractions: San Gorgonio Wilderness, water sports, fishing, extensive views, cool forests, camping.

Location: Southern California on the San Bernardino National Forest. The byway travels a fishhook-shaped route, from Mormon Rocks Fire Station east on Highway 138 to Crestline, continuing east on Highway 18 around Big Bear Lake, then south on Highway 38 over Onyx Summit, and back west to the Mill Creek Ranger Station.

Byway route numbers: California State Highways 138, 18, and 38.

Travel season: Year-round.

Camping: Eight national forest campgrounds on or near the byway, with picnic tables, fire grates, toilets, and drinking water. Numerous other national forest campgrounds within fifteen miles of the byway.

Services: All traveler services in the numerous resort communities along the byway, with limited availability. All services in nearby San Bernardino.

Nearby attractions: Cucamonga Wilderness, Joshua Tree National Monument, ski areas, San Bernardino city attractions, Silverwood Lake.

For more information: San Bernardino National Forest, 1824 S. Commercenter Circle, San Bernardino, CA 92408-3430, (714) 383-5588. Arrowhead Ranger District, (28104 Highway 18, Skyforest) P.O. Box 7, Rimforest, CA 92378, (714) 337-2444; Big Bear Ranger District, North Shore Drive, Hwy 38, P.O. Box 290, Fawnskin, CA 92333, (714) 866-3437; San Gorgonio Ranger District, 34701 Mill Creek Road, Mentone, CA 92359, (714) 794-1123; Cajon Ranger District, Lytle Creek Road, Star Route 100, Fontana, CA 92335, (714) 887-2576.

Description: Rim of the World travels the crest of the San Bernardino Mountains, through historic towns and past lovely lakes. The two-lane highway is paved, with frequent turnouts. Traffic can be heavy on summer weekends, and heavy in winter on Highway 18 to ski areas around Big Bear. The rest of the year traffic is moderately busy.

Summer temperatures range from about fifty to ninety degrees. Afternoon thunderstorms are common. Winter brings rain and snow, with temperatures ranging from below freezing up to the sixties.

Exit Interstate 15 just north of San Bernardino at Cajon Junction. The byway begins at Mormon Rocks Ranger Station, a few miles west on State Highway 138. The area was named for a Mormon encampment near here. The dominant sandstone rocks, called hogbacks, are tilted sandstone containing fossils.

The byway travels east on Highway 138 from Mormon Rocks, crossing Interstate 15 to climb through Crowder Canyon to the top of Cajon Pass. The route then drops down Horsethief Canyon, part of the Old Spanish Trail once used by the Utes to take stolen horses to Utah and New Mexico. Chaparral species like manzanita, chamise, holly-leaved cherry, Joshua trees, and pinyon pine are the primary vegetative species here.

Climbing again, you enter the San Bernardino National Forest. The Lake Silverwood Overlook provides a pretty view of part of the lake, then the route skirts the lake and climbs on a winding road into a forest of ponderosa pine, Jeffrey pine, Douglas-fir, incense cedar, white fir, California black oak, and canyon live oak.

Crestline is a ridgetop resort community in the San Bernardino Mountains. Nearby Lake Gregory is a county-owned regional park, where you can swim and picnic. Anglers fish for rainbow trout, catfish, bluegill, and bass. Hikers can enjoy a two-mile footpath that encircles the lake.

Just south of Crestline, the byway leaves Highway 138 and turns east onto California State Highway 18. Highway 18 has numerous good scenic overlooks as you travel the ridgeline. The Santa Ana and San Jacinto mountain ranges are southwest and southeast, respectively, while to the east San Bernardino Peak's summit reaches 10,649 feet. Baylis Park is named for John Baylis, who had a significant part in getting the Rim of the World drive built in the early 1900s. A half-mile farther, Rim of the World Drive monument commemorates the highway.

Take a side trip from Rimforest on Bear Springs Road to Strawberry Peak Lookout. The fire lookout is staffed by volunteers during the fire season, usually from about May through November. They'll be delighted to show you around. You can see the forest and desert, and on a really clear day you can see all the way out to Catalina Island. Also near Rimforest, Dogwood Campground has ninety-three sites in the dense forest. The dogwood trees

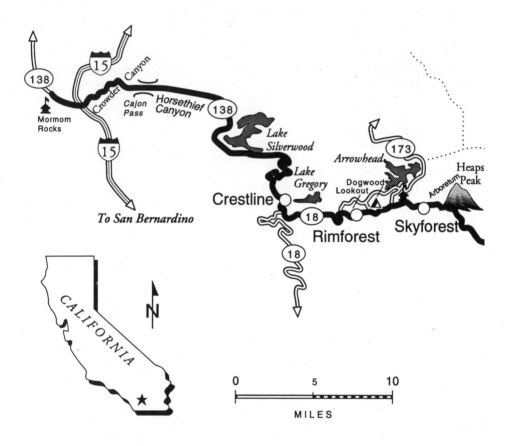

provide an eye-catching display of blossoms each spring in April or May.

The byway passes State Highway 173, which leads to the resort community of Lake Arrowhead. Arrowhead is an enticing lake with opportunities to swim, fish, and boat.

The byway is cut right into the side of a mountain, and the granite faces and rock outcrops are beautiful. Watch for fallen rocks on the road, especially after a rainstorm. Arrowhead Ranger Station, located in Skyforest, has national forest information and maps available.

Stop for information at Heap's Peak Arboretum, and linger on the scenic and informative .7-mile nature trail. Five miles farther east, Deer Lick Ranger Station provides information and maps during the summer fire season.

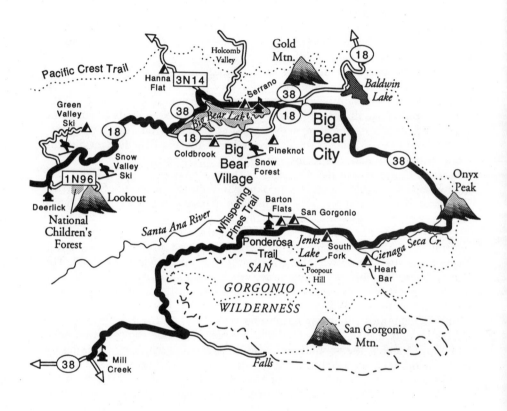

Take a side trip up Forest Road 1N96 to the National Children's Forest, where a nature walk leads through an area devastated by a terrible fire in 1970. It was replanted in 1971 from the contributions of thousands of school children and other people. Return to the Y in the road and go to Keller Peak Lookout, elevation 7,882 feet, where volunteer fire watchers will show you around.

Another side trip, north to Green Valley Lake, leads to downhill and cross-country skiing possibilities, as well as summertime fishing and boating. Green Valley Campground has thirty-six sites in the forest.

In autumn, leaves on the black oaks along the road turn a pretty yellow, or reddish yellow. They look beautiful in contrast to the deeper greens of

Coulter pines, ponderosa pines, and Jeffrey pines. Coulter pines have the largest cones of any pine tree.

The byway passes Snow Valley, another ski area, and crests a small divide which separates waters flowing to the Pacific Ocean from those flowing into the Great Basin. The view from the top includes Big Bear Lake to the east, and San Bernardino Peak and Mount San Gorgonio to the southeast.

The byway twists and turns to Big Bear Lake, through an area so stark locals call it the Arctic Circle. Steep granite walls plunge into the Bear Creek drainage below. At the dam, a side trip on Highway 18 travels by the southern end of Big Bear Lake. Colbrook Campground has thirty-six sites in an open forest of Jeffrey pine and white fir. Pineknot Campground provides forty-eight sites in the trees. Big Bear Lake Village and Big Bear City are resort communities servicing three downhill ski areas and summer tourists. You can fish, swim, boat, canoe, sail, and enjoy other water sports.

The byway turns onto Highway 38 and travels along the north shore of the lake. Driving a few miles north from Fawnskin on 3N14, Hanna Flat Campground has eighty-eight sites in Jeffrey pine and white fir. This campground is usually nice and quiet. A side road (2N09) leads to Holcomb Valley, site of southern California's biggest gold rush. Brochures for the self-guided 'Gold Fever Trail' route are available at the Big Bear Ranger Station, along with other national forest information and maps.

Serrano Campground has 132 sites in the trees between the old and new highways. There are showers, RV hookups and dump station, and five barrier-free sites. It's just a short walk to the lake. Nearby, Meadows Edge Picnic Area is a nice day-use area right by the lake.

A half-mile west of the ranger station, Cougar Crest Trail leads north about two miles up a moderate incline to the Pacific Crest National Scenic Trail. There are some nice views back over the lake from Cougar Crest Trail. The Pacific Crest Trail offers super hiking which is consistently quite easy. East of the ranger station, the very easy Woodland Trail provides a lovely 1.5-mile self-guided nature walk.

Bird watchers can look for numerous waterfowl and shore birds around the lake. Coots, grebes, gulls, and ducks are plentiful. Bald eagles winter here, and a rare species, the spotted owl, also inhabits the area. While looking for birds on the lake, you may notice the dome of a solar observatory.

Take a side trip at the junction of Highways 18 and 38, at the east end of the lake. Stay on 18 east for about seven miles, traveling around the base of Gold Mountain. The road skirts the edge of Baldwin Lake, where one part of the Big Bear Valley Preserve protects the largest group (twenty) of endemic plants in the continental United States. These plants are probably survivors of the last Ice Age and are found nowhere else in the world. Most are very tiny and well adapted to harsh conditions.

Return to the junction of Highways 18 and 38 and follow the scenic byway on Highway 38, which crosses the east arm of Big Bear Lake and turns east again. This more arid countryside supports a mixture of Great Basin sage-brush and rabbitbrush, as well as western junipers and Jeffrey pines. Look for showy blue lupines and scarlet penstemons blooming along the road.

You can learn more about the region's history at the Eleanor Abbott Big Bear Valley Historical Museum, open on summer weekends. Big Bear City offers shops, restaurants, and other traveler services.

The byway climbs to its highest point at Onyx Summit, elevation 8,443 feet.

Mormon Rocks are a prominent feature along the Rim of the World Scenic Byway. San Bernardino National Forest photo.

There are very nice views northeast over the desert as you gain elevation. The route then descends along Cienaga Seca Creek. Heart Bar Campground has ninety-four sites, located on part of the historic Heart Bar cattle ranch. You can drive a little farther down the side road to Fish Creek and walk a short trail to the only aspen grove in southern California. The aspen leaves turn a brilliant gold in autumn. The Fish Creek Trail wanders through meadows and along the stream and makes a very pleasant outing into the San Gorgonio Wilderness.

The Santa Ana River Trail also begins on this side road. When complete, it will stretch from here to the coast.

On the byway, South Fork Campground has twenty-four sites in the riparian vegetation near the river. Look for beavers and cast a line into the creek for trout.

San Gorgonio Campground provides sixty sites in the open forest. Not far away, naturalists present evening programs in the Greyback Amphitheater on summer weekends. Topics include plants, animals, geology, and history of the local mountain area. Nearby, Barton Flats Campground provides forty-seven campsites.

The Barton Flats Visitor Center provides maps, books, backcountry permits, and information on the national forest and nearby San Gorgonio Wilderness. The wilderness encompasses 59,969 acres of forests, meadows, and lakes surrounding San Gorgonio Peak (elevation 11,499 feet), the highest in southern California. There are ninety-six miles of foot trails through this beautiful region.

A side trip on Jenks Lake Road leads to picnicking and several hikes. Jenks Lake is a small day-use lake stocked with rainbow trout. There are picnic tables, a swimming area, and the .4-mile Hidden Cliffs Nature Trail.

Try a hike on South Fork Trail off the Jenks Lake Road. You'll climb a gradual grade through the manzanita about one mile to Horse Meadows and can continue on to a great view of San Gorgonio Peak from Poopout Hill. The overlook has interpretive signs explaining the history of the wilderness. The trail continues beyond Poopout into the wilderness.

Two nature walks are located on the byway, near the western end of Jenks Lake Road. Whispering Pines is a half-mile long, and the Ponderosa Nature Trail is .6-mile long. Both are easy strolls and very interesting.

Four miles west of the visitors center the landslide overlook provides a good view into the canyon of the upper Santa Ana River. Landslides on Slide Mountain left massive scars on the slopes. You can also see old road switchbacks below, part of the original Rim of the World drive before the route over Onyx Summit was completed.

The byway descends farther, and on a clear day you can see San Bernardino. Stop at the scenic overlook just west of Mountain Home Village. This is located right on the San Andreas Fault. Notice how the vegetation changes as elevations change—the hotter, lower slopes support only low-growing shrubs and brush, slightly cooler middle elevations host Douglas-fir and canyon live oak, while the upper reaches are suitable for black oaks and several species of pines.

A side trip east on Forest Falls Road leads past several trailheads into the wilderness and ends at Falls Picnic Area. Big Falls Trail leads .3-mile to an overlook of the pretty waterfall.

The byway ends at the Mill Creek Ranger Station, where visitors can get national forest information, maps, books, and backcountry permits. □

9 LEE VINING CANYON HIGHWAY
Inyo National Forest   California

General description: A twelve-mile climb through rugged Lee Vining Canyon to Yosemite National Park in the high Sierra Nevadas.

Special attractions: Spectacular canyon, Yosemite National Park, Mono Basin National Forest Scenic Area and Visitor Center, Ansel Adams and Hoover wilderness areas, outstanding scenery, hiking, fishing.

Location: East-central California on the Inyo National Forest. The byway travels California State Highway 120 between U.S. Highway 395 and the east entrance to Yosemite National Park.

Byway route number: California State Highway 120.

Travel season: Summer and fall, generally from Memorial Day weekend through early November.

Camping: Five national forest campgrounds on or near the byway, with picnic tables, fire grates, and toilets. Some provide drinking water. No dispersed camping in the canyon. One county campground spread out along Lee Vining Creek. Numerous campsites in Yosemite National Park, available by advance reservation.

Services: All traveler services in Lee Vining and Yosemite National Park, with limited availability. Some services at Tioga Pass Resort.

Nearby attractions: Mono Lake, Devils Postpile National Monument, downhill ski areas, resorts, Pacific Crest Trail, Bodie State Historic Park, June Lake Loop.

For more information: Inyo National Forest, 873 N. Main Street, Bishop, CA 93514, (619) 873-5841. Mono Lake Ranger District, P.O. Box 429, Lee Vining, CA 93541, (619) 647-6525.

Description: Lee Vining Canyon Highway travels from Mono Lake through a spectacular canyon, climbing over 3,200 feet to the high alpine mountains of the Inyo National Forest and Yosemite National Park in the Sierra Nevada Range. The two-lane road is paved with mostly narrow shoulders and has frequent turnouts. Traffic is very heavy, and generally slow moving. Stretches of the road have precipitous slopes, but no guardrails; the highway is safe but this can be a white-knuckle driving experience.

Summer temperatures vary widely from the lower elevations to the higher reaches. Daytime temperatures in the lower part of the canyon go up to about eighty-five degrees; in the upper elevations up to seventy-five. Nights at low elevations dip down to forty or fifty, while up high it can drop down to freezing, but is generally in the high thirties and forties. Expect occasional summer thundershowers in the afternoon. Autumn is colder, ranging from about twenty to fifty-five degrees up high, but remaining warmer, in the sixties, by Mono Lake.

Traveling east to west, the byway begins near the small community of Lee Vining. The Mono Basin National Forest Scenic Area Visitor Center has national forest information, a theater, and exhibits on Mono Basin, tufa formation, brine shrimp, local history, and geology.

Mono Lake is over 700,000-years-old. The lake is cradled in a basin of sagebrush, while the backdrop of steep mountains soar upwards thousands of feet. The tufa spires and knobs are fascinating, and hot springs and steam vents provide evidence of active volcanism. More than a million migrating birds feast on the Mono Lake's abundant brine shrimp and alkali flies. Look for California gulls, Wilson's phalaropes, red-necked phalaropes, eared grebes, and tiny snowy plovers.

You can participate in guided nature walks, attend campfire naturalist programs, and enjoy feeling buoyant when swimming in the mineral- and salt-rich water of Mono Lake. Try the one-mile, self-guided nature trail at South Tufa.

The scenic byway travels west up Highway 120 into Lee Vining Canyon. This is a prehistoric Indian trade route which culminates on the highest vehicle crossing in the Sierra Nevada. The lower section of the canyon has Jeffrey pines and quaking aspens along the stream, while on the slopes are high desert brushland species such as sagebrush, rabbitbrush, and bitterbrush. The ranger station, located on the byway, has national forest information and backcountry permits for wilderness travelers.

The byway then encounters several miles of large meadows, with stands of aspen, red fir, and Jeffrey and lodgepole pines. Wildflower enthusiasts can find leopard lilies in the wet areas and monkshood, larkspur, lupine, and wild iris in the meadows. In early summer the bright yellow blossoms of

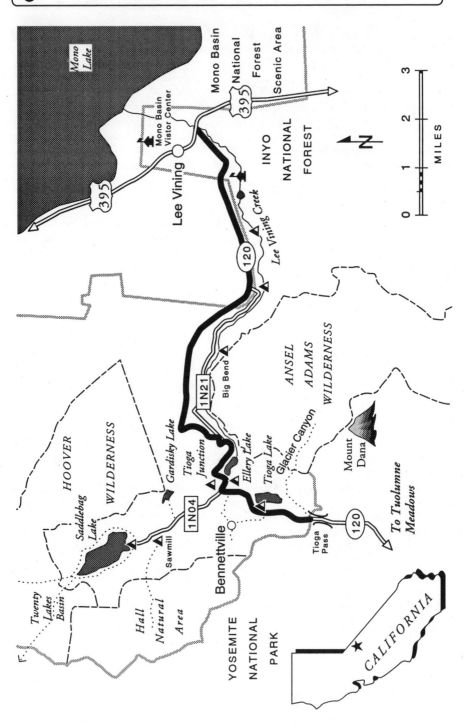

mules-ears and balsamroot brighten the roadside.

Off the byway on Forest Road 1N21, Lee Vining Canyon Campground provides one hundred sites in various spots dispersed along the canyon bottom. Gravel roads lead anglers to rainbow trout in Lee Vining Creek. Big Bend Campground has seventeen sites situated right on a bend in the stream, in a dense stand of firs, pines, and aspens. There is good fishing all along the creek from the pond above the ranger station to the power plant near the campground. Black bears occasionally wander through the campgrounds.

The byway begins its climb up the canyon wall, crossing large talus slopes with precipitous drop-offs. Guardrails are few, and grades are steep. To the south, the boundary of Ansel Adams Wilderness reaches nearly to the canyon floor, and the soaring, barren granite peaks jut skyward. The 228,500-acre wilderness protects many lakes and streams, as well as high-elevation forests and mountain summits.

The road climbs across a rock face, and the view extends down the whole canyon to the Mono Craters. Pullouts along the route allow drivers a chance to sightsee. The route goes around a bend, and Ellery Lake appears like a surprise gem. A waterfall spills out of the outlet when the water is not all diverted through the penstock. The campground has twelve sites best suited to tent camping, near where the creek empties into the lake. Drinking water is available, and brook and rainbow trout inhabit the waters. A nearby resort has lodging, food, a small store, and gas.

Across the road, Junction Campground provides ten sites especially suited for tents. The sites sit on the edge of a meadow near the creek. Wildflowers found at this 9,500-foot elevation include asters, alpine gentians, fireweed, buckwheat, western wallflowers, columbines, and spirea. You can hike from the campground to Bennettville, a historical 1800s mining town. The remnants of just two buildings remain, as well as an old mine shaft and plenty of tailings, but the view all the way up is terrific. Looking south, you can see Mount Dana and the Dana Plateau, and Glacier Canyon. Rangers lead a guided walk up here once a week all summer. You can continue walking all through this beautiful region of high alpine lakes. Mountain heather blooms red, pink, and magenta underfoot.

A side trip north on Forest Road 1N04 gets off the busy highway. The road is generally too steep and narrow for buses and large RVs and towed units. The side road leads along Lee Vining Creek to two more campgrounds and Saddlebag Lake. A trailhead just over a mile from the road junction leads hikers one steep mile up to Gardisky Lake and decent fishing. Gardisky sits in a small basin and offers a great view down the canyon.

Wildflowers are prolific along the byway. Monkeyflowers, swamp onions, and bluebells brighten streambanks, while Indian paintbrush and lupine splash colors across the open meadows. Watch for bighorn sheep on the north side of the canyon between the 8,000- and 9,000-foot elevation signs. Bird watchers can look for pygmy owls, kestrels, flickers, and woodpeckers. Songbirds abound, and overhead golden eagles and many species of hawks ride the thermals rising from the canyon.

Sawmill Campground has twelve walk-in sites just above the creek, in the lodgepole pines. Hikers can walk in to the Hall Natural Area, a pristine environment of lakes and tarns. Researchers here are studying high-elevation vegetation, plant genetics, wildlife, and acid rain.

Saddlebag Lake is surrounded by rock talus slopes. The lake level fluctuates

Tioga Lake is nestled in an alpine meadow along Lee Vining Scenic Byway. Inyo National Forest photo.

greatly according to water releases from the dam. Saddlebag Campground provides twenty-two rustic campsites on a pretty whitebark pine covered knob, with a nice view of the lake. Drinking water is available. A good, easy footpath encircles Saddlebag Lake and provides access into the popular Twenty Lakes Basin, where you can take a half- or full-day loop hike into a region of lovely glacial lakes in the Hoover Wilderness. The remains of old mines make some interesting debris.

The byway climbs again, to shallow Tioga Lake. It sits in a little basin along the road, surrounded by lodgepole, limber, and whitebark pines. Tioga Lake Campground has thirteen sites on a little point between the road and the lake. These sites are also best suited to tent camping, and drinking water is available. Both Ellery and Tioga campgrounds fill quickly.

The byway ends at the Tioga Pass Entrance Station to Yosemite National Park. At 9,945 feet, this is the highest vehicular route across the entire Sierra Nevada Range. Views include glaciated peaks and domes, forests, meadows, and valleys. The headwaters of the Tuolumne River are up here in the alpine reaches of the mountains. A steep, short trail up Glacier Canyon brings you to beautiful alpine lakes and a good view of the glacier on Mount Dana. Listen for the sharp whistle of yellow-bellied marmots on the rock slopes.

Yosemite National Park offers a variety of activities. Drive about eight miles to Tuolumne Meadows, where a visitor center provides information. Nearby is a large campground, lodge, cabins, store, gas, restaurant, mountaineering supplies, and guide service. □

10 FEATHER RIVER SCENIC BYWAY
Plumas National Forest   California

General description: A 130-mile highway over a mountain pass in the Sierra Nevada Mountain Range.

Special attractions: Waterfalls, outstanding vistas, resorts, Bucks Lake Wilderness, Lake Oroville, wildlife viewing opportunities, autumn colors, cross-country skiing, snowmobiling.

Location: Northeast California on the Plumas National Forest. The byway follows California State Highway 70, from the junction of Highways 70 and 191 ten miles north of Oroville to the junction of 70 and U.S. Highway 395 about twenty-five miles north of Reno, Nevada.

Byway route number: California State Highway 70.

Travel season: Year-round.

Camping: Seven national forest campgrounds, with picnic tables, fire grates, and drinking water. Numerous other campgrounds within ten miles of the byway.

Services: All travelers services in Oroville, Quincy, and Portola. All services, with very limited availability, in Belden.

Nearby attractions: Lassen National Park, Lake Tahoe, downhill ski areas.

For more information: Plumas National Forest, P.O. Box 11500, Quincy, CA 95971-6025, (916) 283-2050. Oroville Ranger District, 875 Mitchell Ave., Oroville, CA 95965, (916) 534-6500. Quincy Ranger District, 39696 Highway 70, Box 69, Quincy, CA 95971, (916) 283-0555. Beckwourth Ranger District, P.O. Box 7, Mohawk, CA 96013, (916) 836-2572.

Description: Feather River Scenic Byway offers astounding vistas and scenic diversity. The route begins almost at sea level in the Sacramento Valley on the west and climbs through a remarkable canyon, timbered hills, and a broad valley before topping Beckwourth Pass at 5,228 feet and descending to the arid Long Valley and Sierra Valley. The two-lane road is paved and has scenic turnouts. Weekday traffic is light, but weekend recreation traffic can be moderately heavy. Highway speeds average between forty-five and fifty-five miles per hour.

The weather can be quite different in the lower valleys and the mountains. Fog sometimes fills the valleys in the morning. In the mountains, summer daytime temperatures hover between the seventies and nineties, and evenings sometimes drop to freezing. Expect short, intense afternoon thundershowers in June, August, and September. Winter days range between twenty and fifty degrees but can plunge to zero at night. Snow blankets the ground at higher elevations.

Plan your trip by the sun—its intense rays and glare on the road can make driving into the sun difficult. Drive the byway west to east in the afternoon, or east to west in the morning.

Driving west to east, the byway begins about ten miles north of Oroville, at the junction of Highways 70 and 191. Take 70 east, through green and golden grasslands interspersed with the subtle grey-greens of olive groves. The foothills rise ahead, covered in grasses, oaks, and brush. The byway begins climbing and has the first of many encounters with the Union Pacific Railroad. This route offers many things to interest railroad buffs. A mile east of the byway, ghost town buffs can explore the ruins and big pit at the Cherokee diggings.

Stop at the vista point a few miles past the bridge over Lake Oroville. Manzanita and oaks lead your eye out over an old lava flow into the northern Sacramento Valley. On a clear day you can see the coastal range far to the west.

The byway climbs to Jarbo Gap and winds into the North Fork Feather River Canyon on a very narrow, twisting route. Oaks, digger pines, and brush dot the steep canyon walls on either side of the road.

Train enthusiasts will appreciate the interlacing trusses on a railroad bridge several hundred feet below the highway. To get a good view, cross the highway bridge, then get out and look. The railroad and highway cling to the sides of the canyon wall, while below, the river plunges into a steep gorge.

A series of dams and spillways along this route generate hydroelectric power, providing the name "Staircase of Power." The byway follows a gentle gradient up the canyon, through relatively lush vegetation clinging to the canyon walls. In winter wispy waterfalls cascade off the slopes onto the road.

Watch for rocks on the highway past Pulga. Huge exfoliated slabs of granite create sheer walls of rock. Ferns and weeping springs adorn the area, and California laurel abounds.

Anglers fish for rainbow and brown trout all along this route. Shady Rest Picnic Area is a nice rest stop. Nearby, the road tunnels through solid Arch Rock. Rock climbers enjoy their sport near Elephant Butte, a double tunnel which brings you out at the top of Cresta Dam.

The byway continues past several more powerhouses and crosses Rock Creek on a picturesque and historic steel bridge. The clear waters of the creek mix into the sediment-laden river below the railroad arch trestle. Look for the giant round boulder alongside the road—and watch for fallen rocks through here.

When it was built, the Buck Creek Powerhouse had the tallest penstock in the world—1,800 feet high. It makes an impressive sight.

The community of Tobin was once a popular resort area for railroad travelers. Just beyond, the highway twists and turns alongside the Bucks Lake Wilderness. The wilderness protects diverse habitats ranging from the canyon you are in to 7,017-foot Spanish Peak.

A sign at the Belden Powerhouse relates some interesting history. The Pacific Crest National Scenic Trail intersects the byway at Ebbe Stamp Mill roadside rest area. You can hike a portion of this 2,400-mile trail right from the byway. The trail north meanders along Chips Creek for several pleasantly easy miles, before climbing out of sight. The hike east into Bucks Lake Wilderness Area entails four miles of switchbacks. For an easier family route try Yellow Creek, an easy 1.4-mile creekside trail which dead ends in a box canyon.

Those with a sharp eye may spot Columbian black-tailed deer, or Rocky Mountain mule deer. Other forest inhabitants include California black bear, mountain lion, beaver, gray and red fox, and river otter. Look overhead for bald and golden eagles and on the water for Canada geese and many species of ducks.

The highway travels next to the confluence of the North Fork and the East Branch Middle Fork. A short side trip north on Forest Road 27N26 leads to three campgrounds situated in the oaks and pines along the North Fork.

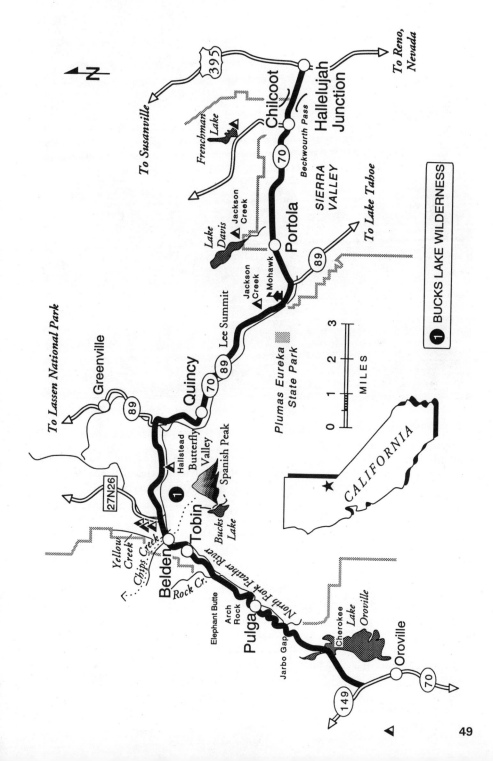

The river, the railroad, and the road all share the canyon near Belden, on the Feather River Scenic Byway. Plumas National Forest photo.

Gansner Bar has fourteen sites, North Fork has twenty sites, and Queen Lily has twelve sites. Look for delicious wild blackberries in the fall. Beyond the campgrounds, the side road leads into a very pretty canyon, with steep, reddish, soft rock and lush vegetation.

The byway now follows the East Branch North Fork into Serpentine Canyon. Hallsted Campground has twenty sites along the river. Farther east on the byway, take a side trip to Butterfly Valley Botanical Area. A path leads through this fertile little valley, home to over 500 species of wildflowers and plants. You may get to see a rare pitcher plant or one of a dozen species of orchids.

Quincy, established in the 1850s, has all travelers services plus a district ranger station and forest supervisor's office for national forest information. The historic courthouse has a two-thousand-pound glass and bronze chandelier lighting the marble staircase, and the grounds outside are lovely. Behind the court house, the Plumas County Museum is very interesting, with numerous displays and a large collection of Mountain Maidu Indian baskets.

About five miles from Quincy, the byway runs by Williams Loop, a rather unique section of the railroad that adjusts an engineering error. Look for the loop just south of the road. Farther along, the byway route runs alongside the Wild & Scenic Middle Fork Feather River. Jackson Creek Campground has fifteen sites, and fishing for rainbows and browns is very popular.

You can get more national forest information at the ranger station in Mohawk. Nearby, Plumas Eureka State Park makes an interesting side trip. The park has historic gold mines, a museum about the 49ers, cross-country and downhill skiing, campgrounds, lakes, and streams. Good family hikes include the Little Jamison Creek Trail and the Madora Lake Nature Walk.

Continuing east on the byway to Portola, you can visit the Railroad Museum and relax at Lake Davis Recreation Area to the north. Just out of Chilcoot, take a side trip up Frenchman Canyon on State Highway 112. Conifers and aspens grow among volcanic rock sculptures, and Frenchman Lake offers campgrounds, picnicking,and fishing.

The byway crosses the Sierra Valley, goes over Beckwourth Summit, and reaches its eastern terminus at Hallelujah Junction. □

11 KINGS CANYON SCENIC BYWAY
Sequoia National Forest   California

General description: A fifty-mile route that climbs through a giant sequoia forest, descends into one of North America's deepest canyons, and travels through a national park.

Special attractions: Giant sequoia trees, the Boole Tree, Chicago Stump, geology, waterfalls, wild & scenic river, Sequoia-Kings Canyon National Park, Boyden Cavern, Monarch Wilderness.

Location: Central California on the Sequoia National Forest. The byway travels California State Highway 180 between the national forest boundary east of Fresno and Cedar Grove in Sequoia-Kings Canyon National Park.

Byway route number: California State Highway 180.

Travel season: The western end is open year round as far as Hume Lake Road. The road east of there is closed by winter snows, generally from about early November through mid-April.

Camping: One national forest campground with picnic tables, fire grates, toilets, drinking water, and dump station. Four additional national forest campgrounds within seven miles of the byway. Seven national park campgrounds, with picnic tables, fire grills, drinking water, garbage cans, and toilets.

Services: Travelers services in Clingan's Junction, Grant Grove, and Cedar Grove, with limited availability. All services in nearby Fresno and Visalia.

Nearby attractions: Jennie Lakes Wilderness, downhill ski areas, Hume Lake, Fresno city attractions.

For more information: Sequoia National Forest, 900 W. Grand Ave., Porterville, CA 93257, (209) 784-1500. Hume Lake Ranger District, 35860 E. Kings Canyon Rd., Dunlap, CA 93621, (209) 338-2251. Sequoia and King's Canyon National Parks, Three Rivers, CA 93721, (209) 565-3456 or 565-3341.

Description: Kings Canyon Scenic Byway traverses an extraordinary cross section of geographical terrain, from deep inner canyons to broad vistas atop rolling mountains. The two-lane road is paved and has scenic pullouts. Traffic in summer can be moderately heavy but tapers off in September.

Temperatures on the byway vary according to elevation. Summer in the lower elevations ranges from sixty to ninety degrees; high elevations have cooler temperatures in the forties to seventies. Expect freezing temperatures around mid-September in the high country and in November at lower elevations.

Traveling the scenic byway from west to east, motorists can stop at the Hume Lake Ranger Station for national forest information. You'll then climb to the national forest boundary at about 3,000 feet elevation. Look for brightly colored hang-gliders soaring above, while around you stretch grassy foothills covered in manzanita, ceanothus, and deerbrush, with scattered California black oak, and some blue oak.

A scenic overlook at 5,000 feet provides views into the Miramonte and Dunlap area 3,000 feet below. Look eastward for giant sequoia thrusting skyward above the mixed conifers.

The byway climbs out of chaparral-type vegetation around Black Oak Flat and enters a coniferous forest of ponderosa pine, incense-cedar, and white fir. Also abundant is mountain misery (bear clover), a low-growing, oily, waxy-leaved aromatic shrub.

Happy Gap provides a view of Sequoia Lake to the north. The lake was developed as a water source for 1870s logging operations; today a YMCA camp operates on its shores. The byway encounters the first big sequoia trees just outside the national park entrance. Many of these sequoia are considered young, about eighty to 100 years old, but you may spot some 2,000-year-old giants.

National Park entrance fees can be waived for travelers who are simply traveling through the park on the scenic byway and are not using the park facilities. However, a complete scenic byway tour includes many park attractions so you should pay the entrance fee and enjoy the recreation opportunities.

Big Stump Grove at the entrance to Kings Canyon National Park affords you the first opportunity to get out and really look at the giant sequoia trees. Sequoias are the among the world's oldest and largest living things. Similar trees were widespread twenty million years ago, but today the giant sequoia is limited to a narrow belt of habitat in the Sierra Nevadas. Protection of these trees versus logging them is very controversial. Two of the largest trees in the world are located right near the scenic byway.

Stop at the Grant Grove Visitor Center, which provides information, exhibits, a slide program, maps, books, and national park personnel to answer your questions. There are three campgrounds and numerous walking trails around Grant Grove.

The General Grant Tree is the third-largest living tree in the world, and our nation's designated Christmas Tree. Its base diameter is over forty feet, its height is 267 feet, and the estimated weight of just the trunk is 1,251 tons. General Grant Tree is probably about 2,000 years old.

Continuing north on the byway, you'll again enter national forest. The McGee Fire Vista affords excellent views west to Delilah Lookout. Verplank and McKenzie ridges frame the vista. The Forest Service has replanted about 12,000 acres after a huge fire that swept through the area in 1954.

Spanish Mountain rises from the deep canyon below Kings Canyon Scenic Byway. Sequoia National Forest photo.

Cherry Gap, elevation 6,804 feet, was named for the abundant choke-cherries. The byway then descends to Converse Basin. Take a side trip into the grove to view the Boole Tree, largest of any tree in any national forest in the United States.

Stump Meadow, in Converse Basin, is an area of gigantic stumps left from the era of massive sequoia logging. In the late 1800s, prior to Forest Service ownership, over 8,000 giant sequoias were cut on this forest district.

Princess Campground provides ninety sites in a second-growth sequoia grove. A nearby wet meadow is full of sedges and rushes, and wildflowers such as shooting stars, wild parsley, and monkeyflowers brighten the edges. Blue jays and gray squirrels abound, mule deer occasionally wander through the campground, and you may see more black bears than you like. Keep all food locked securely away.

A side trip on Forest Road 13S09 leads to Hume Lake, and four additional national forest campgrounds. Hume Lake has a nice sandy beach for swimming, and the lake is stocked with rainbow trout. For a gorgeous view of Kings Canyon, take an easy walk on the east side of the lake, past the dam, and under the gate, on Forest Road 13S06 towards Lockwood Grove.

Back on the byway about two miles east of the Hume Lake turnoff, Bartons Overlook provides a stunning view of Kings Canyon, plus Spanish Peak and other high mountains to the north. The byway descends back into brush and chaparral, and in a wet year the hillsides blaze with the bright colors of poppies, popcorn flowers, and blue-eyed grass.

Junction Overlook looks northeast up the Middle Fork of Kings River towards the granite slabs of Tombstone Ridge, Spanish Mountain, Silver Spur,

11 KINGS CANYON SCENIC BYWAY

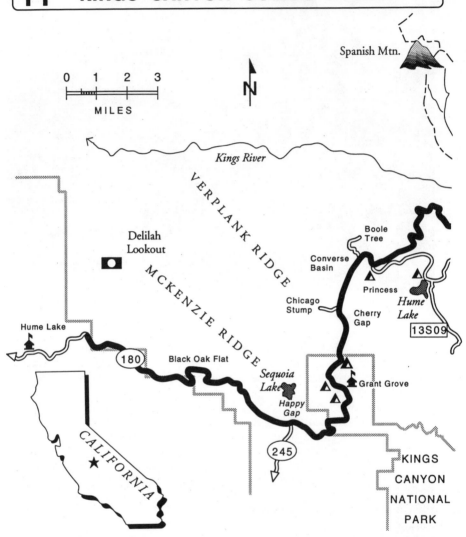

and the Obelisk. From the top of Spanish Mountain to the river is the steepest sustained drop in the continental United States. The summit soars to 10,051, and the river flows by at about 2,000 feet.

Yucca Point provides a fine view into Monarch Wilderness, which extends north and south on both sides of the byway. This 45,000-acre wilderness protects diverse habitats found at elevations between 2,000 and 11,000 feet. The rugged terrain is inhospitable, and includes spectacular and colorful geological formations. The canyon here is little more than a deep crack in the earth, with the highway clinging to the side and the river roaring below. You can hike the switchbacking trail down to the river and picnic or fish for rainbow trout in the river or in Tenmile Creek. Only artificial lures and

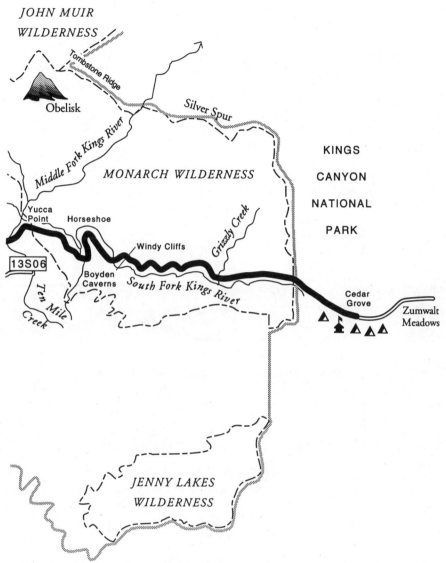

JOHN MUIR
WILDERNESS

Tombstone Ridge

Obelisk

Silver Spur

KINGS

CANYON

NATIONAL

PARK

Middle Fork Kings River

MONARCH WILDERNESS

Yucca
Point

Horseshoe

Grizzly Creek

Windy Cliffs

13S06

Boyden
Caverns

South Fork Kings River

Ten Mile
Creek

Cedar
Grove

Zumwalt
Meadows

JENNY LAKES
WILDERNESS

barbless hooks are permitted in this section of the Kings River.

Just before Horseshoe Bend, Redwood Creek pours over a 250-foot drop, making a lovely waterfall. Horseshoe Bend is a real engineering marvel. The route is cut into the cliffs, half tunneled under the massive rock face. Stop at the overlook and look down—the walls curl away beneath you, while below the river has carved a huge bend in solid rock.

Most of the Sierra Nevada are granite, but one long, continuous dike of limestone occasionally thrusts up. You can see it in Windy Cliffs and at Boyden Cavern. The highway has dropped down alongside the river here, where the canyon widens slightly. Boyden Cavern is a limestone cave, with stalactites, stalagmites, flowstone, and other formations. Tours are available.

The byway travels east through the Monarch Wilderness, in a transition zone of vegetation. Hot, dry south-facing slopes are covered in chaparral, while the cooler north-facing slopes host conifers. Between is the Wild & Scenic South Fork Kings River.

Walk the short, easy trail to Grizzly Falls, a very pretty waterfall just north of the highway. Picnicking is available. A little farther east, you can hike about a mile to Deer Cove, a moderate hike along the shady creek. Listen for mourning doves and various songbirds. Blue jays are abundant and usually raucous. The trail goes on to Wildman Meadow, a steep route well worth the energy.

The byway travels back into a mixed forest of incense-cedars, white firs, and ponderosa pine, and reenters Kings Canyon National Park. This glaciated valley opens up and provides wonderful views into Kings Canyon. Cedar Grove provides four national park campgrounds, numerous hiking trails, and another visitor center. The scenic byway ends at the road's end in Zumwalt Meadows. The return trip provides a new perspective on the route and is very rewarding. □

12 LAMOILLE CANYON ROAD
Humboldt National Forest   Nevada

General description: A twelve-mile road through a magnificent, glacially carved canyon with waterfalls and meadows of wildflowers.

Special attractions: Ruby Mountains Wilderness, sheer-walled cliffs, camping, picnicking, hiking, horseback riding, cross-country skiing, snowmobiling, fishing.

Location: Northeast Nevada on the Humboldt National Forest. The byway travels Route 660 southeast from the national forest boundary just south of Lamoille, to the end of the road.

Byway route number: Forest Road 660.

Travel season: The road is normally open from May through October, then closed by winter snows. The route is then popular with snowmobilers and cross-country skiers.

Camping: One national forest campground, with picnic tables, fire rings, toilets, and drinking water.

Services: All traveler services in nearby Elko. Services, with limited availability, in Lamoille.

Nearby attractions: Ruby Marshes, ghost towns, Southfork State Park.

For more information: Humboldt National Forest, 976 Mountain City Highway, Elko, NV 89801, (702) 738-5171. Ruby Mountains Ranger District, 428 South Humboldt (P.O. Box 246), Wells, NV 89835, (702) 752-3357.

Description: The Lamoille Canyon Road travels into the heart of the Ruby Mountains. The two-lane road is paved and has scenic turnouts. Traffic is very light, and the speed limit is thirty-five mph.

Summer daytime temperatures reach the eighties and nineties, and nights cool to the fifties. Expect afternoon thunderstorms in July and August. Spring and fall daytime temperatures are in the fifties and sixties, with nights down to the thirties and forties. Winter temperatures fall below freezing and snow usually covers the ground from November through May.

To find the byway, exit Interstate 80 in Elko. You can stop at the ranger station for maps, brochures, and national forest information. Ask for the self-guided auto tour to Lamoille Canyon.

Drive southeast on Highway 227. You can see the half-dome summit of 11,350-foot Ruby Dome, highest peak in the Rubies. This summit is more than 5,500 feet above the valley floor. Forest Road 660 begins near Lamoille, and the scenic byway starts at the national forest boundary, about 6,000 feet in elevation.

Lamoille Creek winds between banks lined with aspens and cottonwoods. The stream is stocked with brook and rainbow trout. Bitterbrush and sagebrush dot the slopes. Wildlife watchers may see mule deer, Rocky Mountain bighorn sheep, yellow-bellied marmots, cottontail rabbits, and coyotes in the canyon. Red-tailed hawks often soar on the thermals rising from the canyon floor. Mountain goats inhabit the higher elevations.

There is a picnic area near the old powerhouse, which supplied electricity to Elko and Lamoille between 1911 and 1971. A pressure pipe brought water 3,000 feet down the canyon, creating a water speed of 180 mph. This pressure powered the turbines and produced electricity. A 1971 fire destroyed the power plant, and today all that remains are the powerhouse foundation, pieces of the pipe, and a steel suspension bridge. Lilac bushes planted by powerhouse personnel have escaped and now are naturalized along the stream.

The Ruby Mountains were formed 300 million years ago by folding and faulting of the earth's crust. The range is long and narrow: about one hundred miles long, and only eight miles wide. Glaciers formed on the mountains

Lamoille Creek has cut a deep canyon through the Ruby Mountains of northeast Nevada. Humboldt National Forest photo.

during several ice ages, scouring out U-shaped canyons and leaving hanging valleys. Cirque lakes dot the high elevations, and ten summits reach over 10,000 feet elevation. A band of about one hundred wild horses inhabits the south end of the Ruby Mountains. The mountains were named by fortune-seeking soldiers, who found garnets and thought they were rubies.

The byway climbs the canyon wall above Lamoille Creek. Canyon walls soar thousands of feet overhead. Melting snow creates beautiful waterfalls that plunge down the canyon walls. An overlook provides a good view up Right Fork Canyon. Look for the old scaffolding clinging to the cliff; it supported the water flume for the power plant. The byway continues along the cliff and meets the creek bottom again near Thomas Canyon.

Thomas Canyon is a good example of a hanging valley, and you can hike along the creek and fish for brookies and rainbows. Thomas Creek Campground has forty-two campsites in a grove of aspen trees along the creek. The elevation here is 7,600 feet. The hiking trail is easy, meandering up the gentle canyon, past several waterfalls. It's about two miles to a beautiful meadow of wildflowers, at their peak in June and into July. There are lupine, iris, larkspur, columbine, penstemon, bluebells, Indian paintbrush, and sunflowers.

Bristlecone pines grow in Thomas Canyon. These stunted, gnarled trees are the oldest living things on earth. Some individual bristlecone pines are more than 4,000 years old!

The Changing Canyon Trail is an easy, self-guided path that identifies plant communities. You'll loop around past ponds along the creek, see beaver dams, and learn about lichen.

The byway climbs the canyon wall to Terraces, site of an old Civilian Conservation Corps camp. About two hundred workers lived at the mouth of the canyon in the 1930s and '40s and built the Lamoille Canyon Road. In the mid-'70s an avalanche roared through and wiped out the buildings—today all that remains are an old foundation and some rock stairs. You can picnic here and explore the area.

The byway meets the creek bottom again and travels through big grassy meadows along the wide meanders of the stream. Beavers have been especially busy along here. Sit quietly near a pond and watch them at work.

You'll see numerous avalanche chutes along the west slope as you drive to Roads End. The quaking aspen there are short, twisted, and gnarly from being broken by avalanches. It's particularly evident in the big chute descending from Island Lake, where the surviving trees are somewhat smashed, and have a decidedly downhill lean.

Road's End sits at elevation 10,800 feet, providing spectacular views, picnicking, and super hiking opportunities. The Ruby Mountain Wilderness surrounds you on three sides. You can hike a few miles of the forty-mile-long Ruby Crest National Scenic Trail. It's one mile in to Dollar Lakes and Lamoille Lake, through the tall white pines. A half-mile climb takes you up Liberty Pass, which offers vistas down into cirque lakes and down the length of the Rubies. Another mile of hiking brings you to Liberty Lake, where you can fish for brook trout and enjoy the beautiful mountain setting.

A different trail, also starting at Road's End, switchbacks up two miles to Island Lake, set in a rocky glacial cirque.

Ruby Mountain Wilderness protects about 90,000 acres of the Ruby Mountains. There are over a dozen lakes and about one hundred miles of hiking

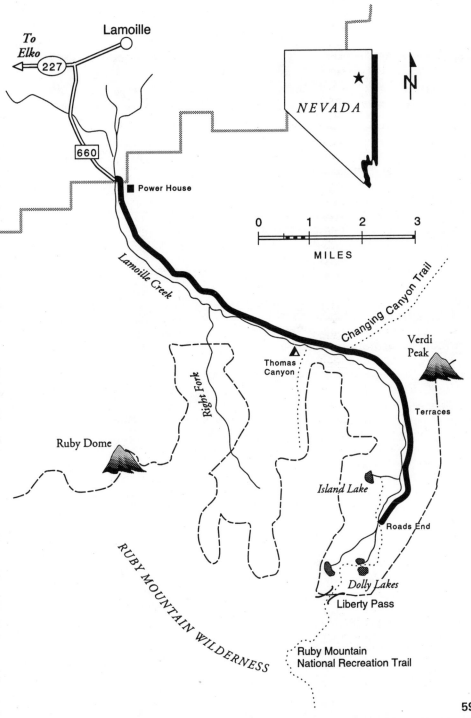

trails. Acres of alpine wildflowers adorn the slopes and meadows. Hikers may see bighorn sheep, mountain goats, mountain lions, mule deer, beavers, Himalayan snow cocks, and ruffed and blue grouse. Do try a hike in this area: the Ruby Mountain Wilderness is the real gem in this mountain range. □

13 PONDEROSA PINE SCENIC ROUTE
Boise, Challis, and Sawtooth National Forests Idaho

General description: A ninety-three mile highway along mountain streams, into the spectacular Sawtooth Mountains Recreation Area.

Special attractions: Outstanding mountain scenery, Sawtooth National Recreation Area, fishing, camping, and hiking.

Location: Central Idaho on the Boise, Challis, and Sawtooth national forests. The byway travels Highway 21 between Idaho City and Stanley.

Byway route number: Idaho State Highway 21.

Travel season: Year-round. Sections may be closed occasionally for snow removal.

Camping: Seven national forest campgrounds on or near the byway, with picnic tables, fire grates, toilets. Most campgrounds provide drinking water.

Services: All traveler services, with limited availability, in Stanley, Lowman, and Idaho City. All services in nearby Boise.

Nearby attractions: Sawtooth Wilderness; Sawtooth, Salmon River, and Payette scenic routes; Lucky Peak and Arrow Rock reservoirs.

For more information: Boise National Forest, 1750 Front Street, Boise, ID 83702, (208) 364-4100. Idaho City Ranger District, P.O. Box 129, Idaho City, ID 83631, (208) 364-4330. Lowman Ranger District, Lowman, ID 83637, (208) 364-4350. Challis National Forest, HC63 Box 1671 Highway 93, Challis, ID 83226, (208) 879-2285. Sawtooth National Forest, 1525 Addison Avenue East, Twin Falls, ID 83301, (208) 622-5371. Sawtooth National Recreation Area, Star Route (Highway 75), Ketchum, ID 83340, (208) 726-8291.

Description: Ponderosa Scenic Route encircles two sides of the magnificent Sawtooth Wilderness while traveling along several beautiful rivers. The two-lane road is paved, and traffic is light. Watch for logging trucks.

Summer daytime temperatures are usually in the sixties or high seventies and drop into the forties at night. Expect occasional short, severe afternoon thunderstorms. Spring and fall temperatures range from below freezing up to the seventies. Winter is generally well below freezing, but can reach the fifties some days or drop down below zero at other times. Most precipitation falls as snow between November and March.

The byway is very scenic driven in either direction. When driving south to north, the byway begins about thirty-eight miles north of Boise, in Idaho City. An interesting, self-guided tour tape increases your enjoyment and understanding of this byway. The tape is available at national forest offices in Boise, Idaho City, and Stanley.

Excluding the 1848 California Gold Rush, Idaho City and the Boise Basin were the West's biggest gold strikes. Mines around Idaho City produced close to thirty million ounces of gold, and the town supported two hundred businesses. The 1875 population was 6,200 people, of which only 360 were women. By 1914 the rush was over and Idaho City was nearly a full-fledged ghost town.

Today you can visit the Boise Basin Museum, look through a miner's cabin, and imagine life in the old Idaho Penitentiary. In winter there is an ice-skating rink in town, as well as nearby cross-country ski and snowmobile trails. The Idaho City Ranger Station has maps, permits, and information available. A community information center in town has seasonal displays about major fires or other events, and general information.

Traveling northeast on Highway 21 from Idaho City, the byway climbs alongside Mores Creek through a forest of ponderosa pine, Engelmann spruce, and Douglas-fir. A side trip east on Forest Road 327 leads to numerous undeveloped recreation opportunities, such as primitive camping, hiking, fishing, and watching wildlife.

On the byway, three campgrounds are within a mile of each other, at an elevation about a mile high. Each is situated in the cool, shady forest and provides drinking water. Ten Mile Campground has fourteen sites; Bad Bear provides eight sites; and Hayfork has six sites.

The route is quite narrow and winding, with switchbacking turns cut into the steep mountainside. Several scenic pullouts provide an opportunity to gaze across the vast, mountainous terrain. About fourteen miles from Idaho City you'll reach Mores Creek Summit, elevation 6,100 feet. As the route descends, you'll pass three cross-country ski trails: Whoop-Em-Up, Gold Fork, and Banner Ridge.

Just north of the ski trails, the byway enters a twenty-four mile stretch of fire-scarred timber. In 1989 lightning from one storm struck more than two thousand times an hour, and the resulting fires burned over 100,000 acres, 46,100 acres of which are the Loman fire. Eight wayside interpretive stops along the byway throughout the burned area explain the fire and its consequences.

Continuing along the scenic byway, Edna Creek Campground provides nine sites and drinking water. A side trip east on forty-two miles of dirt road leads to the town of Atlanta. It takes about an hour and a half to drive there, and you should plan to make a day of it. Call ahead for lodging, food, and various tourist activities. This nearly intact ghost town still has some active mining activities and is an interesting part of the American West.

The byway descends along Beaver Creek to Lowman, through what looks like a moonscape of fire-scarred slopes. The ranger station in Lowman has displays and provides area information, permits, maps, and interpretive materials.

A side trip west from Lowman leads through the South Fork Payette River Canyon. This is possibly the prettiest country in Idaho. Steep evergreen-covered mountains rise above the rocky, pristine white-water river. It's about twenty miles to Garden Valley, and you'll likely see people rafting and kayaking the white-water rapids. If you're interested, commercial outfitters can provide trips down the river.

The byway travels east out of Lowman, along the South Fork Payette River. There are wild bull and rainbow trout, as well as stocked rainbow trout. Fishing is excellent.

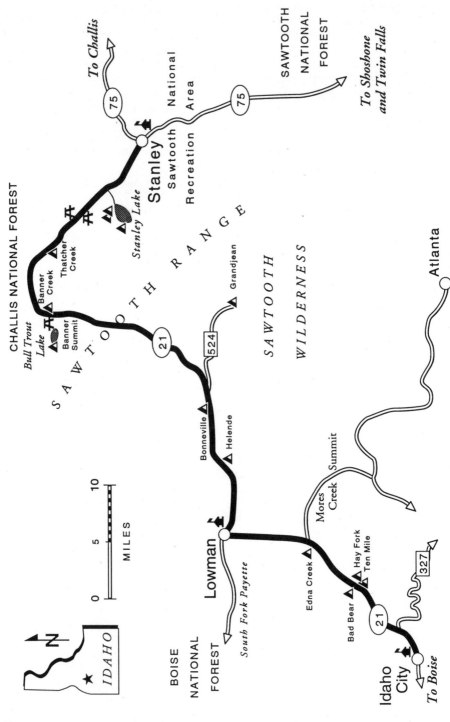

To Challis

75

SAWTOOTH NATIONAL FOREST

75

To Shoshone and Twin Falls

CHALLIS NATIONAL FOREST

Sawtooth National Recreation Area

Stanley

Stanley Lake

Thatcher Creek

Banner Creek

Banner Summit

Bull Trout Lake

S A W T O O T H   R A N G E

21

524

Grandjean

SAWTOOTH WILDERNESS

Atlanta

Bonneville

Helende

Mores Creek Summit

10

5

MILES

0

Lowman

South Fork Payette

BOISE NATIONAL FOREST

Edna Creek

Bad Bear

Hay Fork
Ten Mile

21

327

N

IDAHO

Idaho City

To Boise

The Boise National Forest is rich in wildlife. There are Rocky Mountain elk, mule deer, mountain lions, black bears, bald eagles, and numerous small rodents, along with occasional moose, bighorn sheep, and wolves. Bird watchers can listen for hummingbirds, sapsuckers, flycatchers, peewees, larks, swallows, wrens, catbirds, warblers, orioles, tanagers, and buntings, among many others. Raptors include hawks, ospreys, falcons, merlins, kestrels, and vultures.

Helende Campground provides ten sites in the cool forest and drinking water. Continuing on the highway, you'll get your first view of the spectacularly rugged Sawtooth Mountains. The range is protected by the 217,000-acre Sawtooth Wilderness.

The area traversed by the scenic byway is part of the gigantic Idaho batholith, a volcanic formation over 250 miles long and fifty miles wide. The primary rock type is basalt, a grayish volcanic rock that takes many forms. The Sawtooth Mountains are mostly granodiorite, a granite-like rock. The range was upthrust more than one million years ago. Glaciers have sculpted the dramatic peaks and valleys seen today. There are still some permanent ice fields near the high peaks.

Farther along the byway, Bonneville Campground provides nine campsites in the ponderosa pines. This scenic byway is named for the ponderosa pine, called ponderosa by an early naturalist for its heavy, ponderous wood.

A side trip east on Forest Road 524 leads to a natural hot springs, and a campground near Grandjean. There are numerous trailheads into the Sawtooth Wilderness from this road.

The byway leaves the South Fork Payette River and ascends Canyon Creek to Banner Summit. There is a good viewpoint at the summit, on the border between the Boise and Challis national forests. The highway now drops down alongside Banner Creek into more open countryside with bigger views. A side trip southwest on Forest Road 520 leads to Bull Trout Lake Campground, elevation 6,900 feet. There are nineteen campsites here, drinking water, and fishing opportunities.

On the byway, Banner Creek Campground provides drinking water and three campsites at elevation 6,800 feet. This campground is located at the confluence of Cape Horn and Banner creeks. These small creeks still support wild steelhead and salmon. The fish are born here, migrate nine hundred miles to the Pacific Ocean, spend three to four years growing in the ocean, then return to spawn. Some of the chinook king salmon weigh forty pounds. After spawning, the adults die, their eggs hatch, and the cycle is repeated.

The Frank Church-River of No Return Wilderness is just north of the byway. Combined with the nearby Gospel Hump and Selway-Bitterroot wilderness areas, there are 6,000 square miles of pristine wilderness protecting precious watersheds, wildlife habitat, virgin forests, and untrammeled wildlands.

Big meadows provide extensive views across the forest, to the surrounding mountains. Thatcher Creek Campground provides five campsites and drinking water.

Trap Creek Trailhead is located one mile west of the byway. You can hike three easy miles to Martin Lake or walk another two miles past two other lakes. It's a very pleasant trail.

The byway enters the Sawtooth National Recreation Area, a 756,000-acre area set aside for scenery and recreation. You can camp, hike, fish, backpack, mountain bicycle, float rivers, sail, climb mountains, and water-ski.

Ponderosa Pines.

A few miles south along the byway, a side trip west on Forest Road 455 leads to Stanley Lake, where you'll find three campgrounds, hiking and walking trails, a boat launch, and fishing.

The Ponderosa Pine Scenic Route continues south and ends in Stanley, a small community in the heart of the national recreation area. The views are splendid and recreation opportunities abound. A few miles south of town, the Stanley Ranger Station is located on Highway 75, where you can obtain further national forest information and maps and view the displays.

Every highway out of Stanley is a designated national forest scenic byway. South on Highway 75 is the Sawtooth Scenic Route, and north on 75 is the Salmon Scenic Route. Both scenic byways are described in this book. Enjoy! □

General description: A 161-mile route along the pristine Salmon River, between spectacular mountain ranges.

Special attractions: Frank Church-River of No Return Wilderness, Sawtooth National Recreation Area, Custer Motorway Adventure Road, river rafting, Idaho Centennial Regional Park, Lewis and Clark history, fishing, camping, rugged mountains.

Location: East-central Idaho on the Sawtooth, Challis, and Salmon national forests. The byway follows Highway 75 between Stanley and near Challis; and Highway 93 between Challis and the Idaho/Montana border.

Byway route numbers: Idaho State Highway 75 and U.S. Highway 93.

Travel season: Year-round.

Camping: Fourteen national forest or BLM campgrounds, with picnic tables, fire grates, toilets, drinking water.

Services: Traveler services, with limited availability, in Stanley, Challis, Salmon, and North Fork.

Nearby attractions: Ponderosa Pine and Sawtooth scenic routes; Sawtooth and Frank Church—River of No Return wildernesses; downhill and cross-country skiing; Big Hole National Battlefield.

For more information: Sawtooth National Recreation Area, Star Route (Highway 75), Ketchum, ID 83340, (208) 726-8291. Challis National Forest, HC63 Box 1671 Highway 93, Challis, ID 83226, (208) 879-2285.

Description: The Salmon Scenic Route travels through the spectacular mountains of central Idaho. The two-lane highway is paved and has scenic turnouts. Traffic is generally light, but summers can get busy between Stanley and Yankee Fork. Watch for logging trucks around Salmon.

Summer daytime temperatures are usually in the seventies to high eighties, and drop into the forties at night. Expect occasional short, severe afternoon thunderstorms. Spring and fall temperatures range from below freezing up to the seventies. Winter is generally well below freezing, but can reach the fifties some days, or drop down below zero at other times. Most precipitation falls as snow between November and March.

The byway is very scenic driven in either direction. When driving southwest to northeast, begin in Stanley, an old mining town now geared to tourism and recreation. The ranger station just south of town has national forest information, maps, and permits, as well as some interpretive displays and books to buy. You may wish to get the tour brochure for the Custer Motorway Adventure Road, a route located just off the scenic byway. Commercial outfitters in Stanley offer numerous recreation opportunities, including white-water and scenic floats, and backcountry trips.

Drive northeast on Highway 75, through the steeply incised Salmon River canyon. The scenic byway closely follows the winding course of the river. North-facing slopes are covered in Douglas-fir trees, while the hotter south-facing slopes support scattered Douglas-fir, grasses, and sage. Granite rock outcrops and sheer rock walls soar above the river bottom.

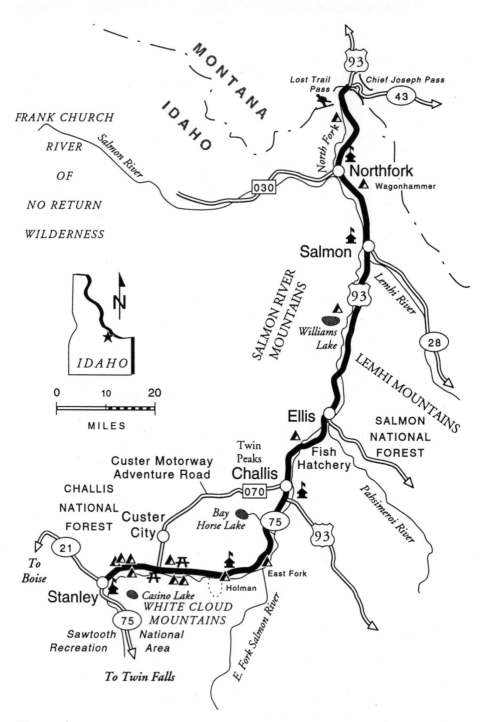

14 SALMON RIVER SCENIC ROUTE

MONTANA

IDAHO

FRANK CHURCH

RIVER

OF

NO RETURN

WILDERNESS

Salmon River

Lost Trail Pass

Chief Joseph Pass

93

43

North Fork

030

Northfork

Wagonhammer

Salmon

93

Lemhi River

SALMON RIVER MOUNTAINS

Williams Lake

LEMHI MOUNTAINS

28

N

IDAHO

0   10   20

MILES

SALMON NATIONAL FOREST

Ellis

Fish Hatchery

Pahsimeroi River

Twin Peaks

Cuser Motorway Adventure Road

CHALLIS NATIONAL FOREST

Challis

070

Custer City

Bay Horse Lake

75

93

To Boise

21

Holman

East Fork

Stanley

Casino Lake

WHITE CLOUD MOUNTAINS

75

Sawtooth Recreation   National Area

E. Fork Salmon River

To Twin Falls

Four campgrounds are situated within a few miles of each other along the river. Salmon River has thirty-two campsites; River Side provides eighteen; and Mormon Bend and Basin Creek each have seventeen. The campgrounds provide good fishing access for stocked rainbow trout. From winter through spring anglers may hook a steelhead; in late summer you may see spawning chinook salmon in the shallows. The salmon must come about 850 miles from the Pacific Ocean to their traditional spawning grounds here in the Salmon River. The elevation here is 6,100 feet above sea level. Mosquitoes can be brutal in mid-summer: bring repellent.

Hikers will enjoy an easy outing up Casino Creek. For a day trip, go the full six miles to Casino Lake. You could also do a nine-mile point-to-point hike, up Little Casino Creek and down Sunny Gulch. (Leave a vehicle at the Sunny Gulch Trailhead south of Stanley.) You'll get fantastic views of the Sawtooth Mountains, the White Clouds, and the Salmon River Canyon.

Sunbeam Dam is located about eleven miles east of Stanley. An interpretive display there explains some of the local history. This dam was originally built to provide power for the mines up Yankee Fork, but the mining operations were abandoned before the dam was ever used. However, it was a severe block for migrating fish and a portion of the dam has been blown out twice, perhaps by concerned fishermen?

You'll likely see lots of elk in this area in wintertime. About a mile west of the dam, Sunbeam Hot Springs pours 107-degree water into the river. An old CCC-built bathhouse is there, and bathers have piled rocks to create wonderful little hot pools next to the river. It's a delightful, rustic spot.

You might take a short or else day-long side trip on the Custer Motorway Adventure Road. This road follows the Yankee Fork into historic mining districts and ghost towns, and past a gold dredge, millsites, and cemeteries. Look for mountain goats on the slopes northwest of Bonanza. Custer City is just eight miles north of the scenic byway and has a historic walking tour and many interesting displays.

The forty-three-mile Custer Motorway Adventure Road is kept open during the summer months. The route from Sunbeam to Custer is paved or well-maintained gravel suitable for passenger cars. Between Custer and Challis is a narrow dirt road best suited for high-clearance vehicles. That stretch of road is not recommended for low-clearance autos, large motorhomes, or towed trailers.

Continuing east on the byway, Dutchman Flat Campground has five campsites in the forest of lodgepole pines. Across the river, Upper O'Brien and Lower O'Brien campgrounds each have fourteen campsites.

The byway twists and turns along the river. The canyon widens around Snyder Springs, and views open up to include the high peaks to the north. Continue east to Torrey's Hole, a popular takeout for river floaters. Farther along, Holman Creek Campground has twelve sites. There are lots of elk and deer inhabiting this area. A good hiking loop here leads up Holman Creek, across the ridge, and down Mill Creek. A few miles east of the campground, Yankee Fork Ranger Station has maps, books, displays, permits, and national forest information.

Bird watchers will find abundant birdlife in this byway region. Bald eagles and rough-legged hawks are here in winter. Osprey, Swainson's, and red-tailed hawks, and kestrels are here spring through fall. Migrating waterfowl include Canada geese, green-winged teals, mallards, northern pintails, goldeneyes, mergansers, and American wigeon. Songbirds here spring through fall include mountain bluebirds, northern flickers, broad-tailed hummingbirds, tree and barn swallows, western meadowlarks, robins, yellow warblers, and mourning doves.

A few hardy birds spend the entire year here: look for great horned owls, golden eagles, Cassin's finches, dark-eyed juncos, American dippers, black-billed magpies, and Clark's nutcrackers.

The byway turns north around East Fork Campground, a BLM area with eight campsites located right at the confluence of the East Fork Salmon and Main Salmon rivers. Spring and fall are good times to try a hike up Malm Gulch to the petrified forest located a few miles up the rough dirt road. Continuing along the course of the Salmon River, the valley widens and supports ranching and farming activities. BLM's Bay Horse Campground provides nine sites along the edge of the river, elevation 5,400 feet. Highway 75 continues north, and ends at the junction of Highways 75 and 93.

The scenic byway now follows U.S. Highway 93 north. However, a two-mile side trip south on Highway 93, then four miles north, brings you to a delightful little hot springs. Challis Hot Springs is a developed area, with a hot pool, picnicking, and camping opportunities.

An interpretive center at the junction of Highways 75 and 93 provides area information, local mining history, and maps. Keep your eyes open for Rocky Mountain bighorn sheep in this area. Follow 93 north into Challis, a small community offering backcountry and river expeditions, charter plane rides, lodges, and small shops. A side trip west on Forest Road 070 is part of the Custer Motorway Adventure Road. This narrow dirt road is best suited for high clearance vehicles.

Twin Peaks rise to the northwest. These are volcanic cones, once hidden

Autumn is a beautiful time to travel the Salmon River Scenic Route. Osborn photo.

in a huge caldera. The caldera has eroded, leaving the twin mountains jutting up prominently.

North of Challis the byway runs through more open ranching country. Warm springs keep the ground a bit swampy and clear of snow in winter. Bright oranges and reds of the sandstone river bluff brighten the landscape. A BLM campground provides a few campsites along the river.

Take a short side trip at Ellis to the fish hatchery on the Pahsimeroi River. You can see the salmon and steelhead operations, and learn about these interesting, anadromous fish. Continue south up the Pahsimeroi Valley for a lovely drive through an isolated, rural mountain valley.

The byway continues north along the Salmon River, through a dry, arid region of hills and mountains. The Salmon River Mountains rise to the west; the Lemhi Mountains to the east. A side trip west leads to Williams Lake Campground, with fifteen sites in the Douglas-fir and ponderosa pines along the lake. A resort and marina are also located on Williams Lake.

The community of Salmon is located at the confluence of the Lemhi and Salmon rivers. The national forest headquarters provides national forest information, maps, permits, and interpretive materials and displays. Salmon is home to a number of river runners and backcountry outfitters. A small museum informs you about local history. For a taste of the real ranching west of today, take a very pretty side trip up Highway 28, through the rural Lemhi River valley.

Continuing north on the byway, you travel through a dry, arid region, very hot in sumertime. Wagonhammer Springs has four campsites on a little bench above the springs. The water there is excellent: fill your jugs.

As you continue north, ponderosa pines, Douglas-fir, sagebrush, and grasses grow on the slopes above the river canyon. Located at the confluence of the North Fork and Main Salmon rivers, the tiny community of Northfork is geared to river rafting. The ranger station provides national forest information, maps, permits, and interpretive materials. You could take a side trip west on Forest Road 030, following the river past a number of picnicking and camping areas. This is a very popular and busy rafting area.

The byway now climbs alongside the tiny North Fork, past residences scattered in the heavily timbered steep slopes. The forest is predominately Douglas-fir, subalpine fir, and Engelmann spruce. Watch for logging trucks in this narrow canyon.

You're following the route of Lewis and Clark, who crossed Lost Trail Pass on their 1804-5 exploration of the West. Chief Joseph also used a portion of this route, leading his people on the historic and tragic Flight of the Nez Pearce.

Twin Creek Campground provides forty-six sites in the forest. Anglers can cast for little rainbow and cutthroat trout. The byway ascends the final leg of Lost Trail Pass, elevation 6,995 feet. The byway ends at the Idaho/Montana border.

At the top a historic marker is informative. Nearby, Lost Trail Ski Area provides excellent downhill skiing. Numerous cross-country ski areas are found atop both Lost Trail Pass and nearby Chief Joseph Pass. If you continue down Lost Trail Pass a short ways, you can end your byway tour with a relaxing soak in Lost Trail Hot Springs. □

15 SAWTOOTH SCENIC BYWAY
Sawtooth National Forest   Idaho

General description: A sixty-one-mile route from volcanic desert sagebrush lands into spectacularly rugged mountains.

Special attractions: Sawtooth National Recreation Area, Sawtooth Wilderness, downhill and cross-country skiing, camping, lakes and streams, historic mining areas, fishing, hiking, geology.

Location: South-central Idaho on the Sawtooth National Forest. The byway travels Highway 75 between Shoshone and Stanley.

Byway route number: Idaho State Highway 75.

Travel season: Year-round.

Camping: Fifteen national forest campgrounds, with picnic tables, fire grates, toilets, drinking water.

Services: All traveler services, with limited availability, in Shoshone, Bellevue, Hailey, Ketchum, and Stanley. All services in nearby Twin Falls.

Nearby attractions: Craters of the Moon National Monument; Salmon River, Payette River, and Ponderosa Pine scenic routes.

For more information: Sawtooth National Forest, 2647 Kimberly Road East, Twin Falls, ID 83301-7976, (208) 737-3200. Sawtooth National Recreation Area, Star Route (Highway 75), Ketchum, ID 83340, (208) 726-7672. Stanley Ranger Station - SNRA, Stanley, ID 83278, (208) 774-3681. Ketchum Ranger District, Sun Valley Road (Box 2356), Ketchum, ID 83340, (208) 622-5371.

Description: The Sawtooth Scenic Byway traverses a wonderland of rugged alpine peaks and deep glaciated valleys. The two-lane highway is paved, with frequent scenic turnouts. Traffic is moderately busy in summer and light the rest of the year.

Summer daytime temperatures are usually in the sixties or high seventies, and drop into the forties at night. Expect occasional short, severe afternoon thunderstorms. Spring and fall temperatures range from below freezing up to the seventies. Winter is generally well below freezing, but can reach the fifties some days, or drop below zero at other times. Most precipitation falls as snow between November and March.

The byway is very scenic driven in either direction. When driving south to north, begin in Shoshone, just north of Twin Falls. Sawtooth Scenic Route follows Highway 75 north, through black volcanic flows and a sage-covered high desert landscape.

In summer you can visit the Shoshone Ice Caves, which are volcanic lava tubes in the middle of these vast lava plains. Tour guides explain the year-round ice, prehistoric Indian history and wildlife, and the geologic significance of this formation.

A side trip west on U.S. Highway 20 leads to Magic Reservoir, very popular with those who enjoy boating, water-skiing, windsurfing, and fishing.

The highway travels through the Big Wood River Valley, cradled between the Smoky Mountains to the west, and the Pioneer Mountains to the east. To the northeast you can see 12,078-foot Mount Hyndman, the highest peak on the Sawtooth National Forest.

Sawtooth Scenic Byway offers abundant outdoor recreation.

The communities of Ketchum and nearby Sun Valley offer multiple recreation opportunities. Bald Mountain Ski Area is world-renowned for downhill skiing. If you're visiting in summer and in good shape, hike or bicycle the strenuous Centennial Trail, from the base of the ski mountain to the top.

Byway information is available at the district ranger's office in Ketchum. They have maps, general information, and self-guiding automobile tour tapes. You can tour the historic Ore Wagon Museum, which houses mining wagons used to haul ore in the late 1800s. Once a year these wagons are brought out for the Labor Day parade.

Ketchum was a favorite getaway for Ernest Hemingway. He'd likely be surprised at the Ketchum of today. Resorts provide lots of activities, there are numerous festivals and celebrations, shops and restaurants, as well as a year-round skating rink.

The byway enters the Sawtooth National Forest about eight miles north of Ketchum. Four miles farther north, stop at the Sawtooth National Recreation Area (SNRA) Headquarters and Visitor Information Center. Here you'll find abundant recreation and visitor information, including displays on multiple resource use, wildlife, and recreation, as well as books on history, flora, and fauna, and a video screening room with a large library of videos for children and adults. A self-guiding automobile tour tape guides you from here to Stanley, and is a wealth of information. You can buy the tape at the visitor center, or borrow it.

The SNRA encompasses 756,000 acres and includes three mountain ranges and the headwaters of five major Idaho rivers. Recreation opportunities include camping, float boating, swimming, picnicking, interpretive sites, hiking, bicycling, fishing, cross-country skiing, horseback riding, and snowmobiling.

Across from the visitor center, North Fork Campground provides thirty sites in an aspen grove along the Big Wood River. Anglers cast for rainbow trout in the river. The elevation here is 6,280 feet. Nearby, Wood River Campground has thirty-two campsites. Naturalists present summer programs in the amphitheater. Topics include plants and animals, history, and geology. A short, self-guiding interpretive trail leads you through the wetlands along the river. The Cave Trail is great for kids, and ends at a cave carved out by the river.

The SNRA is home to more than three hundred species of wildlife, including several endangered species. Big game includes mule deer, elk, pronghorn antelope, mountain goats, bighorn sheep, and black bears. There are also coyotes, snowshoe hares, blue grouse, spruce grouse, numerous waterfowl, martens, mink, beavers, and other animal species.

The byway climbs up to Easley and Boulder View campgrounds. Each provides ten campsites scattered amongst the willows and aspen trees. You can swim and fish in the river, or go soak in the natural hot water plunge.

Continuing up the byway, the Smoky Mountains rise to the west. This range was named because of careless settlers and campers who started forest fires. To the north, the Boulder Mountains are rich in silver, gold, lead, zinc, and copper. Mining activities have occurred in the Boulders from 1879 into this century. The mineral-rich soils affect the quaking aspen trees, which provide spectacular autumn colors. Normally, aspens are a yellow-gold color in autumn, but here at the base of the Boulder Mountains they turn gold, yellow, orange, and red.

Baker Creek is a popular winter snowmobile area. A few miles farther, Prairie Creek has several groomed cross-country ski trails. In summer you can drive the Prairie Creek Road to Mill Lake trailhead. Roundtrip, this is a 4.5-mile hike with just over 1,000 feet elevation gain. The canyon and peaks are beautiful. For a day hike, try the 10.7-mile loop on the Miner and Prairie Lakes trails. This route provides great views of the canyon and out to the high peaks.

The byway continues along the Big Wood River. The lodgepole and subalpine fir forest is interspersed with open meadows and views of the Boulder Mountains. As the route climbs, you'll travel through an open riparian area, thick with red- and gold-stemmed willows, and quaking aspen. Beavers have been very busy through here, and the ponds provide good trout fishing. Engelmann spruce and Douglas-fir grow on the slopes above the river bottom.

Galena has a historic lodge and numerous recreation opportunities, including mountain bicycling trails. This near-ghost town is named for the kind of lead ore taken from the mountains.

Wildflowers are abundant in this area. Look for flowers such as mariposa, fireweed, shooting star, penstemon, cinquefoil, elephanthead, sulphur flower, lupine, camas, and arrowleaf balsamroot.

The byway twists and turns along a terraced hillside. An old sheep driveway severely eroded the hill here, and the terraces are part of a rehabilitation effort. They stabilize the hillside from erosion and allow the vegetation a chance to grow. A quarter-mile south of Galena Summit you can hike 2.5 miles to Titus Lake. There are scenic views of the peaks along the trail, and you'll be well away from any civilization. Try a refreshing plunge into the cold water! From there, turn around and climb back to your car, or continue down the more challenging 3.5 miles along Titus Creek to Galena Lodge. This makes a great day hike.

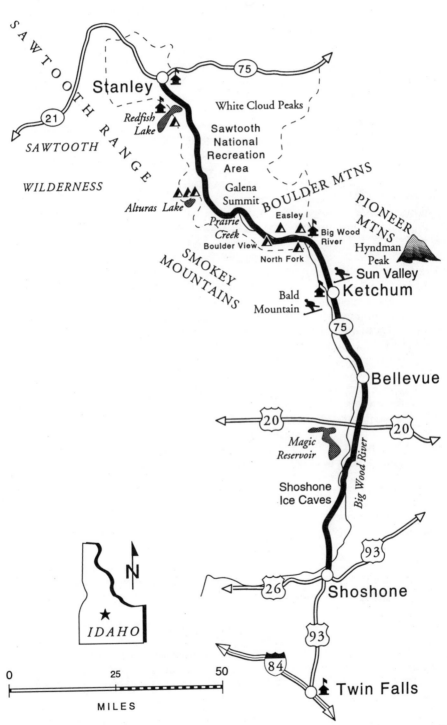

Galena Summit lies at 8,701 feet. This is a subalpine environment, supporting only hardy subalpine firs, Douglas-firs, and whitebark pines, as well as low-growing forbs and grasses. Dead trees, called snags, are evidence of the harshness of winter at this high elevation. Galena Summit divides the Big Wood River and Salmon River drainages. You can see numerous avalanche chutes from the road.

Galena Overlook is located about a mile west of the pass. You'll get an incredible view of the Sawtooth Mountain Range and Valley. The range is about thirty miles long and fifteen miles wide. The valley below has big, rounded glacial moraines covered with timber. Also visible from the overlook are the headwaters of the Salmon River. Signs at the overlook explain the features of the area.

The scenic byway descends into the valley, headwaters of the Salmon River. Chinook and sockeye salmon come nine hundred miles from the Pacific Ocean—up the Columbia, Snake, and Salmon rivers—to spawn here in the place of their birth. They travel about twelve miles a day, upriver against the current, rapids, and numerous manmade obstacles.

In springtime keep your eyes open to see greater sandhill cranes in the wet meadows around Sawtooth City. A little farther along the byway, take a side trip to Alturas Lake. A natural sand beach is a good place for swimming. You can also camp, fish, boat, picnic, day hike, and sail. The three campgrounds have a total of sixty campsites available.

The byway continues north, through pastoral ranchlands and scattered buildings. The Sawtooth Range rises to the west. The pinkish rocks at this northern end of the range are part of the Sawtooth Batholith, which intruded twenty-five million years ago into the grayish 110-million-year-old Idaho Batholith. About one million years ago, the area was uplifted into these mountains, then eroded and sculpted by glaciers. Some small icefields still remain in the high peaks.

The Sawtooth Wilderness protects most of the Sawtooth Range. There are forty-two peaks over 10,000 feet in the wilderness, as well as the headwaters for four major rivers. Nearly 300 miles of trails traverse the wilderness, which is a wonderland of lakes, waterfalls, timbered slopes, grassy meadows, rugged peaks, deep gorges, and glacial basins.

Continuing north on the byway, the White Cloud Peaks are visible to the east. In summer stop to tour the interesting Sawtooth Hatchery. The hatchery raises chinook and sockeye salmon, as well as steelhead trout. Annually, this operation collects four million steelhead trout eggs for other hatcheries, and raises three million steelhead right here. Each steelhead female carries between 4,500 to 6,000 eggs. The young steelhead are released, in an attempt to replace the multitudes killed during migration.

The visitor center at Redfish Lake has exhibits explaining area history and prehistory, geology, and fisheries. Picture windows provide a fantastic view across the lake to the Sawtooth Wilderness. Naturalists present evening interpretive programs in the amphitheater, and a .25-mile barrier-free interpretive trail winds through a wetland ecosystem.

There are eight campgrounds scattered along Redfish and Little Redfish lakes, with a total of 201 campsites. You'll find a store, restaurant, lodging, boat tours and rentals, horseback riding, and fishing for Dolly Varden, rainbow trout, and small landlocked kokanee salmon. Hikers can choose from many trails. Try the easy Fishhook Creek Trail, which winds two miles through the forest along the creek. The Bench Lakes Trail makes a perfect long afternoon hike and provides outstanding views down to the lake, and up to the high peaks.

Back on the byway, you'll drive through the forest of lodgepole pines and emerge into the sage flats and rolling hills around Stanley. The Salmon River is beautiful. Stop at the Stanley Ranger Station for maps and information, then continue into Stanley, the end of the scenic byway.

Stanley is a historic mining town, still full of little cabins and old buildings. Additionally, there are modern services available. The views of the mountains surrounding the town are spectacular.

The two other highways out of Stanley are also designated national forest scenic byways: the Salmon River Scenic Route runs east on Highway 75; and the Ponderosa Pine Scenic Route travels west on Highway 21. □

16 TETON SCENIC BYWAY
Targhee National Forest   Idaho

General description: A twenty-mile route from pastoral valley ranchlands up through a narrow river gorge, and across a mountain pass.
Special attractions: Wildlife, fishing, camping.
Location: Eastern Idaho on the Targhee National Forest. The byway follows Highway 31 between Swan Valley and Victor.
Byway route number: Idaho State Highway 31.
Travel season: Year-round.
Camping: One national forest campground, with picnic tables, fire rings, toilets, drinking water.
Services: All traveler services, with limited availability, in Swan Valley and Victor.
Nearby attractions: Palisades Reservoir, Grand Tetons, cross-country and downhill skiing, South Fork Snake River, Mesa Falls National Forest Scenic Byway.
For more information: Targhee National Forest, 420 North Bridge Street (P.O. Box 208), St. Anthony, ID 83445, (208) 624-3151. Palisades Ranger District, P.O. Box 398B Route 1, Idaho Falls, ID 83401, (208) 523-1412.

Description: The Teton Scenic Byway travels through rural Idaho and crosses a mountain pass. The two-lane highway is paved and has occasional turnouts. Traffic is moderately light. Snow tires or chains are advised in winter.

This designated national forest scenic byway is part of the longer, state-designated Teton Scenic Route, which travels between Idaho Falls and Ashton. The following description covers only the designated national forest scenic byway.

Summer temperatures are generally in the seventies to eighties, and nights can drop to the forties. Spring and fall days are often into the fifties and sixties, but may also drop below freezing. Winter highs average in the twenties to

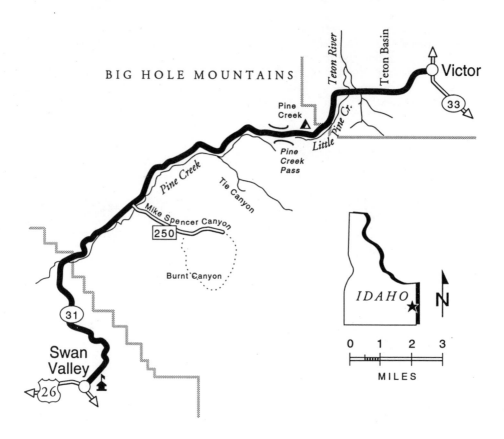

thirties, dropping below zero at times. Most precipitation falls as snow between October and April.

The byway is very scenic driven in either direction. When driving southwest to northeast, begin in the small community of Swan Valley. You can obtain national forest information, maps, and other publications at the Swan Valley Work Center. Drive north on Highway 31, through agricultural lands. The primary crops through here are wheat, barley, and hay, along with cattle and horses. The southern end of the Big Hole Mountains rise out of the forested background.

The Targhee National Forest begins about five miles from Swan Valley. You'll immediately enter the mouth of Pine Creek Canyon. The byway crosses

The Teton Scenic Route meanders through agricultural lands as well as wild lands.

the bridge over a deep and very narrow rocky gorge, and winds for a mile through the narrow canyon. Douglas-fir and lodgepole pines grow on the north and northwest-facing slopes, while mountain mahogany, juniper, and aspens grow on the south and southeast-facing slopes. Willows and dogwoods line the creek bottom, with chokecherry and hawthorns scattered throughout.

The highway emerges from the gorge into a narrow, flat canyon bottom of small meadows. You can pull off and fish for rainbow and cutthroat trout in Pine Creek or have a picnic along the stream. A short side trip east up Mike Spencer Canyon (Forest Road 250) brings you to opportunities for primitive, dispersed camping and hiking. You could walk a moderately strenuous eight-mile loop hike, up Burnt Canyon and back down Mike Spencer Canyon.

The byway begins to climb in earnest around Tie Canyon. The road is steep and winds through the forest, composed primarily of lodgepole pine and Douglas-fir. Patches of aspen break up the evergreens. While ascending the pass, you'll get several good views to the west, over open sagebrush ridges to the forested mountains beyond. Pine Creek Pass reaches 6,800 feet elevation. A pullout allows you a leisurely view over the surrounding area.

Wildflowers along the byway include buttercups, Indian paintbrush, and mules-ear. Elk, mule deer, moose, black bears, and coyotes inhabit the region. Bird watchers can look for ravens, bluebirds, hawks, and grouse.

The highway descends from the pass. En route, Pine Creek Campground provides eleven campsites in the forest. You'll follow the gentle drop along Little Pine Creek, leave the national forest and drive into Teton Basin. Hay, cows, and horses, and wheat and barley are raised here. Numerous creeks combine to form the headwaters of the Teton River, which offers excellent fishing and good bird-watching opportunities. The byway ends in the small community of Victor. □

General description: A seventy-mile highway through the mountains, forests, and ranchlands of central Montana.

Special attractions: Limestone canyons, historic mines and buildings, fishing, hunting, camping, snowmobiling, downhill and cross-country skiing.

Location: Central Montana on the Lewis & Clark National Forest. The byway travels U.S. Highway 89 between the junction of Highways 89 and 12 near White Sulphur Springs and the junction of Highways 89 and 87, near Belt.

Byway route number: U.S. Highway 89.

Travel season: Year-round.

Camping: Four national forest campgrounds, with picnic tables, fire grates, toilets, and drinking water. Numerous opportunities for dispersed, primitive camping.

Services: All traveler services in White Sulphur Springs, with limited availability. Lodging in Neihart and a cafe near Monarch. All services in nearby Great Falls.

Nearby attractions: C.M. Russell Museum, Giant Springs State Park, natural hot springs, Missouri River.

For more information: Lewis & Clark National Forest, P.O. Box 871, Great Falls, MT 59403, (406) 791-7700. Kings Hill Ranger District, P.O. Box A, White Sulphur Springs, MT 59645, (406) 547-3361.

Description: Kings Hill Scenic Byway crosses the Little Belt Mountains with their beautiful mountain vistas and limestone outcrops. The two-lane route is paved and has frequent pullouts; most of it has wide shoulders. Traffic is light to moderate.

Summer weather in central Montana is very pleasant. Daytime temperatures are usually in the seventies or eighties, and nights are cooler, down to the forties and fifties. Spring and fall often have days in the fifties and sixties and nights down to freezing. Winter is cold, but frequent sunny days make the freezing temperatures quite tolerable. Deep snow generally covers the ground from December through March.

The byway is scenic when driven from either direction. When driving north, begin in White Sulphur Springs. A visit to the natural hot springs is always a pleasure, and you can tour the historic Castle.

The byway begins at the junction of Highways 12 and 89. Drive north on 89, through productive ranchland and hay meadows. The Castle Mountains rise to the east, the Big Belt Mountains form the western skyline, and the Little Belt Mountains dominate the north. Douglas-fir and ponderosa pine dot the hillsides.

A mile and a half from Butler Hill, a side road leads west to Newlan Creek Reservoir, stocked with rainbow trout. The byway follows Newlan Creek, which offers decent fishing for small cutthroat and brook trout. The byway enters national forest lands about ten miles from its beginning.

A side trip northwest on Forest Road 119 leads to Sheep Creek's dispersed

78

primitive camping, in a large meadow about six miles from the byway. Bring your own drinking water.

On the byway, Jumping Creek Campground provides eleven sites sheltered under big Engelmann spruce. Mosquitoes can be thick at times. Some sites are barrier-free.

The highway runs through a corridor of lodgepole pines and Douglas-firs, with scattered stands of aspen that are very pretty in autumn.

Kings Hill Pass is the highest pass open all winter in Montana. The elevation at the pass is 7,393 feet, and annual snowfall in this area averages twenty-three feet. Nearby, Showdown Winter Sports Area offers downhill skiing. In summer you can drive to the top of the ski area and enjoy the view from Porphyry Lookout at 8,192 feet. The lookout is open in July and August and provides great views of the surrounding Little Belt Mountains, including Big Baldy Mountain (9,175 feet) to the northeast, Yogo Peak (8,801 feet) to the east, and Black Butte (6,795 feet) to the west. On a clear day you can see south to the Absaroka Range near Yellowstone National Park.

On the west side of the road, Kings Hill Campground has fifteen sites in the shady lodgepole pine forest. Across the highway, a forest service cabin is available to rent. Make arrangements to rent the cabin in advance at the ranger station in White Sulphur Springs. You can cross-country ski from the top of the pass on the Ranch Creek and Deadman trails.

A few miles north of the pass, snowmobilers and cross-country skiers have separate trail systems which begin at the snowmobile parking lot. The Silvercrest Cross-Country Ski Trail System provides about eleven miles of groomed ski trails. Snowmobilers can follow over a hundred miles of groomed trails on both sides of the highway.

A side trip on Chamberlain Road, Forest Road 3328, connects with the Jefferson Creek Road, Forest Road 267. This eighteen-mile loop gets you up to some nice scenic views and many recreation opportunities, such as dispersed camping, fishing, hunting, and finding solitude.

The byway now follows the gentle grade of Belt Creek. Many Pines Campground has twenty-three sites in the lodgepole pines. Anglers usually have good luck fishing for small rainbow trout.

Less than a mile from the Jefferson Road turnoff, turn east off the highway onto a very short road. The trailhead to Memorial Falls leads an easy .5 mile to the base of this very pretty falls.

The byway reaches Neihart, a small community founded when silver and lead were discovered in 1881. Sapphires worth more than three million dollars were taken from nearby mines. Today mining has ceased, and a few old historic buildings remain, such as one housing Wu Tang Laundry and Drugs. Neihart has some lodging and one cafe. You can still find interesting rocks and minerals in the old mine dumps. North of town, big outcrops of limestone jut above the highway. Roadcuts have exposed Precambrian basement rocks, part of our continental crust. Some are very interesting, such as quartz, pink and white feldspar, and black mica.

About five miles north of Neihart, Aspen Campground has six sites in the lodgepoles. A half-mile farther north, the Belt Creek Information Station is open year round and has national forest information. Trailheads lead east and west from the station; hike east about ten miles to Big Baldy Mountain, the highest on the district. The route goes through the timber and follows Pioneer Ridge to the summit. For an easier stroll, the trail west of the information station

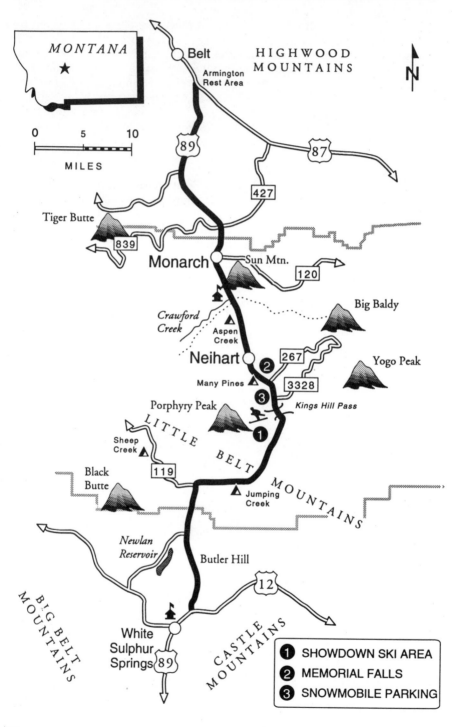

MONTANA

0   5   10
MILES

N

Belt
HIGHWOOD MOUNTAINS

Armington Rest Area

89

87

427

Tiger Butte

839

Monarch
Sun Mtn.
120

Crawford Creek

Big Baldy

Aspen Creek

Neihart
267
Yogo Peak

Many Pines
3328

Porphyry Peak
Kings Hill Pass

LITTLE

Sheep Creek

119

BELT

Black Butte

MOUNTAINS

Jumping Creek

Newlan Reservoir
Butler Hill

12

BIG BELT MOUNTAINS

White Sulphur Springs
89

CASTLE MOUNTAINS

1 SHOWDOWN SKI AREA
2 MEMORIAL FALLS
3 SNOWMOBILE PARKING

Kings Hill Scenic Byway travels alongside pretty streams, through the forested mountains of central Montana. Lewis & Clark National Forest photo.

wanders a few miles up Crawford Creek. You can enjoy the forest, fish for little brookies, and watch for wildlife such as mule deer and elk. Some black bears also inhabit the region.

Look overhead for soaring raptors such as golden eagles, red-tailed hawks, and goshawks. Wildflowers such as pasqueflower, trillium, and ladyslippers brighten the meadows and forest along the byway.

The byway continues through ponderosa pine, lodgepole pine, and quaking aspens. Lodgepoles are so-named because their straight, narrow trunks made excellent teepee poles. Sun Mountain dominates the foreground.

Monarch is nearly a ghost town, but once was the scene of frantic silver mining. Many of the limestone outcroppings around Monarch contain interesting fossils. A side trip east on gravel Forest Road 120 opens up opportunities for dispersed camping and recreation.

The byway leaves national forest lands and travels through the steep white cliff walls of Monarch Canyon, past a challenging stretch of springtime white water known as the Belt Creek Sluice Boxes. The highway enters agricultural lands in the prairie-type environment. Tiger Butte dominates the western countryside.

You can watch beavers near the Isaac Walton Rest Area. The byway ends a little farther north at Armington Rest Area, at the junction of Highways 89 and 87. □

18 NORTH FORK HIGHWAY
Shoshone National Forest   Wyoming

General description: A 27.5-mile canyon highway along the North Fork Shoshone River to the east entrance of Yellowstone National Park.

Special attractions: North and South Absaroka wilderness areas, Washakie Wilderness, unusual rock formations, beautiful river, camping, downhill and cross-country skiing.

Location: Northwest Wyoming on the Shoshone National Forest. The byway travels Highways 14/16/20 west from the national forest boundary near Cody to the Yellowstone National Park boundary.

Byway route numbers: U.S. Highways 14, 16, 20.

Travel season: The scenic byway is open year-round. The continuation of the highway into Yellowstone National Park is open from about April through mid-November.

Camping: Ten national forest campgrounds, with picnic tables, fire grates, toilets, drinking water.

Services: All traveler services in Cody.

Nearby attractions: Yellowstone National Park; Buffalo Bill State Park, Reservoir, Historic Center, and Old Trail Town; Chief Joseph Scenic Highway; Beartooth National Forest Scenic Byway.

For more information: Shoshone National Forest, 225 West Yellowstone Avenue, P.O. Box 2140, Cody, WY 82414-2140, (307) 527-6241. Wapiti Ranger District, 203A West Yellowstone Avenue, P.O. Box 1840, Cody, WY 82414, (307) 527-6921.

Description: The North Fork Highway travels through a wide canyon carved by the pristine North Fork of the Shoshone River. President Theodore Roosevelt called this the fifty most beautiful miles in America. The two-lane highway is paved and has numerous scenic turnouts. Traffic in summer is fairly constant and light the remainder of the year. The North Fork Highway is open year round to Pahaska Tepee, but the continuation of the highway in Yellowstone National Park is plowed and open only from about April through mid-November.

Weather in this region is highly variable, but bright sunshine is the norm. Frost and snow could occur any day of the year. Generally, summer temperatures range from highs in the eighties down to the mid-fifties. Afternoon thunderstorms are common, especially in the high elevations. Spring and fall often have days in the forties to sixties and nights below freezing. Winter is very cold and can dip well below zero.

The byway is very scenic driven from either direction. Driving east to west, begin with a stop in Cody. There you'll find quite a few interesting places. The Buffalo Bill Historical Center is a complex which includes the Whitney Gallery of Western Art and the Buffalo Bill, Plains Indian, and Winchester museums. Old Trail Town has historic buildings and a museum with Indian relics and frontier guns. Rodeos run every night of the summer. You can do the walking tour of town, and art galleries and shops make interesting browsing.

The huge, tilted anticline of Rattlesnake Mountain dominates the western horizon, and the highway tunnels through the core of the mountain to emerge at Buffalo Bill Dam, built in 1910. Buffalo Bill State Park provides numerous recreation opportunities to fish, swim, boat, and camp. A multi-agency visitor center should be complete in 1993.

The highway crosses to the south side of the river, and the Chinese Wall is prominent on the north side of the canyon. This geologic formation is actually a long volcanic dike. Molten rock, or magma, was squeezed sideways into sedimentary rock, the magma hardened, and the softer rock eroded, leaving this vertical wall of volcanic rock.

The scenic byway begins at the national forest boundary. Signal and Flag peaks stand as sentinels on either side of the Wapiti Valley. Wapiti is the Indian word for elk. Sagebrush, juniper, and other dryland plants dot the hillsides, and cottonwoods along the river provide a cool oasis in this arid region. Public campgrounds, private resorts, and summer homes are located along the byway.

You'll see unique rock formations while touring this byway. Repeated volcanic eruptions poured lava over the multicolored clays and sandstone. Soupy mudflows from eruptions formed rocks called breccia, which have eroded into fantastic shapes called hoodoos, spires, and pinnacles. Old cobblestones from the river sit like caps atop tall, thin chimneys. With a little imagination, you can pick out formations such as Camel Rock, Goose Rock, Slipper Rock, Laughing Pig, and Anvil Rock. An interpretive sign at a pulloff by Holy City rock formation explains more about these geologic processes. You'll also find other national forest information posted on the information board.

The canyon begins to narrow slightly, and conifers such as lodgepole pine, Douglas-fir, and Engelmann spruce dot the hillsides. Subalpine fir grows at the higher elevations. Big Game Campground provides seventeen sites in the cottonwoods along the river, at elevation 5,900 feet. Mosquitoes can be annoying but the fishing is good. Anglers cast for cutthroat, rainbow, and brown trout.

The Shoshone was the country's first timber reserve, designated by President Harrison in 1891. Wapiti Ranger Station was built in 1903—the very first national forest ranger station to be built with appropriated funds. It is now listed on the National Register of Historic Places. Nearby, Wapiti Campground has forty-one sites in the shade of the cottonwoods. A big herd of elk winters in this area every year.

Elk Fork Campground provides horse corrals and thirteen campsites. Stretch your legs on an easy hike up Elk Fork Creek. Fishing is pretty good, and you can hike along the creek bottom up to eleven miles before the trail gets steep. The trails along this byway receive heavy horseback use, so watch where you step.

Wildlife viewing in the North Fork Shoshone Canyon is quite rewarding. There are black bears, elk, moose, mule deer, bighorn sheep, coyotes, and beavers, as well as an occasional mountain goat. This area has one of the highest concentrations of grizzly bears in the lower forty-eight; follow regulations and take suitable precautions when hiking and camping along this byway. It is the bear's home, not yours.

Clearwater Campground was the site of a Civilian Conservation Corps Camp until 1941. Today there are thirty-two campsites and a foot trail to

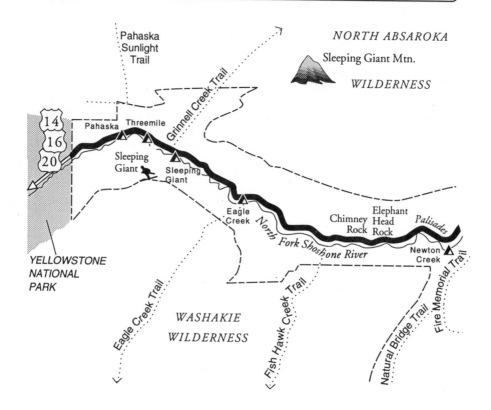

the north up Clearwater Creek. You can hike about four miles on maintained trail into the North Absaroka Wilderness. The wilderness is a land of stunning glacier-carved volcanic mountains. Two hundred and seventeen miles of trails lead through the 350,488 acres of wildlands.

Continuing west on the byway, stop at Mummy Cave. This cave provided shelter for hunters from about 7200 B.C. to 1580 A.D. At least eleven different cultures used the cave during that time. The mummified body of a prehistoric human who died around 734 A.D. was found here, giving the cave its current name.

Rex Hale Campground sits at elevation 6,100 feet. There are eight campsites. A very short side trip south on Forest Road 435 brings you to two trailheads. The Natural Bridge Trail leads to a view of a natural bridge in the Washakie Wilderness. The five-mile Blackwater Fire Memorial National Recreation Trail follows the creek, then climbs to some outstanding views atop the summit of Clayton Mountain. Firefighters memorials on the highway and on Clayton Mountain commemorate the twenty-seven firefighters killed during the 1937 Blackwater Fire.

Newton Creek Campground has thirty-one sites, at elevation 6,300 feet. Interesting rock formations jut out through here. The Palisades dominate the

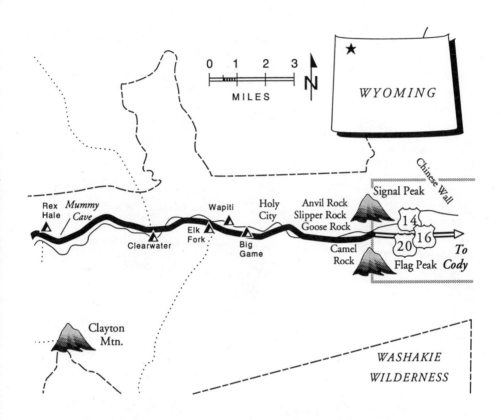

northern side of the canyon, while to the south the rock formation called Henry Ford sits holding a steering wheel (if you have an active imagination). Elephant Head Rock is another interesting formation—and Chimney Rock is obvious and easy to pick out.

Fishhawk Creek and Eagle Creek trails take you south into the Washakie Wilderness. The Washakie protects 704,529 acres of volcanic mountains cleft by deep, steep drainages. The Washakie was named for Chief Washakie of the Shoshone Indians. At low levels, you can ford the river at Fishhawk or go through the Boy Scout Camp. Fishhawk is a fairly strenuous climb. Eagle Creek has a footbridge across the river and climbs along the creek on a moderate grade.

You are now in the very heart of bear country and should exercise extreme caution when camping and hiking. Eagle Creek Campground has twenty sites along the river. Sleeping Giant Campground provides six sites at elevation 6,600 feet. A steep trail north leads along Grinnell Creek, into the North Absaroka Wilderness.

Sleeping Giant Winter Sports Area is a small downhill ski area. Nearby, Threemile Campground has thirty-three sites. The byway now leaves the North Fork and follows Middle Creek. A mile or so west, Pahaska Tepee was Buffalo

The North Fork Highway travels through a region of ranches, rivers, and mountains. Photo by Dewey Vanderhoff/Cody, WY.

Bill Cody's hunting lodge, now listed on the National Register of Historic Places. Pahaska Campground has twenty-four campsites in the evergreens along the creek. This is a popular starting point for snowmobilers and cross-country skiers into Yellowstone National Park. The Pahaska-Sunlight Trail is very diverse and climbs very gently for about four miles before the grade increases. If you hike up Jones Creek or up the North Fork drainage, you can see the extensive burns from the big forest fires of 1988. The vegetation is coming back, and in summer the magenta blossoms of fireweed brighten the charred slopes.

The scenic byway ends at the east entrance to Yellowstone National Park, elevation 6,951 feet. Look back east to find the Sleeping Giant Mountain, reclining on his back with his hands folded. □

NEBO LOOP SCENIC BYWAY
Uinta National Forest · Utah

General description: A thirty-eight mile highway through the Wasatch Range, past mountain lakes and unique geologic features.

Special attractions: Devil's Kitchen Geologic Area, Payson Lakes Recreation Area, Mount Nebo Wilderness, camping, fishing, autumn foliage.

Location: Central Utah on the Uinta National Forest. The byway travels Forest Road 015, between Payson and Highway 132 just east of Nephi.

Byway route number: Forest Road 015.

Travel season: From around Memorial Day until around Thanksgiving, then closed by winter snows.

Camping: Four national forest campgrounds, with picnic tables, fire grates, toilets, and drinking water.

Services: All traveler services in Nephi and Payson.

Nearby attractions: Huntington Canyon and Eccles Canyon national forest scenic byways, Little Sahara Sand Dunes, Salt Lake City urban activities, Timpanogos National Monument.

For more information: Uinta National Forest, 88 West 100 North, Provo, UT 84601, (801) 377-5780. Spanish Fork Ranger District, 44 West 400 North, Spanish Fork, UT 84660, (801) 798-3571.

Description: Nebo Loop Scenic Byway provides magnificent views and lots of recreation opportunities. The two-lane highway is paved and has frequent scenic turnouts. Weekend traffic is moderately heavy and slow moving. Weekdays are less busy.

Temperatures vary considerably by elevation. The byway climbs from about 5,300 feet elevation to about 8,200 feet. Generally, summer days reach the seventies and eighties at the higher elevations and cool to the fifties or sixties at night. Expect afternoon thunderstorms in August and September. Spring and fall have freezing temperatures at night and may reach the fifties or sixties on sunny days. Winter temperatures are usually around freezing but may go below zero. Cross-country skiing and snowmobiling are popular in winter.

The byway is very scenic driven in either direction. Driving north to south, begin in Payson, a full-service community, and drive south on 100 North Street. Bear left at the Y in the road, past a big tan water tank and the Payson power plant. The byway follows Peteetneet Creek through the riparian vegetation of Payson Canyon. Gray rock outcrops jut out, and glimpses of rolling mountaintops beckon you up out of the smog.

Maple Bench Campground is located up a steep paved road. There are ten sites in the stand of Rocky Mountain maples. It's very secluded and a lovely getaway. Bright rust-colored lichens grow on the maples, and wild roses bloom in the clearings. Maple Lake is another mile up a dirt road. Anglers cast for brook and rainbow trout. You can hike three miles to Red Lake and try your fishing luck there, too.

The byway climbs alongside the pretty cascades and drops off the creek into a forest of white fir, Douglas-fir, and aspens. Watch for elk in the mornings

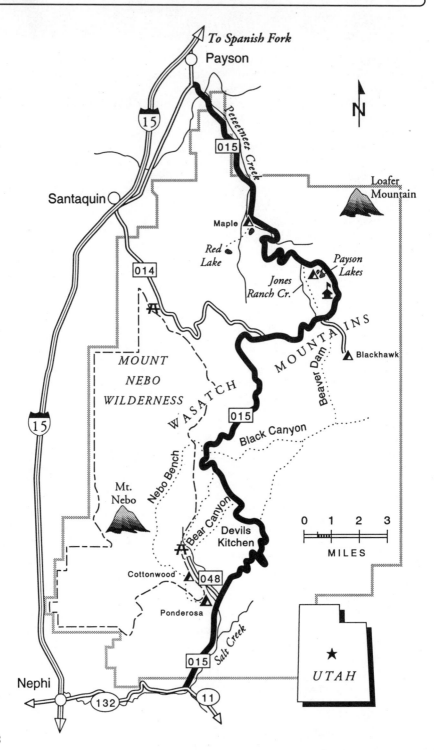

To Spanish Fork

Payson

I-15

015

Peteetneet Creek

Loafer
Mountain

Santaquin

Maple

Red
Lake

Payson
Lakes

014

Jones
Ranch Cr.

Blackhawk

MOUNT
NEBO
WILDERNESS

WASATCH

MOUNTAINS

Beaver Dam Cr.

015

Black Canyon

I-15

Nebo Bench

Mt.
Nebo

Bear Canyon

Devils
Kitchen

0 1 2 3

MILES

Cottonwood

048

Ponderosa

Salt Creek

015

UTAH

Nephi

132

11

Nebo Loop travels through the forest atop the Wasatch Mountains. Uinta National Forest photo.

and evenings. Other wildlife species inhabiting this region include black bears, bighorn sheep, mule deer, coyotes, beavers, marmots, porcupines, and a variety of squirrels, chipmunks, mice, and voles. Bird watchers can look for warblers, flycatchers, woodpeckers, hummingbirds, sparrows, juncoes, bluebirds, and raptors such as golden eagles, and Cooper's, sharp-shinned, and red-tailed hawks.

Stretch your legs on a short hike along Jones Ranch Creek. Children will delight in the little frogs in the boggy areas, and you may see elk and mule deer.

The byway reaches about 8,000 feet elevation and rolls for many miles across the undulating ridges and hilltops. Stands of aspen trees are pretty against the deep green hues of white firs.

The Payson Lakes Recreation Area is very popular. No motors are allowed on the water, so you can enjoy peaceful, quiet surroundings for camping, fishing, canoeing, and hiking. Campgrounds provide a total of one hundred sites, many barrier-free. Deer flies can be pesky during the summer. You can hike on several trails in the area.

Payson Guard Station has national forest maps, trail guides, and general information about the byway. Nearby, you can hike various loops from the Blackhawk area. You'll share the trails with horseback riders. Try the Beaver Dam loop, or walk out to Mount Loafer.

The views across the top of Nebo Loop Scenic Byway are tremendous. On a clear day you can see out into the western desert. Other landmarks visible from the byway include Thistle Slide, the nation's seventh largest mud slide; Skyline Drive in Sanpete County; and Utah Lake.

You could return to Payson by following Forest Road 014 down Santaquin Canyon. This steep, beautiful canyon has a fast-moving trout stream, campground, picnic area, and rugged rock outcrops.

Nebo Bench Trail is a great twelve-mile day hike with spectacular views. The entire route is fairly easy, and if you're really energetic the trail connects with a path that ascends Mount Nebo. Have someone pick you up at the other end of the trail on Forest Road 048, near Ponderosa Campground.

Mount Nebo Wilderness protects 28,500 acres of wilderness surrounding Mount Nebo. Nebo reaches 11,877 feet and is the highest peak in the Wasatch Range. It's a beautiful area of razorlike ridges and very steep terrain, especially beautiful viewed from the east side, on the byway. The word Nebo means "sentinel of God."

Stop at Devil's Kitchen Geologic Interest Area. A very short interpretive walk identifies the vegetation and leads to a surprising view of hoodoos, cones, and columns. The Price River Formation is a multi-colored conglomerate of easily eroded rock, which has weathered here into fascinating shapes. Ravens glide overhead on the thermals, while swallows zoom around catching insects. It's a delightful place to spend some time.

The Wasatch Mountains are mostly limestone, formed from the remains of marine organisms that lived in a huge inland sea. The region was thrust upward and folded, and lava flowed out from cracks in the ground. Glaciers scraped and scoured the mountaintops, then melted and created the Great Salt Lake in the basin below.

The byway provides views of Mount Nebo as you descend via a series of switchbacks into low, rolling hills. Dominant tree species here are Gambel oak and Rocky Mountain maple. A side trip on Forest Road 048 leads north to two campgrounds and a picnic area. Ponderosa has twenty-eight campsites in the cottonwoods and ponderosa pines along the creek. Cottonwood provides eight campsites. Bear Canyon Picnic Area sits in a beautiful, big grassy bowl surrounded by mountains.

The byway follows Salt Creek and ends at Highway 132, just east of Nephi, a full-service community. □

Red maple and quaking aspen add brilliant splashes to the fall colors along Minnesota's four national forest scenic byways—Avenue of Pines Scenic Byway, North Shore Drive, Northwood Scenic Byway, and Scenic Highway. Minnesota's fall pallete also includes red pine, paper birch, and tamarack as well as sugar maple and redcedar.

The still waters of Redfish Lake reflect Grand Mogul, a peak in one of the three mountain ranges in the Sawtooth National Recreation Area. This 756,000-acre national recreation area encompasses a portion of south-central Idaho's Sawtooth Scenic Byway, and offers diverse recreation on its lakes and rivers—including camping, fishing, float boating, bicycling, and picnicking.

Indian paintbrush
and monkeyflower
flourish around
Hershberger Moun-
tain Lookout on the
Rogue-Umpqua
Scenic Byway in
Oregon. This
lookout has been
completely refur-
bished to its
original 1925
condition and is
listed on the
National Register
of Historic
Lookouts. Visitors
to this historic site
are rewarded with
clear views of
Highrock and Fish
mountains, Mount
Bailey, and Mount
Thielsen.

Airplanes have always been a popular way to view Alaska's
incredibly beautiful and diverse scenery and wildlife. The
Seward Highway, however, runs 127 miles through the
Chugach National Forest and State Park, from Anchorage to
Seward, and provides another way to travel the state. Tourists
on this route can see sparkling glaciers, mighty whales,
colorful mountains and lakes, and floating icebergs, in addition to outstanding scenery like the Kenai Mountains, pictured
here from Bear Lake.

Island Lake sits in a rocky glacial cirque in the heart of the Ruby Mountains. Verdi Peak, behind the lake, shows evidence of the glacial activity that shaped this range. Island Lake can be reached by a two-mile trail beginning at Road's End on Nevada's Lamoille Canyon Road.

PHOTOGRAPHING AMERICA'S NATIONAL FOREST SCENIC BYWAYS

The exquisite color photographs in *Scenic Byways II* were shot by Larry Ulrich, a nationally known outdoor photographer whose work has appeared in *Audubon, Sierra,* and *Wilderness,* and Audubon and Sierra Club calendars.

Ulrich's photo expeditions have taken him through America's national forests for more than twenty years. He has explored these public lands from the Alaska to Texas and from Washington to Georgia—there are few national forests he has not photographed.

Many of Ulrich's photo expeditions have taken him along the Forest Service's designated scenic byways. When shooting the byways, Ulrich "looks at everything from a photographer's eye," but he also appreciates the fact that these lands along the byways are being preserved for generations to come.

"I love to explore places where I've never been," Ulrich says, "and anytime I hear of a new scenic byway, I travel it." Ulrich's dedication to shooting the best of the national forests has led him along many byways. His favorites include the San Juan Skyway, featured in *Scenic Byways,* and the Sawtooth Scenic Byway (page 70 of *Scenic Byways II).*

Azalea and flowering dogwood add to the spectacular spring blossom display, which begins in April along Mississippi's Natchez Trace Scenic Byway. Wildflower enthusiasts can also look for agave, jack-in-th-pulpit, golden club, iris, wild hyacinth, and fawn lily.

"National Forests serve a good
purpose as playgrounds for people.
They are used. . .by campers, hunters,
fishermen, and thousands of pleasure
seekers from nearby towns. They are
great recreation grounds for a large part
of the people of the West, and their value
in this respect is well worth
considering."

Gifford Pinchot
First Chief of the Forest Service, 1907

A summer storm captures the colors of sunset over the Markaguant Plateau, which stretches north from Brian Head Peak. Utah's breathtaking Brian Head-Panguitch Lake Scenic Byway traverses this 11,315-foot peak providing extensive views of the surrounding country from Markaguant Plateau in the north to the Great Basin and Nevada in the west to Arizona in the south.

''Working closely with our friends at the local level—the highway departments, the chamber of commerce and private businesses—we have become partners in bringing the American people closer to the beauty of their National Forests and sharing the cultural heritage of the country. At the same time, we are providing new opportunities to enhance and strengthen local economies through understanding of multiple-use forest and rangeland management.''

F. Dale Robertson
Chief of Forest Service on
National Forest Scenic Byways

Sunset silouettes cattails at the edge of 700,000-year-old Mono Lake, along east-central California's Lee Vining Canyon Highway. Visitors to the lake can enjoy guided nature walks, campfire naturalist programs, and a swim in the mineral- and salt-rich water.

General description: A seventeen-mile route up Beaver Canyon, with beautiful mountain scenes and interesting geologic formations.

Special attractions: Elk Meadows Ski Area, camping, picnicking, fishing.

Location: West-central Utah on the Fishlake National Forest. The byway begins in Beaver and travels east on Highway 153 to Elk Meadows Ski Area.

Byway route number: Utah State Highway 153.

Travel season: Year-round. Snow tires or chains required November 1 through March 31.

Camping: Three national forest campgrounds, with picnic tables, fire rings, toilets, and drinking water.

Services: All traveler services in Beaver, and at the ski area.

Nearby attractions: Brian Head-Panguitch, Cedar Breaks, Markaguant, and Fishlake National Forest scenic byways; Cedar Breaks National Monument.

For more information: Fishlake National Forest, 115 East 900 North, Richfield, UT 84701, (801) 896-9233. Beaver Ranger District, 190 North 100 East, Beaver, UT 84713, (801) 438-2436.

Description: Beaver Canyon Scenic Byway travels through a lovely canyon alongside the Beaver River. The two-lane road is paved, with frequent scenic and recreation turnouts. Chains or snow tires are required in winter. Traffic is light.

Summer temperatures range from about sixty to ninety, with very low humidity. Expect afternoon thunderstorms in July and August. Spring and fall are very pleasant with temperatures in the sixties and seventies, dipping sometimes to freezing at night. Snow blankets the ground in the higher elevations from November through April.

The byway begins in Beaver, a full-service community. The Beaver Ranger District office has national forest information and maps. Beaver's historic district features more than thirty buildings with unusual pioneer architecture. In summer you can visit the Old Courthouse Museum to see pioneer and Indian artifacts and attend live theatre in the Old Opera House.

The byway enters the canyon at the national forest boundary. The steep volcanic slopes host pinyon pines, junipers, and a few ponderosa pines, mixed with various desert shrubs such as manzanita, sagebrush, rabbitbrush, mountain mahogany, Mormon tea, and bitterbrush. Cottonwoods line the river bottom, creating lovely cool pockets in the desert.

The power plant a few miles into the canyon is one of a series that generate electricity for the city of Beaver. You'll see several water pipes and penstocks at 6,500 feet elevation, along the byway. Near the power plant, Little Cottonwood Campground has fourteen sites along the river. Two barrier-free campsites and a barrier-free fishing path are located in the campground.

The highway begins a gentle ascent, and you'll see plenty of evidence of rock slides along the road. Beaver Canyon bisects the Tushar Mountains, a series of stratovolcanoes that erupted with incredible violence in Tertiary

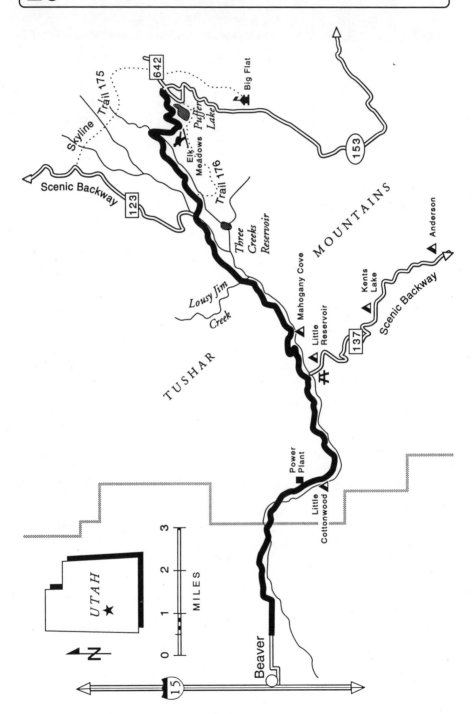

time (about twenty-four million years ago). In road cuts and rock outcrops you can find breccia from the massive mud flows, volcanic ash, and lava.

A summer side trip on Forest Road 137 leads to numerous recreation opportunities. About a mile up the road, Little Reservoir is stocked with rainbow and brown trout. The campground has eight sites and a barrier-free fishing path. Four miles farther, Kents Lake Campground is situated at an elevation of 8,800 feet. There are seventeen campsites, and fishing is good in Kents Lake. Anglers cast for brook and rainbow trout. You can continue along 137 another four miles to Anderson Meadow Reservoir, elevation 9,350 feet, for brookies and rainbows. A ten-site campground is situated near the lake. There are also numerous opportunities for primitive, dispersed camping along this route, and you can follow 137 past LaBaron Reservoir (rainbows and brookies) out to Highway 153 and on to Junction in the Marysvale Valley east of the Tushar Mountains.

The byway begins a steep, switchbacking climb. Mahogany Cove Campground is located right in the crook of a hairpin turn. There are seven camp-

Tremendous geologic uplift and folding are evident in this outcrop in Beaver Canyon. Beverly Magley photo.

sites amongst the mountain mahogany and pinyons, with a nice view of the mountains. The big penstock on the mountain brings water from the reservoir to the power plant below.

Wildlife on the Fishlake National Forest includes moose, elk, mule deer, mountain goats, bobcats, and mountain lions. Bird watchers can look for raptors such as eagles, hawks, and falcons. Flycatchers, nuthatches, kingbirds, flickers, warblers, hummingbirds, and woodpeckers flit through the trees.

The byway continues to climb, and the forest is composed of aspens, Engelmann spruce, and subalpine and white fir. There is good fishing in the Merchant Valley Reservoir and dispersed camping possibilities along Lousy Jim Creek. There are a few ATV trails in the area, and a scenic backway, for high clearance four-wheel-drive vehicles, follows Forest Road 123 north.

The Tushar Ridge Trail 176 is very level and easy. It wanders through the forest and out across the ski runs. Much of the route goes across private property, so please stay on the trail. Begin at the trailhead near the junction of Three Creeks and Highway 153 and hike east. If you hike the full 5.5 miles, you can connect to the Puffer Lake Trail 175 and follow it to the end of the scenic byway.

Elk Meadows Ski and Summer Resort has good downhill skiing in winter and summertime resort-type activities. The scenic byway continues on for a few miles and ends at the Puffer Lake Resort Road. In summer you could continue east on 153, on a dry-weather-only road, out to U.S. Highway 89.

Try a hike north on the Skyline National Recreation Trail #225, starting at Big Flat. You'll follow a ridgeline that's above timberline, where you can see a long distance into the peaks and valleys east and west of the ridge. Wildflowers are especially prolific in late July. You can walk about five miles north and have someone pick you up at the trailhead on Forest Road 129 or Forest Road 642 or loop back on Puffer Lake Trail 175 through the aspens and evergreens. □

21 FISHLAKE SCENIC BYWAY
Fishlake National Forest   Utah

General description: A thirteen-mile route across a high plateau, along the shores of beautiful Fish Lake.

Special attractions: Far-ranging vistas, fishing, boating, camping, waterfowl, wildflowers.

Location: Central Utah on the Fishlake National Forest. The byway begins at the junction of Highways 24 and 25 and follows Highway 25 northeast to Johnson Reservoir.

Byway route number: Utah State Highway 25.

Travel season: Year-round.

Camping: Five national forest campgrounds, with picnic tables, fire grates, toilets, drinking water.

Services: Gas, food, and lodging, with limited availability, at Fish Lake resorts. Traveler services in nearby Loa.

Nearby attractions: Capitol Reef National Park, Beaver Canyon National Forest Scenic Byway, Otter Creek Reservoir.

For more information: Fishlake National Forest, 115 East 900 North, Richfield, UT 84701, (801) 896-4491. Loa Ranger District, 150 South Main Street, Loa, UT 84747, (801) 836-2811 or 836-2800.

Description: Fishlake Scenic Byway is a delightful drive to a mountain lake surrounded by scenic mountains. The two-lane road is paved, and traffic is moderate.

Summer temperatures range from the sixties to nineties, with very low humidity. Expect afternoon thunderstorms in July and August. Spring and fall are very pleasant, with daytime temperatures usually between fifty and seventy. Snow covers the ground from November through April.

Driving the route west to east, the byway begins at the junction of Highways 24 and 25. A few small groves of aspen trees spring out of the sage and juniper surroundings. Here you're up high above Grass Valley, and the views extend west over the valley and the small community of Greenwich.

The highway travels northwest, past summer homes and scattered development. Near the national forest boundary, Hancock Flat Road leads south to dispersed, primitive camping opportunities. Another side road, Mytoge Mountain Road, has some wonderful scenic overlooks along its length.

The byway enters more extensive stands of aspen, which are very colorful in autumn. Road cuts expose the extensive volcanic origins of this high plateau. Ash, breccia, and lava covered a region seventy miles across, and the Fish Lake Hightop Plateau is part of Utah's largest volcanic region.

Leaves are just ready to burst out as the ice melts from Fish Lake in early spring. Beverly Magley photo.

Fish Lake is cradled in a "graben," or down-faulted valley. The Fremont River heads in Fish Lake, and the waters flow east and eventually empty into the Colorado River at Glen Canyon. Fish Lake is located at an elevation of 8,800 feet. The lake is about 5.5 miles long and hosts lake (Mackinaw) trout, rainbow trout, wild brown trout, and splake. Mytoge (my-TOE-gee) Mountain fills the eastern skyline, and there are picnic areas, three resorts (two have RV sites), a trailer dump station, boat launches, and three campgrounds.

Doctor Creek Campground provides twenty-nine sites at the south end of the lake. Mackinaw Campground has fifty-three sites in the aspens, with a view of the lake. Bowery Campground has thirty-one sites near the lake.

The Lake Shore Trail runs along the west side of Fish Lake, between the shore and the road. It's a pleasant path to bicycle or walk, and it allows you to poke along and admire the scenery and vegetation.

Fishlake National Forest personnel are stationed in the Fish Lake Lodge during the summer. You can obtain national forest information, maps, and other publications there. Weekend evening programs are presented by naturalists at Twin Creeks amphitheater. Topics cover wildlife, geology, archaeology, history, and other natural history areas.

If you're interested in geology, the Fish Lake self-guided auto tour is very informative. Pick up a brochure at the lodge.

Broad, flat Pelican Point juts into the lake, and the red stems of willows are pretty against the blue water. Looking northeast over the lake, Mount Marvine keeps its cap of snow well into the summer.

Nearby, an endangered species success story can be observed. The Utah prairie dog was an endangered species. A small population was transplanted here into the highest-elevation area of its traditional habitat. The impoundment here and other places around the state have been successful, and today the Utah prairie dog is no longer considered endangered.

Stretch your legs on the Pelican Canyon Trail, a moderately difficult 1,500-foot climb through aspens and conifers into a steep-walled canyon. It's about four miles to the gorgeous views from Tasha Spring. You can return on the same trail, or make a twelve-mile loop by following Tasha Creek down to its trailhead near Frying Pan Campground, then walking the road back to your vehicle.

The byway crosses a marshy area at the north end of the lake. Bird watchers will have a great time here. Look for white pelicans, great blue herons, snowy egrets, and numerous kinds of ducks, such as pintail, mallard, bufflehead, gadwall, and canvasback. There are Canada geese, loons, and mergansers on the lake, as well as numerous songbirds in the lands surrounding the lake.

Just north of Fish Lake, there are nice walking trails to the east leading to Crater Lakes and beyond. Frying Pan Campground has eleven sites in the aspens, on the slopes of a big ridge. About a half-mile beyond, Rock Canyon Trail gains about 1,800 feet elevation as it winds through the glaciated water pockets atop the high plateau. It's well worth the climb.

The scenic byway terminates at the end of Fish Lake. Just three miles north, Johnson Valley Reservoir is stocked with rainbow and cutthroat trout and has a few brookies, too. It's a nice place to cross-country ski or snowmobile, and ice fishing is popular. Piute Parking Area has RV sites with a view of the reservoir.

Wildflowers are abundant in the Fish Lake region. Alpine buttercups, columbine, Rocky Mountain iris, horsemint, larkspur and blue flax brighten the wetter meadows, while dryland flowers such as asters, Indian paintbrush, skyrockets, and globeflowers are found higher up. One of the best wildflower spots is in "the garden," found by driving up Sevenmile Creek Road almost to Mount Terrell Guard Station. Blossoms are usually most abundant from the middle of July into early August.

You can take Forest Road 036 to its junction with Highway 72, near Loa. There are stunning views as you descend the Fremont River. □

21 FISHLAKE SCENIC BYWAY

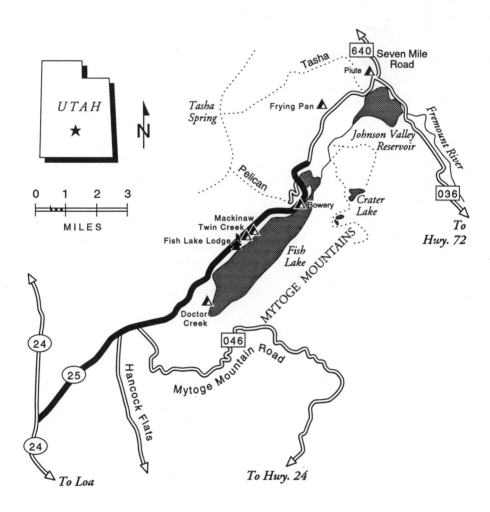

General description: A twelve-mile highway from the Salt Lake Valley up through a narrow canyon to high mountain resorts.

Special attractions: Twin Peaks and Lone Peak wilderness areas, Snowbird and Alta ski and summer resorts, rock climbing, camping, picnicking, hiking.

Location: Central Utah on the Wasatch-Cache National Forest. The byway travels Highway 210 between Salt Lake City and Albion Basin just past Alta.

Byway route number: Utah State Highway 210.

Travel season: Year-round between Salt Lake City and Alta. Snow tires or chains required November 1 - May 1. The last three miles of road past Alta closed by winter snows, usually from November through May.

Camping: Two national forest campgrounds, with picnic tables, fire grates, toilets, and drinking water.

Services: All traveler services in Salt Lake City, Snowbird, and Alta.

Nearby attractions: Big Cottonwood Canyon National Forest Scenic Byway, Salt Lake City urban activities, downhill skiing, Mount Olympus Wilderness.

For more information: Wasatch-Cache National Forest, 8226 Federal Building, 125 South State Street, Salt Lake City, UT 84128, (810) 524-5030. Salt Lake Ranger District, 6944 South 3000 East, Salt Lake City, UT 84121, (801) 524-5042.

Description: Little Cottonwood Canyon Scenic Byway traverses a narrow, sheer-walled canyon up into high mountain meadows. The two-lane road is paved as far as Alta and has numerous scenic turnouts. The steady stream of traffic can move slowly. Watch for bicyclists and joggers on the shoulders. From Alta to Albion Basin the road surface is gravel.

Weather can vary dramatically from the lower elevations to the upper mountains. Generally, summer days range from the sixties to the nineties, with periodic afternoon thunderstorms. Spring and fall temperatures range from about forty to seventy degrees in the lower elevations, and from freezing to the sixties at the upper elevations. Winter up high hovers from the teens to the thirties, but can drop below zero. Most moisture falls between October and May as snow; this area gets twice the snow of the mountains south and north.

To find the byway, exit Interstate 15 on 9000 South, and drive east to Highway 210 and the mouth of the canyon. Massive granite blocks were quarried here to build the Salt Lake Temple. Early settlers used the canyon for water, silver and lead mining, lumber, and hunting.

Cross into the national forest, and within a mile start looking for colorfully-clad rock climbers scaling the granite walls. Several waterfalls adorn the route. The Wasatch Range through here is predominantly granite and Precambrian rocks. This is difficult to erode, and consequently the water often has to plunge over and down a wall, rather than wearing a groove into the rocks. In the higher elevations, multi-colored bands of softer sandstone and limestone are visible.

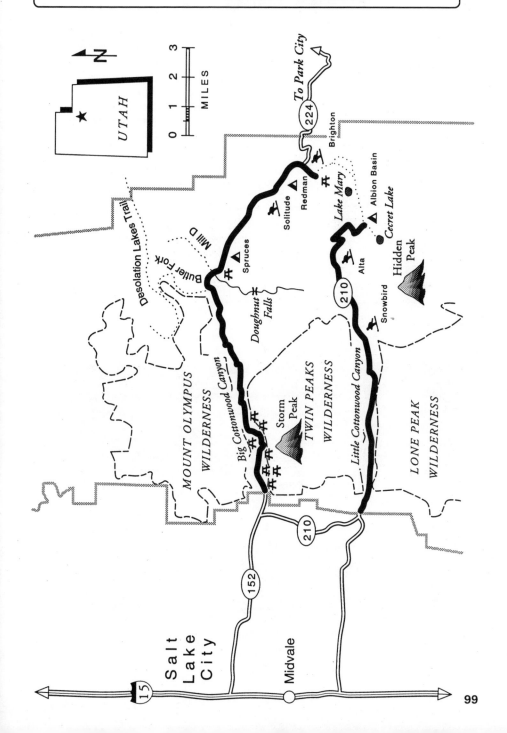

22 & 23

LITTLE COTTONWOOD AND BIG COTTONWOOD CANYON SCENIC BYWAYS

UTAH

N

MILES

0 1 2 3

To Park City

224

Brighton

Redman

Solitude

Lake Mary

Albion Basin

Cecret Lake

Hidden Peak

Alta

Spruces

Desolation Lakes Trail

Mill D

Butler Fork

Doughnut Falls

Snowbird

210

Big Cottonwood Canyon

Storm Peak

TWIN PEAKS WILDERNESS

Little Cottonwood Canyon

MOUNT OLYMPUS WILDERNESS

LONE PEAK WILDERNESS

210

152

Salt Lake City

Midvale

15

The byway runs right between two wilderness areas: Twin Peaks Wilderness on the north, and Lone Peak Wilderness on the south. Twin Peaks Wilderness protects 11,796 acres of the extremely steep, rugged ridge separating Big and Little Cottonwood canyons. Lone Peak Wilderness encompasses 30,088 acres of dramatically steep canyons running off a major ridgeline. It's a popular backcountry ski area for experts.

The Tanner Slide Area is a series of avalanche chutes that create dangerous conditions in winter and spring. Tanner Flat Campground has thirty-nine sites in a grove of canyon live oaks. Mosquitoes are rarely a problem, but no-see-ums, black flies, and yellow jackets can be annoying. Little Cottonwood Creek is stocked with rainbow trout.

A variety of wildlife species inhabit the Wasatch-Cache National Forest. There are elk, moose, mule deer, bobcat, mountain lion, marmot, pine marten, coyote, badger, skunk, snowshoe hare, porcupine, ground squirrel, and beaver. Bird watchers can look for gray jays, red-breasted nuthatches, hairy woodpeckers, pine siskins, yellow-bellied sapsuckers, warbling vireos, mountain bluebirds, water pipits, MacGillivray's warblers, green-tailed towhees, black-throated gray warblers, vesper sparrows, robins, magpies, golden eagles, red-tailed hawks, and great horned owls.

The byway climbs steadily up along Little Cottonwood Creek, past Snowbird and Alta ski areas. Snowbird has a year-round aerial tram to the top of 11,000-foot Hidden Peak. The view is glorious. You can see the wildly tilted, colorful rock layers of the Twin Peaks summit ridge and beyond across much of northern Utah. To the south, Mount Timpanogas and its surrounding wilderness are very impressive.

Alta was a rip-roaring mining town in the 1860s and '70s, then followed

The year-round tram at Snowbird provides a bird's-eye view of the surrounding mountains and canyons. Wasatch-Cache National Forest photo.

the route of most boom-and-bust industries. Alta's ghost town status ended in 1938 when Utah's first ski area was built there.

Continue on the highway to the end of the road in Albion Basin. The campground has twenty-eight sites near a little stream. Engelmann spruce and subalpine fir trees surround the mountain meadows. Wildflowers in the basin are a photographer's dream, including asters, bluebells, marigolds, cinquefoils, clematis, columbines, elephantheads, phlox, gentian, fireweed, primroses, and calypso orchids.

Numerous interconnecting trails wind through this area, and into the adjacent wilderness and backcountry. An easy 3.4-mile hike leads from Albion Basin to Brighton, on the Lake Mary Trail. You'll wander past lakes and beautiful alpine meadows. Listen for the high whistle of pikas and marmots. Another easy hike leads just .8-mile to Cecret Lake, set in a glacial basin and surrounded by peaks. It's absolutely beautiful.

Returning west on the same highway is a delight. The views look different from this perspective, and the narrow canyon walls frame a view of the distant Oquirrh (O-ker) Mountains rising above the Utah Valley. □

For map, see page 99.

23 BIG COTTONWOOD CANYON SCENIC BYWAY
Wasatch-Cache National Forest   Utah

General description: A fifteen-mile highway up a beautiful, sheer-walled canyon, opening into a forested, glaciated high mountain valley.

Special attractions: Mount Olympus and Twin Peaks wilderness areas, Solitude and Brighton ski areas, camping, interesting geology, hiking.

Location: Central Utah on the Wasatch-Cache National Forest. The byway travels Highway 152 between Salt Lake City and the end of the road at Brighton Ski Area.

Byway route number: Utah State Highway 152.

Travel season: Year-round. Snow tires or chains may be required Nov. 1 - May 1.

Camping: Two national forest campgrounds, with picnic tables, fire grates, toilets, and drinking water.

Services: All traveler services in Salt Lake City. Services, with limited availability, at the ski areas.

Nearby attractions: Little Cottonwood Canyon National Forest Scenic Byway, Salt Lake City urban activities, downhill skiing, Lone Peak Wilderness.

For more information: Wasatch-Cache National Forest, 8226 Federal Building - 125 South State Street, Salt Lake City, UT 84128, (810) 524-5030. Salt Lake Ranger District, 6944 South 3000 East, Salt Lake City, UT 84121, (801) 524-5042.

Description: Big Cottonwood Canyon Scenic Byway follows a stream through a beautiful canyon, up into the high mountains. The two-lane road is paved and has numerous scenic turnouts. Traffic is very steady and may move slowly. Watch for joggers and bicyclists on the highway.

Weather is extremely variable from the low elevations at the west end to the high elevations at the east end. Generally, expect summer daytime temperatures in the sixties to nineties, with periodic afternoon thunderstorms. Spring and fall temperatures range from the forties to seventies in the lower canyon and from freezing to about the fifties up high. Snow generally remains at the high elevations until late June but melts off down below by early May. Expect winter temperatures from below zero to the forties up high and between the twenties and forties at the low elevations. Most of the year's precipitation falls as snow between October and May.

To find the byway, exit Interstate 15 at 7200 South, then drive east, following the signs to Solitude and Brighton ski areas.

The byway begins at the national forest boundary, amid the chokecherry bushes and cottonwood trees along Big Cottonwood Creek. There are several nice picnic areas along the creek, and rock climbers seem to be everywhere on the sheer canyon walls. At Birches Picnic Area you can see a big water flume on the north canyon wall. Big Cottonwood Creek is used to generate power and is a primary source of water for Salt Lake City.

A geology exhibit explains the Storm Mountain Slide Area. The Wasatch Front lies along a huge fault zone, and the region is still moving. Layers of sedimentary rock tilt at wild angles, exhibiting the tremendous folding, upthrust, and faulting that created the Wasatch Mountain Range. A half-mile farther east on the byway, another exhibit points out quartzites, sandstones, and mudstones. It's easy to envision the geologic history displayed on the canyon walls.

The byway ascends alongside the cascading creek, switchbacks up steep terrain, and passes through another landslide area. You learn that limestone is compressed into marble and see fossils in the limestone at the next road-side exhibit. Beavers are busy in this meandering stretch of stream, and the pretty red and gold stems of willows decorate the banks.

You can hike a number of trails into the wildernesses and adjacent back-country on either side of the byway. The trails are generally moderately strenuous and climb steadily out of the canyon. The Butler Fork Trail connects to Mill D Basin or Desolation Lake Trail, for good long day hikes.

Spruces Campground provides ninety-seven sites along the creek in the forest. The elevation here is 7,500 feet. Nearby, off the Cardiff Fork Road, you can take a short walk on Doughnut Falls Trail to an unusual waterfall, which drops through a hole in a rock. Watch for shy mule deer along the trail.

The highway climbs into a forest of Engelmann spruce, subalpine fir, Douglas-fir, and stands of aspen. Golden aspen leaves in autumn sparkle against the deep green backdrop of the conifers. The valley widens here, and you can learn about glaciation at the next exhibit. Glaciers covered the Wasatch Range in the last Ice Age, and only a few of the highest peaks jutted up out of the ice. The melt-water drained down the canyons along the Wasatch Front, carrying sediments out to the valley below.

Redman Campground has thirty-eight sites in the forest, at elevation 8,300 feet.

Solitude Ski Area provides winter downhill skiing and summertime mountain bicycle trails. A side trip on Highway 224 makes it possible to loop through Park City and return to Salt Lake City on the interstate. Highway 224 is a

Big Cottonwood Creek cut a canyon through the rugged, twisted rock layers of Storm Mountain. Beverly Magley photo.

well-maintained gravel road which gets you up high into the cool mountains, offers views of the surrounding mountains, and provides access to several good mountain bicycling trails. It can get quite busy on summer weekends.

The high mountain meadows bloom from spring through fall with wildflowers. Columbine, monkshood, bluebells, monkeyflowers, violets, pussytoes, and phlox are prolific and easy to identify.

Brighton Ski Area lies at the end of the scenic byway. Numerous hiking trails crisscross the area. Try the short, easy Dog Lake Trail through meadows of wildflowers, with good views of the surrounding peaks. An easy loop begins on the barrier-free Silver Lake Loop Trail, then follows the Brighton Lakes Trail and Lake Mary Trail back to Brighton. The panoramic views are great. You'll probably see marmots, pikas, chipmunks, ground squirrels, and blue grouse. You might also be lucky enough to spot golden eagles, coyotes, or even a bobcat. A visitor center and nordic rental shop at Silver Lake will be completed in 1992. □

General description: A thirty-three-mile route up a colorful, narrow canyon to a pretty reservoir and on up into the mountains.

Special attractions: Pineview Reservoir, autumn foliage, fishing, cross-country skiing, snowmobiling, interesting geology, far-ranging vistas.

Location: North-central Utah on the Wasatch-Cache National Forest. The byway travels Highway 39 between Ogden and the national forest boundary west of Woodruff.

Byway route number: Utah State Highway 39.

Travel season: Year-round between Ogden and the junction of Highways 39 and 242. Road closed by winter snows from the junction of Highways 39 and 242 east to the national forest boundary. That section usually open from late April through mid-December.

Camping: Ten national forest campgrounds, with picnic tables, fire grates, toilets, drinking water.

Services: All traveler services in Ogden. All services, with limited availability, in and around Huntsville and Eden.

Nearby attractions: Bird refuges along Great Salt Lake, downhill skiing, Logan Canyon National Forest Scenic Byway, Salt Lake City urban attractions, Wellsville Mountain Wilderness.

For more information: Wasatch-Cache National Forest, 8226 Federal Building, 125 South State Street, Salt Lake City, UT 84128, (801) 524-5030. Ogden Ranger District, 507 25th Street, Suite 103, Ogden, UT 84402, (801) 625-5112.

Description: Ogden River Scenic Byway travels through a very diverse region, from a narrow canyon to a large reservoir and up into mountain meadows. The two-lane highway is paved and has scenic turnouts. Traffic is constant in summer and on winter ski weekends. The remainder of the year, traffic is moderate. The byway east of the reservoir and campgrounds gets very light use.

Summer temperatures generally range from the fifties to the nineties. Expect afternoon thunderstorms in the high elevations in July and August. Spring and fall may drop to freezing at night but rise to the sixties and seventies during the daytime. Snow can fall from mid-September through April, and the upper section of the byway road is usually closed by snow from mid-December through late April. The closed road is used as a snowmobile route.

Beginning in Ogden, stop at the Visitor Center in Union Station for pamphlets, books, national forest information, and maps. While there, browse through the Utah State Railroad Museum. Ogden has been a center of intermountain railroading since the 1890s. It was also the meeting place for annual mountain men rendezvous in the 1820s. The community is named for Peter Skiene Ogden, a fur trapper.

Travel east on Highway 39, through a residential area. Big gray rock outcrops jut out of the forested slopes. Narrowleaf cottonwoods line the river, along with gambel oak, box-elder, and bigtooth maple. Douglas-fir and

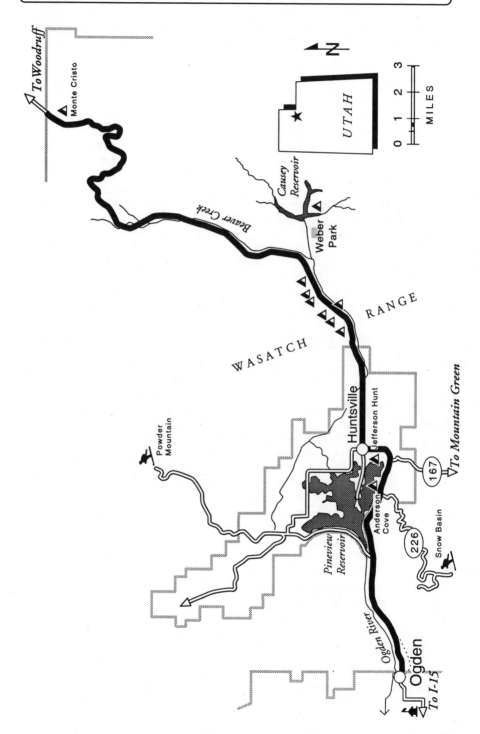

subalpine fir grow on the cooler, north-facing canyon slopes.

The byway through the canyon is quite narrow, with sharp curves. Most of the rock comprising this part of the Wasatch Mountain Range is very old and hard, and difficult to erode. These Precambrian rocks are about 2.6 billion years old and are primarily metamorphic rocks—quartzite, schist, and gneiss. Consequently, the canyon is steep and narrow, except at the top where softer layers of limestone and shale are streaked with colors ranging from red to pink to white.

A great family hike starts at the Smokey the Bear sign about three miles up the canyon. The path leads about five miles back to 22nd Street in Ogden, following an old Indian trail over ridges and through small canyons. There are some wonderful viewpoints along the route.

The byway climbs up to Pineview Reservoir and multiple recreation opportunities. The lake lies in a broad valley ringed by mountains. This popular area gets the most use of any lake its size in Utah. It can be tough to find an open campsite. You can boat, windsurf, swim, and fish for bass and crappie in the reservoir. Anderson Cove Campground has seventy-six sites on a knoll above the lake. There is a small national forest information station with maps and brochures, and campground hosts can answer many of your questions. Jefferson Hunt Campground is more primitive and provides twenty-nine sites in the cottonwoods along the lakeshore.

Wildlife watchers can look for Canada geese, mallards, great blue herons, and sandhill cranes. Bald eagles winter here. A wildlife viewing area on the North Arm of the reservoir is a good place to take your binoculars and field guides for a rewarding outing.

Two side trips offer splendid scenery: south on Highway 226 to Snow Basin Ski Area or south on Highway 167 to Mountain Green. Both routes wind through big green valleys and gorgeous mountain terrain. In summer the wildflowers are abundant.

Another side trip winds around the north shore of the reservoir through pastoral countryside and residential areas. Powder Mountain Ski Area lies north of this route.

Utah's only Trappist monastery is about four miles east of Huntsville. Just west of town, drive out the little peninsula to the swim beach, boat launch, and picnic area. It's a photographer's delight.

Continue east on Highway 39, past residences and farms. A series of seven campgrounds sit under the cottonwood trees along the Ogden River, providing a total of one hundred and fifty campsites. Mosquitoes can be annoying at times. Be careful of shy rattlesnakes in the rocky areas around camp. They don't like to be surprised.

Just past the campgrounds, a side trip east leads to Weber County Memorial Park and Causey Reservoir. The reservoir is very pretty, lying between forested slopes and big red rock outcrops. You can picnic, swim, and fish for rainbows, kokanee, and cutthroats in the reservoir. The park has areas developed for picnicking and playing softball, volleyball, and horseshoes. Skullcrack Trail circles the reservoir and is a very nice family hike.

The byway now follows Beaver Creek, which winds through dense willows, aspens, and cottonwoods. You may see moose or mule deer or beavers at work on their dams. Look overhead for soaring goshawks, sharp-shinned and red-tailed hawks, or watch for the bright blue of a mountain bluebird. The highway climbs up into a more open area, with wide-ranging vistas. The forst is almost

Pineview Reservoir is a popular summer recreation area along the Ogden River Scenic Byway. Wasatch-Cache National Forest photo.

continuous stands of aspen trees, which are especially beautiful in autumn when the leaves turn gold. You'll see open meadows full of wildflowers and high peaks all around. Lomatium, balsamroot, and mules-ears are very showy in July. The view changes continually as the road winds along. Engelmann spruce and subalpine fir provide deep green hues as a backdrop to the showy aspen trees. There are lots of moose and elk in this area.

The byway reaches its highest elevation at about 8,400 feet. Take time to get out of your car and savor the views, the solitude, and the fresh air. You can see west to Willard and Ben Lomond peaks, northwest into the Wellsville Mountain Wilderness, and southwest to Snow Basin.

Monte Cristo Campground provides fifty-three sites at this high elevation. The byway ends at the national forest boundary. Highway 39 continues east to Woodruff, down a small canyon, past ranchland and low rolling hills dotted with Utah juniper and sagebrush. Watch for pronghorn antelope grazing in the fields. □

General description: A sixty-five mile mountain route, with beautiful lakes and far-ranging vistas.

Special attractions: High Uintas Wilderness, alpine lakes, wildlife, autumn foliage, outstanding views, camping, fishing, hiking.

Location: North-central Utah on the Wasatch-Cache National Forest. The byway travels Highway 150 between Kamas and the national forest boundary just south of the Utah-Wyoming border.

Byway route number: Utah State Highway 150.

Travel season: Usually from Memorial Day through mid-October, then the road between Soapstone and Bear River is closed by winter snows.

Camping: Twenty-three national forest campgrounds, with picnic tables, fire rings, and toilets. Some provide drinking water.

Services: All traveler services, with limited availability, in Kamas. Gas in Bear River. All services in nearby Heber City, and in Evanston, Wyoming.

Nearby attractions: Downhill skiing, Rockport State Park, Wasatch Mountain State Park.

For more information: Wasatch-Cache National Forest, 8226 Federal Building - 125 South State Street, Salt Lake City, UT 84128, (801) 524-5030. Kamas Ranger District, Kamas, UT 84036, (801) 783-4338. Evanston Ranger District, Evanston, WY 82980, (801) 642-6356 summer only, (307) 789-3194 year round.

Description: Mirror Lake Scenic Byway traverses a stunning region of alpine lakes, high mountains, and beautiful views. The two-lane road is paved, and has frequent scenic turnouts. Traffic is moderately heavy, except on popular holiday weekends when it is very busy. Watch for bicyclists on the highway.

Weather in the mountains is variable. Byway elevations range from 6,437 feet at Kamas up to 10,715 feet on Bald Mountain Pass. Generally, July and August temperatures at the high elevations range from the forties to the seventies. Expect intense afternoon thunderstorms in August. June and September are usually dry, with freezing nighttime temperatures and days in the fifties or sixties. Snow usually blankets the ground between October and May and winter temperatures remain below freezing. The byway serves as a snowmobile route in winter.

The byway is beautiful driven in either direction. Traveling south to north, begin at the ranger station in Kamas to obtain maps, brochures, and general information. Follow Highway 150 in an easterly direction, through the pinyon-juniper vegetation, which includes flowering shrubs such as bitterbrush and rabbitbrush, and wildflowers such as globemallows, poppies, lilies, and herons-bill. Notice the gray rock outcrops between mileposts 2 and 3—Mississippian limestone. This rock formation was once an enormous sea. It's full of marine fossils and extends from the Grand Canyon north to Michigan.

You can walk through the Kamas Fish Hatchery and see how trout are raised for release into streams and lakes around Utah. They raise rainbow trout, including the hybrid albino trout, which has coloration almost like a sunfish.

The highway follows Beaver Creek, a lovely meandering stream lined with willows. The gold and red willow stems are very pretty against winter's white snow. In summer, you can fish for rainbow and brook trout. Just inside the national forest boundary, Yellow Pine Campground has thirty-three sites in the open forest of Utah junipers and ponderosa pines.

Look for beaver dams along the creek as you continue along the byway. Beaver Creek Campground provides fourteen sites amidst the aspen trees, near the creek. Taylors Fork Campground has eleven sites, and nearby Shingle Creek Campground provides twenty-one sites. These campgrounds supply drinking water and are popular with ATV users.

Stretch your legs on the Shingle Creek Trail. It's fairly level for a couple of miles, meandering through the Douglas-fir and aspen trees along the creek. The trail then climbs gradually, through a jumbled talus slope called the "golden stairs" and ends near several pretty lakes.

The byway leaves Beaver Creek and begins its ascent into the mountains. Less than a mile from the highway, Lower Provo Campground has drinking water and ten sites in the evergreens along the Provo River. The forest here is composed primarily of ponderosa pines and white firs.

The byway crosses the North Fork Provo River, which has good fishing for rainbows and brookies and opportunities for dispersed primitive camping, and now follows the Provo River, another good fishing stream.

Soapstone Campground has drinking water and thirty-three sites in an aspen and lodgepole pine forest. The elevation here is 8,200 feet. In mid-summer, you can usually find tasty thimbleberries a short ways up Soapstone Basin Road.

Shady Dell Campground supplies drinking water and has twenty sites situated in the trees along the river. The byway travels past the west portal of six-mile-long Duchesne Tunnel, a Bureau of Reclamation water project which carries six hundred cubic feet of water per second.

Duchesne Tunnel Campground is quite primitive and best suited for self-contained units. A few miles east, Cobblerest Campground provides drinking water and eighteen sites in the trees along the river.

The byway turns north, still on Highway 150 along the Provo River. A very short trail leads to Slate Gorge Overlook, which offers a view of sandstones and dark gray, reddish, and black shales. These are Precambrian rocks, deposited in a big gorge cut into the earth about a billion years ago. The gorge is about fifty feet deep here, and the water cascades below.

Upper Provo Bridge Campground has five sites in the trees along the river, at 9,200 feet elevation. Walk the short, paved trail to Provo River Falls Overlook. This cascading falls was in a Disney movie.

The byway provides glimpses of the high mountain summits in the High Uintas Wilderness. Climbing steadily, you'll drive into a region of high mountain meadows surrounding numerous glacially carved lakes. The Uinta Mountain Range is a huge arching fold in the earth called an anticline. Repeated glaciation and melting carved big U-shaped valleys for drainage and left pothole lakes at the top. Glacial moraines, the loose rock pushed into mounds and ridges by the movement of those glaciers, are evident all along the byway. The big white quartzite boulders strewn around were plucked from the high peaks by glaciers.

There are numerous recreation opportunities along the top, at this 10,000-

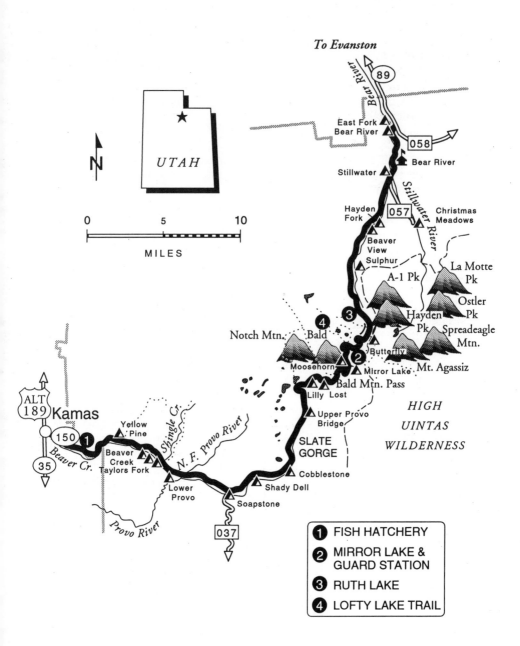

To Evanston

89
Bear River

East Fork
Bear River

058

Bear River

Stillwater

Stillwater River

Hayden
Fork

057

Christmas
Meadows

Beaver
View
Sulphur

A-1 Pk

La Motte
Pk

Ostler
Pk

Hayden
Pk

Spreadeagle
Mtn.

Notch Mtn.

3

4

Bald

Butterfly

Mt. Agassiz

Moosehorn

2

Mirror Lake

Bald Mtn. Pass

Lilly Lost

HIGH
UINTAS
WILDERNESS

UTAH

N

0   5   10

MILES

ALT
189

Kamas

150

1

Yellow
Pine

Shingle Cr.

35

Beaver Cr.

Beaver
Creek
Taylors Fork

N. F. Provo River

Upper Provo
Bridge

SLATE
GORGE

Cobblestone

Lower
Provo

Shady Dell

Soapstone

037

Provo River

1 FISH HATCHERY

2 MIRROR LAKE &
GUARD STATION

3 RUTH LAKE

4 LOFTY LAKE TRAIL

Wildlife along Mirror Lake Scenic Byway includes the regal elk. Photo by Michael S. Sample.

foot elevation. Bring repellent, because mosquitoes can be annoying from about mid-June through early August. Lakes and streams are stocked with brook trout and albino rainbow trout from the hatchery near Kamas. Hiking trails and other non-motorized recreation routes abound. This is a popular area for mountain bicycling, walking, horseback riding, fishing, camping, wildlife viewing, and just plain relaxing.

A side trip on Forest Road 041 brings you to the Notch Mountain and Notch Lake trailheads. You can hike this well-marked route through the alpine lakes area up to ten miles, ending on the highway at Bald Mountain Pass. To make a shorter loop, hike out the Notch Mountain Trail, then return to Forest Road 041 on the Crystal Lake trail.

Lilly Lake Campground provides drinking water, and fourteen sites on the lakeshore, in the forest of subalpine firs and lodgepole pines. Lodgepoles were named because they grow straight and narrow and make ideal poles for tipis. Nearby, Lost Creek Campground has drinking water and thirty-four camp-sites along the creek.

An overlook allows you to stop and admire 11,947-foot Bald Mountain. The grayish-green rock is shale, and the orange is quartzite. Look southeast to see the jumbled, granite boulders comprising the summit of Murdock Mountain, elevation 11,212 feet. You can also see the Provo River Basin, Mount Timpanogas on the Uinta National Forest, Haystack Mountain, and the beautiful lakes country surrounding Bald Mountain. This region west of the byway is a semiprimitive area, primarily for nonmotorized recreation.

The byway tops Bald Mountain Pass, elevation 10,715 feet. Right at timberline, Icelandic poppies brighten the ground between the twisted, gnarly shapes of "krummholtz," or subalpine fir, and various tough, low-growing shrubs. The headwaters for four rivers originate on Bald Mountain Pass: Provo, Weber, Bear, and Duchesne rivers. You'll see into Moosehorn Lake, Hayden Peak, and Mount Agassiz in the High Uinta Wilderness. A good family hike from the pass leads two miles to the summit of Bald Mountain. You'll gain 1,228 feet in elevation, and the panoramic view from the top is outstanding. Look for Hayden and Agassiz peaks to the east, and enjoy the surrounding peaks and lakes to the west. Lucky hikers may spot bighorn sheep or moun-tain goats here.

The byway descends the pass, offering views into the High Uintas Wilder-ness. Moosehorn Campground has drinking water and thirty-three sites in the trees around the lake. Bald Mountain juts up just to the west. Stop at the Mirror Lake Guard Station to look at the bulletin board. There you'll find informa-tion on weather, birds, and flowers, along with other regional tidbits.

Inhabitants of this byway region include elk, mule deer, moose, mountain goats, bighorn sheep, yellow-bellied marmots, coyotes, black bears, bobcats, mountain lions, pine martens, badgers, skunks, snowshoe hares, porcupines, ground squirrels, and beavers.

Bird watchers can look for golden eagles, gray jays, magpies, robins, vesper sparrows, red-tailed hawks, great horned owls, red-breasted nuthatches, pine siskins, yellow-bellied sapsuckers, hairy woodpeckers, warbling vireos, moun-tain bluebirds, water pipits, MacGillivray's warblers, green-tailed towhees, and black-throated gray warblers.

Mirror Lake Campground has a picnic area, drinking water, and eighty-five campsites near the lake. Several horse and hiking trails lead into the wilder-ness from here. A mile north on the byway, you can walk one of the nicest ·

four-mile loops in this area. Follow the Lofty Lake Trail past Kamas, Lofty, and Scout lakes for some beautiful views into Bear River Basin, Cutthroat, Jewel, and Teal lakes, then return to the trailhead via Picturesque and Pass lakes. It's a moderate hike with a few steep rocky sections, well worth the effort.

A mile farther along the byway, Butterfly Campground provides drinking water and twenty campsites. Walk a few miles of the Highline Trail into the High Uintas Wilderness to Scudder Lake. The lake sits in a pretty basin surrounded by subalpine fir forest, and fishing is pretty good.

Hayden Pass reaches 10,347 feet elevation. You can see Hayden Peak and the whole ridgeline which forms the westernmost boundary of the wilderness. Stretch your legs on a .7-mile trail into Ruth Lake, a lovely forested alpine lake with brook trout and nice solitude.

The byway descends through the forest along the Hayden Fork of the Bear River, another glaciated U-shaped valley. The High Uintas Wilderness is east of the byway. Engelmann spruce and subalpine fir are the primary tree types here.

A historical monument commemorates Richard K. A. Kletting, who was instrumental in creating Utah's first forest reserve in 1897. Two miles north, Sulphur Campground provides drinking water and has twenty sites at the upper edge of a meadow. The Hayden Fork is stocked with rainbow and cutthroat trout. Look for moose in the early morning or late evening. The north slope of the Uintas hosts Utah's largest population of moose.

The byway now travels along the bottom of the canyon, where willows and wet meadows are interspersed with trees. Wildflowers in these wet meadows include shooting star, monkshood, Indian paintbrush, lupine, rose, elephanthead, yellow monkeyflower, fairyslipper, bog orchid, dogtooth violet, marsh marigold, bluebell, geranium, corn lily, yarrow, columbine, cinquefoil, and fireweed.

Beaver View Campground has drinking water and sixteen campsites. If you're quiet, you can watch the beavers at work on their dams. Hayden's Fork Campground offers drinking water and nine campsites along the edge of a river in a lodgepole pine forest. Stillwater Campground has drinking water, picnicking, and eighteen campsites near the confluence of the Hayden Fork, Stillwater Fork, and Main Fork.

Take a side trip on Forest Road 057 to Christmas Meadows. Here the Stillwater Fork really is still water, meandering slowly through a big beautiful meadow. There are eleven campsites, picnic tables, and drinking water. You can see up the Stillwater Fork into the High Uintas Wilderness. The rugged summits of Ostler Peak and Spreadeagle Mountain jut up. A walk into the wilderness follows the canyon bottom through the forest, and you may see moose and deer.

Farther along the byway, Bear River Ranger Station is open from Memorial Day to the end of October. Stop in for maps and national forest information. The view is stunning; the north slope of the Uinta Mountains dominates, and numerous summits are visible: Reids, Kletting, LaMotte, Ostler, and A-1 peaks. Snow forms an "A" over the number "1" on A-1 Peak. Most of these mountains hold snow into early August.

Near the national forest boundary on the banks of the river, Bear River Campground has four sites and East Fork Campground eight sites. Both supply drinking water.

Hayden Peak juts above Moose Horn Lake, along the Mirror Lake Scenic Byway. Wasatch-Cache National Forest photo.

A side trip east on Forest Road 058, the North Slope Road, is a thirty-eight mile scenic backway suitable for high-clearance or four-wheel drive vehicles.

The byway ends at the national forest boundary. The highway continues north to Evanston, Wyoming, through ranchland, meadows, and hayfields. Sulphur Creek Reservoir has a historical plaque commemorating the old railroad community called Bear Town. In the 1870s, lumber was floated down a flume from the Uintas to the reservoir. You can still find the remains of old kilns that made charcoal for the engines. ☐

General description: A six-mile drive, with riveting views of the cliffs and amphitheaters of Cedar Breaks National Monument.

Special attractions: Outstanding geologic formations, beautiful views, wildflowers, Ashdown Gorge Wilderness, hiking, camping.

Location: Southwest Utah on the Dixie National Forest and Cedar Breaks National Monument. The byway travels Highway 148 from its southern terminus on Highway 14, through the national monument, to its northern terminus at the junction of Highways 143 and 148.

Byway route number: Utah State Highway 148.

Travel season: Open from about June through mid-October, then closed by winter snows.

Camping: One national park campground, with picnic tables, fire grills, restrooms, and drinking water.

Services: No traveler services on the byway. Traveler services available in nearby Brian Head resort with limited availability, or full services in Cedar City.

Nearby attractions: Brian Head-Panguitch Lake, Markaguant, and Beaver Canyon national forest scenic byways; Bryce Canyon and Zion national parks; Red Canyon; Pine Valley Mountains Wilderness.

For more information: Dixie National Forest and Cedar City Ranger District, 82 North 100 East (P.O. Box 580), Cedar City, UT 84720, (801) 865-3700 Supervisor's Office; (801) 865-3200 District Ranger. Cedar Breaks National Monument, P.O. Box 749, Cedar City, UT 84720, (801) 586-9451.

Description: Cedar Breaks Scenic Byway combines a unique blend of national forest and national monument. The paved two-lane highway, is open from about June through mid-October, and has frequent scenic pulloffs and overlooks. Traffic is constant and slow-moving. The speed limit through the monument is thirty mph.

Summer daytime temperatures are often in the seventies and eighties but drop into the forties and fifties at night. Expect afternoon thunderstorms in July and August. Spring and fall temperatures can be quite brisk at this 10,000-foot elevation, and roads are often slick with ice or snow.

Cedar Breaks Scenic Byway is connected to two other scenic byways: the Markaguant on the south and the Brian Head-Panguitch Lake on the north. Driving from south to north on the Cedar Breaks Scenic Byway, you climb through sagebrush meadows and rolling hills, up into ponderosa pines and aspen, and culminate in the high-elevation spruce-fir forest on the plateau. Autumn colors are beautiful.

Take a side trip west on Forest Road 277 to the electronic site at the top of Mount Blowhard. An excellent five-mile downhill hike leaves from Mount Blowhard and drops through Ashdown Gorge Wilderness to Highway 14.

About two miles from its start, the byway leaves the Dixie National Forest and enters Cedar Breaks National Monument. Early settlers mistakenly called

Four separate overlooks each offer a unique perspective on Cedar Breaks National Monument. Dixie National Forest photo.

junipers "cedars," and breaks is a term for badlands, or highly eroded areas.

Stop at the visitor center in the park to get information and maps and to view the excellent exhibits on geology, wildlife, wildflowers, and history. Walk the two-mile Wasatch Ramparts Trail out to Spectra Point and on through forests and wildflower meadows along the rim. A stand of bristlecone pines are on Spectra Point. Individuals of this species are the oldest living things on earth; some trees are over 4,000 years old. Treat them all with care.

Cedar Breaks is a huge amphitheater on the edge of the Markaguant Plateau. The limestone here is over 1,300 feet thick and the beautiful reds, yellows, and purples result from oxidation of minerals, mostly iron and manganese. This soft rock erodes easily, and thirteen million years of uplift, frost, snow, ice, and wind carved the spires, ridges, columns, arches, and canyons. It's an unforgettable scene. The amphitheater itself is over 2,000 feet deep and more than three miles in diameter.

The campground provides thirty sites and a picnic area. Naturalists present evening programs in the amphitheater.

The Rim Drive winds five miles through the park. Stop at the scenic overlooks for different perspectives on the amphitheater. Each is different and unique. From Chessmen Ridge Overlook, you can walk the Alpine Pond Trail. This is a short, easy, self-guided nature walk loop along the rim.

Wildlife watchers can look for elk, mule deer, black bears, coyotes, foxes, mountain lions, bobcats, jackrabbits, and pikas, as well as numerous species of squirrels, gophers, mice, and voles. Bird watchers may spot golden eagles, goshawks, red-tailed hawks, or kestrels soaring overhead. Rufous hummingbirds, flickers and woodpeckers, violet-green swallows, gray jays, mountain chickadees, juncoes, grosbeaks, finches, and warblers are commonly seen in the area.

The byway ends at the junction of Highways 148 and 143. Highway 143 is another national forest scenic byway described in this book, called Brian Head-Panguitch Lake. □

26 CEDAR BREAKS SCENIC BYWAY

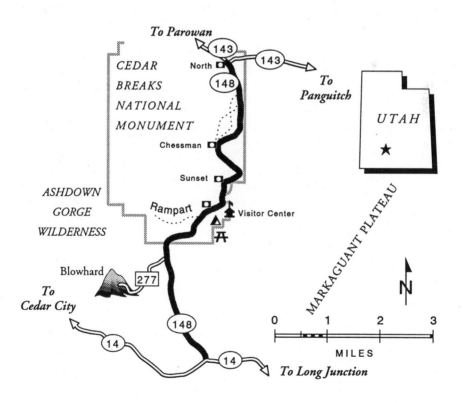

General description: A forty-mile highway across the Markaguant Plateau, with stunning views, lakes, and wilderness.

Special attractions: Fascinating geology, extensive views, Ashdown Gorge Wilderness, lakes, camping, hiking, fishing.

Location: Southwest Utah on the Dixie National Forest. The byway travels Highway 14 between Cedar City and Long Valley Junction.

Byway route number: Utah State Highway 14.

Travel season: Year-round.

Camping: Five national forest campgrounds on or near the byway, with picnic tables, fire grills, toilets, and drinking water.

Services: All traveler services in Cedar City. Gas, phone, food, with very limited availability, in Long Valley Junction.

Nearby attractions: Cedar Breaks National Monument; Cedar Breaks, Brian Head-Panguitch Lake, and Beaver Canyon national forest scenic byways; Bryce Canyon and Zion national parks; Red Canyon; Pine Valley Mountain Wilderness; Coral Pink Sand Dunes.

For more information: Dixie National Forest and Cedar Breaks Ranger District, 82 North 100 East (P.O. Box 580), Cedar City, UT 84720, (801) 865-3700 Supervisor's Office; (801) 865-3200 District Ranger's office.

Description: The Markaguant (MAR-ka-gunt) Scenic Byway traverses the lakes and forests of a massive plateau. The two-lane highway is paved and has frequent scenic turnouts. Traffic is constant. Watch for logging trucks.

Summer daytime temperatures are usually in the seventies and eighties but can reach the nineties. Expect severe afternoon thunderstorms in July and August. Spring and fall daytime temperatures hover in the sixties, and nights drop to the thirties and forties. Winter is cold, with plenty of snow cover and temperatures from below zero to just above freezing.

The byway is very scenic driven in either direction. You may wish to plan your trip according to the time of day, to minimize sun glare. Drive west to east in the afternoon, and east to west in the morning.

When driving west to east, begin in Cedar City, a full-service community. You can obtain maps and national forest information at the ranger station.

The byway travels east up Cedar Canyon on Highway 14. The mouth of the canyon marks the Hurricane Fault, where the east side was lifted several thousand feet above the west side to create the Hurricane Cliffs. Cedar Canyon is one of the few openings in the Hurricane Cliffs. Exposed slopes show colorfully banded red, white, and tan sandstone, siltstone, and mudstone. Wind and stream erosion have carved spires and columns into the soft rock.

Ashdown Gorge Wilderness lies just north of the byway. The wilderness protects about 7,000 acres of steep, beautiful terrain adjacent to Cedar Breaks National Monument. Elevations range from around 6,000 to 10,000 feet. It's known for the beautiful views of red cliffs and ledges, and natural arches and small waterfalls at the lower elevations. About fifteen miles of maintained

Strawberry Point, just off the Markaguant Scenic Byway, provides a stunning view of southern Utah. Dixie National Forest photo.

trails wind through the wilderness. Most are considered strenuous.

Big cut banks, piles of debris, and piles of rocks are evidence of the huge spring floods that roar through here. After spring run-off, Coal Creek is very mild or even dried up.

A scenic backway takes off from the byway and goes into the Kolob area of Zion National Park. This route is suitable for high clearance four-wheel drives.

There are several beaver dams along the creek. Sit quietly until the beavers get used to your presence, and then you can watch them at work.

About eight miles from Cedar City, you can see a black cap of lava crowning the sheer, tan cliffs. This is part of the volcanic explosion that covered most of the Markaguant Plateau thirty million years ago. At the national forest boundary, the first breathtaking view of pink eroded cliffs lies ahead. This same formation is in Cedar Breaks National Monument. Silted limestone deposits from an ancient freshwater lake are colored by the oxidation of minerals, mostly iron and manganese. The soft rock erodes into scenic and interesting patterns.

Cedar Canyon Campground offers seventeen sites in the aspen and fir along

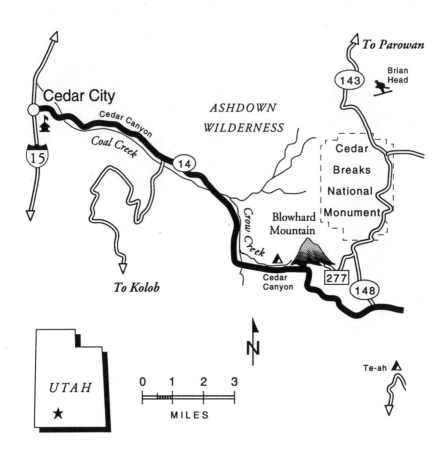

the creek. Traveling east, the view opens up to the south and looks over aspens, mountains, and valleys into Zion National Park. The byway rolls across the forested Markaguant Plateau to its junction with Highway 148. In summer, a side trip north on this road, another national forest scenic byway, leads into Cedar Breaks National Monument. It's well worth the trip.

Another side trip leads west from Highway 148. Follow Forest Road 277 to the electronic site at the top of Mount Blowhard. The Mount Blowhard Trail winds about five miles downhill, through Ashdown Gorge Wilderness and comes out on Highway 14. You'll descend through several life zones, from high elevation Engelmann spruce and subalpine fir, through Douglas-fir, and

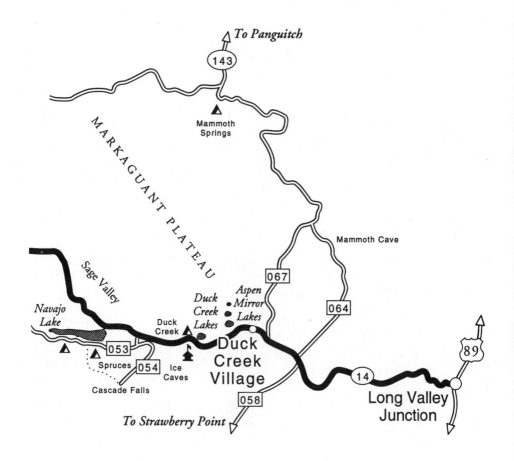

into the oaks and aspens at the bottom. There are extensive vistas to the west and great views into Cedar Breaks.

Continuing east on 14, the route travels through fields of wildflowers adjacent to lava beds. Blossoms brightening the meadows include larkspur, lupine, penstemon, columbine, and Indian paintbrush. Wildlife on the national forest includes black bears, elk, mule deer, mountain lions, bobcats, coyotes, gray and red foxes, jackrabbits, and a variety of mice, voles, squirrels, shrews, and bats. You'll definitely see lots of grazing sheep.

A side trip on Forest Road 053 descends to Navajo Lake. There you'll find three national forest campgrounds, two resorts, and opportunities to swim and canoe. Anglers fish for rainbow and brook trout.

Spruces Campground, elevation 9,200 feet, has twenty-eight campsites in the dense forest of Engelmann spruce. Take a hike on the Rim Trail, for spectacular views into Zion National Park. The trail extends about three miles from Spruces Campground to Cascade Falls National Recreation Trail.

Just west of Spruces, Navajo Lake Campground provides twenty-eight sites right on the lakeshore. West of Navajo Lake, Te-Ah Campground has forty-two sites in a stand of aspen trees. Te-ah is the Navajo Indian word for deer.

You can drive to Cascade Falls on Forest Road 054. At the end of the road, a .5-mile self-guiding nature trail leads to the cascading waterfall. The falls is very interesting geologically. It is one of two outlets for Navajo Lake, whose waters descend through lava tubes and percolate into the surrounding limestone. The water pops out from the red rock cavern and drops down Cascade Falls. The other outlet for Navajo Lake is a spring which forms Duck Creek Lake, a few miles northeast of here.

Back on the byway, the Duck Creek Visitor Center is located near milepost 28. Stop in summertime for national forest information, books, materials, and maps. Nearby ice caves in a lava tube are interesting.

Duck Creek Campground has eighty-one sites in the forest of spruce, pine, and aspen near Duck Creek Lake. Water from here flows a short distance then disappears into the porous volcanic sinkhole near Duck Creek Village, to re-emerge farther east. Eventually it drains into the Sevier River. Duck Creek Lake is a popular place to fish for planted rainbow and brown trout. There are some big fish in the little pond.

Duck Creek Village caters to cross-country skiers and snowmobilers. Nearby, Aspen Mirror Lake is planted with rainbow trout. A side trip northeast on Forest Road 067 leads through lava flows and pretty vistas along Mammoth Creek. The source of the creek is visible at Mammoth Springs, a lava tube near the small, primitive campground.

The byway descends through a thick ponderosa pine forest. Another side trip, south on Forest Road 058, takes you to Strawberry Point, where you have extensive views of the Pink Cliffs and Zion National Park.

The byway offers big views of the pink cliff formations on the Paunsaugunt Plateau to the east. The vegetation changes as you drop down into the drier, lower elevations. There are oaks, pinyon pines, junipers, and mountain maples. The maples turn bright red in autumn.

Markaguant Scenic Byway ends at Long Valley Junction, at the intersection of Highways 14 and 89. You could return to Cedar City via the Brian Head-Panguitch Lake National Forest Scenic Byway, just to the north. □

General description: A fifty-five mile route up and over a high rolling plateau, with wide-ranging views.

Special attractions: Panguitch Lake, Brian Head Ski Area, Cedar Breaks National Monument, Ashdown Gorge Wilderness, interesting geology, hiking, camping.

Location: Southwest Utah on the Dixie National Forest. The byway travels Highway 143 between Panguitch and Parowan.

Byway route number: Utah State Highway 143.

Travel season: Year-round.

Camping: Three national forest campgrounds, with picnic tables, fire grates, toilets, and drinking water.

Services: All traveler services in Parowan and Panguitch, with limited availability. Food, lodging, boat rentals, gas at Panguitch Lake resorts.

Nearby attractions: Cedar Breaks, Markaguant, and Beaver Canyon national forest scenic byways; Bryce Canyon and Zion national parks; Pine Valley Mountain Wilderness; Red Canyon Scenic Byway.

For more information: Dixie National Forest, 82 North 100 East (P.O. Box 580), Cedar City, UT 84720, (801) 865-3700. Cedar City Ranger District, 82 North 100 East, Cedar City, UT 84720, (801) 865-3200.

Description: Brian Head-Panguitch Lake Scenic Byway traverses a high plateau, offering some stunning views and plenty of recreation opportunities. The two-lane road is paved and has frequent pulloffs. Traffic is steady all summer and light the rest of the year, except between Parowan and Brian Head on winter weekends.

Weather on the high plateau can vary considerably from the valleys below. Summer daytime temperatures are usually between seventy and ninety degrees. Expect severe afternoon thunderstorms in July and August. Spring and fall daytime temperatures hover around sixty, and nights drop to the thirties and forties. Winter is cold, with plenty of snow cover and temperatures from below zero to around freezing.

The byway is very scenic driven in either direction. When driving east to west, begin in Panguitch, which has some lovely pioneer-era homes. Follow Highway 143 west, climbing gradually through the pinyon-juniper vegetation. About thirteen miles from town, White Bridge Campground provides twenty-nine sites in the cottonwoods along Panguitch Creek. The creek is stocked with rainbow trout and is very popular with anglers.

A few miles farther on the byway, Panguitch Lake sits in a sagebrush basin. Aspens and pine trees cover the hills surrounding the lake. There are several resorts, and opportunities to fish for planted rainbow and brown trout. Two campgrounds provide sixty-seven campsites. Naturalists present summer weekend programs in the amphitheater. Topics cover natural history, wild-life, geology, archaeology, and area attractions.

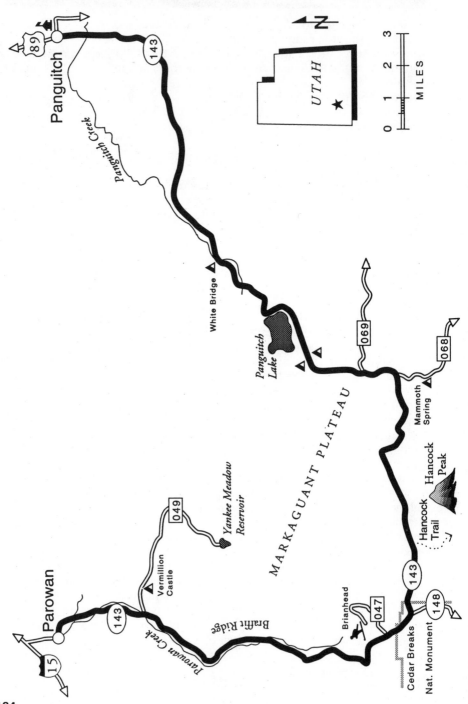

A few miles beyond the lake, a side trip on Forest Road 069 (Birch Spring Knoll) is well worth your time. The road is rough and you may prefer to walk, but by all means go at least a mile, through an immense flow of chunky basalt. Bright green lichens cling to the rocks, aspen grow out of nooks and crannies, and tenacious wildflowers shoot out of cracks in the rocks. It's a fascinating place.

The geologic history here is easy to see and understand. This part of Utah was composed of freshwater limestone and silts that were upthrust into plateaus. Geologists conjecture that thirty million years ago, that thrusting action opened vents and lava streamed out. The lava is hundreds of feet thick in places, and it filled and blocked many stream channels. The lava didn't cover other areas of the plateau, and this is obvious around Panguitch Lake.

Two miles father along the byway, another side trip presents an opportunity to see more beautiful vistas. Forest Road 068 (Mammoth Creek Road) rolls through the aspen and ponderosa pine forest to the top of the plateau, where spruce and fir dominate. The creek has some nice brown trout. Meadows have wildflowers like Indian paintbrush and asters. You can see the lava flows throughout the area.

Continue along the byway, across the rolling terrain of the plateau. Hancock Peak Trail is a delightful walk across the plateau. Follow the cairns (piled rocks) through a wide sagebrush valley, across streams, into the spruce/fir forest, and along a pretty pond. The trail goes 6.5 miles and ends on Forest Road 240.

The byway cuts through a corner of Cedar Breaks National Monument and offers a riveting view of the breaks from Mammoth Summit. Continuing on Highway 143, Brian Head Ski Area offers prime winter downhill skiing opportunities, and good summer mountain bicycle trails. Brian Head Peak is the highest point on the Markaguant Plateau, at elevation 11,315 feet. You can

Snow blankets the high, rolling Markaguant Plateau, and provides excellent winter skiing opportunities. Dixie National Forest photo.

drive to the top in summer and see the Great Basin and Nevada to the west, Arizona to the south, and the Markaguant Plateau stretched out immediately around you. Cinder cones jut up here and there, evidence of volcanic activity. The summit of Brian Head is composed of lava that is hundreds of feet thick.

The byway descends in a series of hairpin turns, not recommended for towed units. Braffit Ridge's white rocks dominate the eastern horizon. Near milepost 10, Dry Lakes Scenic Backway is a high-clearance, four-wheel-drive route.

Vermillion Castle Campground has sixteen sites adjacent to Bowery Creek. Douglas-fir and pinyon-juniper vegetation adorn the steep slopes. You can fish for planted rainbows in the little pond. The reddish-orange cliffs are brilliant at sunset, and you can find interesting shapes eroded into the limestone. Keep going out 049 to Yankee Meadow Reservoir to fish for rainbows and brookies.

The byway meanders through the narrow canyon created by Parowan Creek, and ends in the small community of Parowan. □

29 ECCLES CANYON SCENIC BYWAY
Manti-La Sal National Forest   Utah

General description: A sixteen-mile highway across a mountain plateau, then down a narrow canyon in a major coal-producing region.
Special attractions: Boating, fishing, camping.
Location: Central Utah on the Manti-La Sal National Forest. The byway travels the entire length of Highway 264, between its junctions with Highways 31 and 96.
Byway route number: Utah State Highway 264.
Travel season: Year-round.
Camping: One national forest campground, with picnic tables, fire grates, and toilets, drinking water.
Services: No traveler services on the byway.
Nearby attractions: Huntington Canyon National Forest Scenic Byway, Price Canyon Recreation Area.
For more information: Manti-La Sal National Forest and Price Ranger District, 599 West Price River Drive, Price, UT 84501, (801) 637-2817.

Description: Eccles Canyon Scenic Byway travels down a narrow canyon of the Wasatch Plateau, dropping from about 10,000 feet elevation down to 7,500 feet. The two-lane highway is paved, and traffic is generally light except during hunting season in autumn. Speed limits vary from thirty-five to fifty-five mph. Watch for large trucks year round.

Summer temperatures at the top generally range from the fifties to the eighties. Expect short-lived, intense afternoon thunderstorms in July and August. Spring and fall temperatures range from below freezing up to the fifties or sixties. Snow blankets the ground from November to May and accumulates to ten feet deep at the top. Check road conditions before driving this route in winter. Snow tires or chains are required between October 1 and April 30.

Traveling west to east on the byway, you'll begin on the Huntington Canyon Scenic Byway, described in this book. Eccles Canyon Scenic Byway begins atop the Wasatch Plateau at the intersection of Highways 31 and 264 and follows 264 below Fairview Lake. Meadows of wildflowers line the banks of meandering streams. Blossoming flowers include lupine, columbine, larkspur, penstemon, Indian paintbrush, Jacobs ladder, and mustard.

Flat Canyon Campground has twelve sites in a dense stand of Engelmann spruce and subalpine fir trees. Tiny Boulger Reservoir is stocked with rainbow trout. A mile east, a boat ramp on Electric Lake provides access to this larger reservoir. Fishing on the reservoir and its tributaries is closed from January 1 to July 1 for the Yellowstone cutthroat trout spawning season. Cutthroat transplants from this fishery are used to stock other lakes and streams in Utah.

Anglers find good fishing opportunities along Eccles Canyon Scenic Byway. Manti-La Sal National Forest photo.

29 ECCLES CANYON SCENIC BYWAY

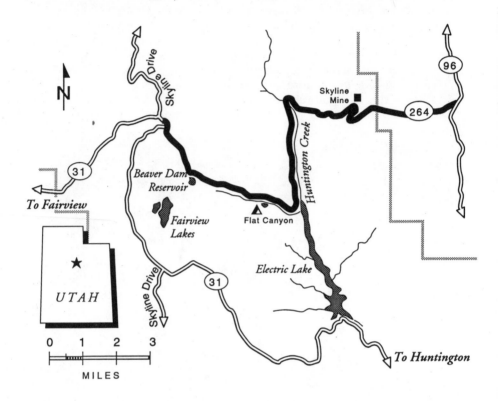

The byway ascends alongside the sinuous course of Huntington Creek. A fenced enclosure helps naturalists monitor the sedimentation in the stream to see the impacts of moving a natural gas pipeline.

A steep climb brings you up a forested high ridge, then you'll drop down Eccles Canyon. The Skyline Mine is a major coal mine, producing between 3.5 and five million tons of coal annually. Production is expected to increase and this could become the largest underground coal mine in the world. Seventy percent of Utah's coal production comes from public lands on the Manti-La Sal National Forest.

The byway leaves the national forest and ends at the junction of Highways 264 and 96, near a big loadout area where trucks empty coal into waiting trains. North on Highway 96 takes you to Scofield Lake State Recreation Area, where there is boating, fishing, hiking, camping, and picnicking. □

HUNTINGTON CANYON SCENIC BYWAY
Manti-La Sal National Forest   Utah

General description: A forty-eight mile drive over the Wasatch Plateau, in the heart of the coal region.

Special attractions: Lakes, fishing, camping, far-ranging vistas, picnicking, Eccles Canyon National Forest Scenic Byway.

Location: Central Utah on the Manti-La Sal National Forest. The byway travels Highway 31 between Fairview and Huntington.

Byway route number: Utah State Highway 31.

Travel season: Year-round.

Camping: Three public campgrounds, with picnic tables, fire grates, toilets, drinking water.

Services: All traveler services in Fairview and Huntington.

Nearby attractions: Prehistoric Museum in Price, Cleveland Lloyd Dinosaur Quarry, Mount Nebo National Forest Scenic Byway, Price Canyon Recreation Area.

For more information: Manti-La Sal National Forest and Price Ranger District, 599 West Price River Drive, Price, UT 84501, (801) 637-2817. Sanpete Ranger District, 150 South Main, P.O. Box 6-4, Ephraim, UT 84627, (801) 283-4151.

Description: Huntington Canyon Scenic Byway climbs atop the Wasatch Plateau and provides some far-ranging views. The two-lane road is paved and has frequent scenic turnouts. Traffic is generally light to moderate, except during the fall hunting season when it gets very busy. Watch for big trucks going to and from the mines.

Summer temperatures at the top generally range from the fifties to the eighties. Expect short-lived, intense afternoon thunderstorms in July and August. Spring and fall temperatures range from below freezing up to the fifties or sixties. Snow blankets the ground from November to May and accumulates to ten feet deep at the top. Check road conditions before driving this route in winter. Snow tires or chains are required between October 1 and April 30.

The byway is very scenic driven in either direction. Elevations vary from about 6,000 feet up to 10,000 feet. Traveling west to east, begin in Fairview. You can tour the Museum of Natural History and Arts and stroll through town to see the nice-looking pioneer-era buildings. Head east on Highway 31 up Fairview Canyon, along Cottonwood Creek. The steep slopes are dotted with aspen, Engelmann spruce, and Douglas-fir, and the highway climbs up an eight percent grade.

Take a side trip north on Skyline Drive, for beautiful views and dispersed, primitive camping opportunities. The meadows are full of grasses, herbaceous sages, and wildflowers such as lupine, columbine, larkspur, and Indian paintbrush. In winter this is a popular snowmobiling route.

The scenic byway remains on Highway 31, past the junction of Highways 31 and 264. (Highway 264 is the Eccles Canyon Scenic Byway, described in this book.) Huntington Canyon Scenic Byway rolls across the plateau, and

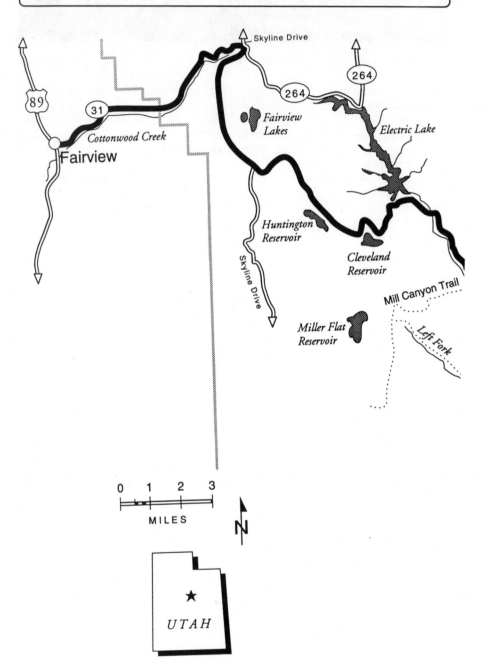

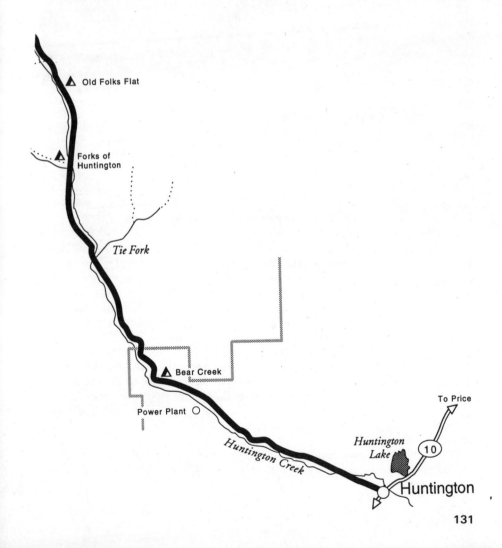

Old Folks Flat

Forks of
Huntington

Tie Fork

Bear Creek

Power Plant

Huntington Creek

Huntington
Lake

To Price

10

Huntington

Huntington Canyon Scenic Byway travels through the forest up Huntington Canyon, then crosses the Wasatch Plateau. Manti-La Sal National Forest photo.

provides a beautiful view of Fairview Lakes. Continuing along, the views broaden to include the verdant San Pitch River Valley to the west and the San Pitch Mountains and Mount Nebo Wilderness to the northwest.

The byway enters a region of reservoirs which store water for irrigation in the Castle Valley. Huntington Reservoir is a popular winter recreation area. Winter sports include snowmobiling, tubing, and cross-country skiing. The complete skeleton of a 9,500-year-old Columbian woolly mammoth was discovered just below the dam site. Mastodon, ancient horse, and shortfaced bear remains were also found in this area, or in sinkholes along Skyline Drive.

Nearby, Cleveland Reservoir is a popular fishery for stocked rainbow trout. The setting is beautiful—rolling hills, meadows, and forest. Electric Lake contains native Yellowstone cutthroat trout. Boat access to the lake is from Highway 264.

The byway descends along Huntington Creek, which has beaver dams, still pools, and rushing waters. This is a blue-ribbon stretch of water, for fly fishing only. There are rainbow, cutthroat, and brown trout.

Deer and birds may share the willow-lined streambank with you. Other mammals include elk, black bear, porcupine, blue grouse, mountain lion, and moose. Look overhead for golden eagles, red-tailed hawks, goshawks, and kestrels. Bald eagles migrate through in late fall and spring.

Old Folks Flat Campground has group picnicking and some family camp-sites in a stand of spruce and fir trees. There are two horseshoe pitch areas and good access for fishing the creek.

Continuing on the byway, Forks of Huntington Canyon Campground has family sites in the spruce and willows along the creek. The sagebrush community of vegetation covers the south-facing slopes, while conifers and aspens grow on the cooler, north-facing side. You can fish in both Huntington Creek and the Left Fork.

A wonderful National Recreation Trail ascends the Left Fork. It gains only 500 feet elevation in just over four miles. You can fish the creek and enjoy a cool walk in the forest of aspens, Engelmann spruce, and subalpine fir.

A few miles south of the campground, walk the Tie Fork Canyon Road and see how many of the twenty-two species of trees you can identify. To name just a few: quaking aspen, water birch, alder, cottonwood, and several species of junipers, firs, and pines.

The byway exits the national forest and travels by county-managed Bear Creek Campground, which has twenty sites in the cottonwoods along the creek. Just south is the coal-burning Huntington Power Plant. A conveyor belt brings coal from the Deer Creek mine to the two-unit plant, each of which burns 8,000 tons of coal each day.

The byway ends in Huntington, a full-service community. Nearby, Huntington Lake State Beach provides opportunities to fish, swim, camp, and boat. □

31 HIGHWAY OF LEGENDS
San Isabel National Forest   Colorado

General description: An eighty-two mile paved highway through a moun-tainous region rich in history.
Special attractions: Splendid mountain scenery, autumn colors, legends, mining history, resorts, camping, fishing, hiking, mountain biking, downhill and cross-country skiing.
Location: South-central Colorado on the San Isabel National Forest. The byway is a horseshoe-shaped route connecting Trinidad and Walsenburg.
Byway route numbers: U.S. Highway 160 and Colorado State Highway 12.
Travel season: Year-round.
Camping: Four national forest campgrounds within four miles of the byway, with picnic tables, fire grates, toilets, and drinking water. Campgrounds also at one state park, one state recreation area, and one municipal park.
Services: All traveler services in Trinidad and Walsenburg.

Nearby attractions: Great Sand Dunes National Monument, Fort Garland State Museum.

For more information: San Isabel National Forest, 1920 Valley Drive, Pueblo, CO 81008, (719) 545-8737. San Carlos Ranger District, 326 Dozier Street, Canon City, CO 81212, (719) 275-4119.

Description: Highway of Legends climbs from the plains through the scenic Sangre de Cristo Mountains, crosses a mountain pass and descends back to the plains. The route is two-lane paved highway. Newer sections have wide shoulders. Traffic is moderately heavy in summer and autumn and light the remainder of the year.

Weather on the plains may be radically different than that found in the mountains on the same day. Generally, expect summer in the mountains to bring daytime temperatures between eighty and ninety. Afternoon thunderstorms are frequent. Spring and fall are cooler, in the fifties to seventies, with plenty of spring rain and snow showers. Snow generally covers the ground between December and April, and daytime temperatures may reach the forties but dip below freezing at night.

Scenery on the byway is good when driven from either direction, but counterclockwise is considered best. If traveling counterclockwise, begin the scenic tour in Walsenburg, located just off Interstate 25.

The Walsenburg Mining Museum's displays and simulated coal mine shaft explain what life was like for local coal miners between 1880 and 1940. Remains of over fifty mines are still in evidence around Walsenburg.

Traveling U.S. Highway 160 west out of town, you pass huge slag heaps and more mining ruins. About three miles from downtown, Lathrop State Park offers recreation on two lakes, along with golfing, camping, and picnicking. Anglers fish for rainbow trout, channel catfish, bass, and crappie. Swimming is pleasant, and ducks and deer inhabit the area. Watch for shy rattlesnakes hunting in the tall grass or sunning among rocks. They don't like to be surprised.

Two short hiking trails let you stretch your legs. One, less than two miles long, climbs up the Hogback to gain views of the surrounding buttes and mountains, including Pikes Peak to the north. To the south, the Spanish Peaks are riveting. Indians named the two prominent peaks Wahatoya, or breasts of the world. They believed rain from those peaks fed and nurtured the land below. Spaniards later spelled them Huajatolla.

The byway continues west on 160, through pinyon-juniper vegetation and grasslands. About eleven miles from Walsenburg, bear left onto Colorado State Highway 12. The road heads south and in a few miles provides a beautiful view of the Spanish Peaks above, and La Veta and the Cuchara Valley below.

La Veta is a lovely tourist town with an active arts community. Visit the Fort Francisco Museum, lodged in the original 1862 adobe plaza built by two ranching partners. Next door, check out a play at the Fort Francisco Center for the Performing Arts. It's easy to spend several hours strolling through the exhibits and buildings and visiting galleries and shops. Just east of town, Daigre and Wahatoya lakes provide pleasant fishing, picnicking, and hiking opportunities.

Farther up the valley, 500-foot-high Goemmer Butte is a unique volcanic cone. Other interesting volcanic features are Profile Rock and the Devil's

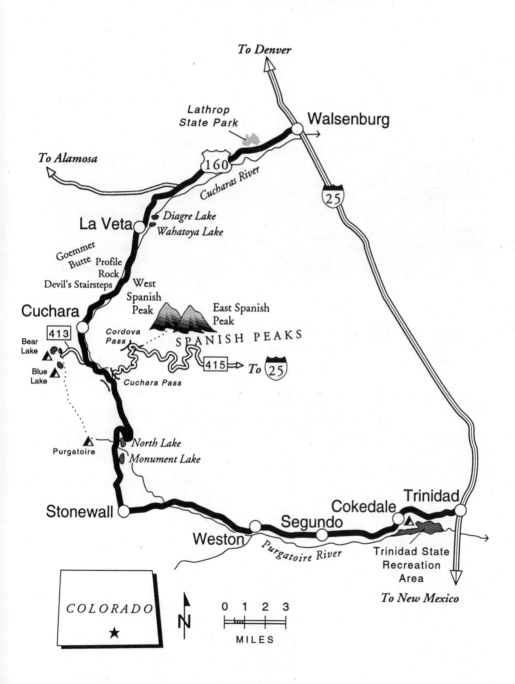

To Denver

Lathrop
State Park

Walsenburg

To Alamosa

160

Cucharas River

25

La Veta

Diagre Lake

Wahatoya Lake

Goemmer
Butte
Profile
Rock

Devil's Stairsteps

West
Spanish
Peak

East Spanish
Peak

SPANISH PEAKS

Cuchara

413

Cordova
Pass

Bear
Lake

415 ⇨ To 25

Blue
Lake

Cuchara Pass

Purgatoire

North Lake

Monument Lake

Trinidad

Cokedale

Stonewall

Segundo

Weston

Purgatoire River

Trinidad State
Recreation
Area

To New Mexico

COLORADO

N

0 1 2 3

MILES

Highway of Legends encircles the spectacular Spanish Peaks, reflected here in a serene lake. Gordon Kelley photo.

Stairsteps. The Spanish Peaks region differs from the rest of the Rockies by its geology. About thirty-five million years ago, huge masses of molten rock pushed into the cracks and folds of existing sedimentary rock. The softer sedimentary rock gradually eroded away, leaving the hard dikes exposed today. The dikes radiate out from the center like bicycle spokes and create walls of rock popular with rock climbers.

A gap was eroded into one of the dikes by the Cucharas River, and the highway passes through alongside the river. You'll pass this same geologic "wall" on the south side of the pass, at Stonewall. Twelve miles from La Veta is the resort community of Cuchara. Travelers can find all services here, as well as winter downhill skiing. A few miles south of Cuchara, turn west on Forest Road 413 past Cuchara Picnic Area to Blue Lake Campground. Fifteen sites sit next to the lake in the spruce and fir at this 10,500-foot elevation. Nearby, and 200 feet higher, Bear Lake Campground has fourteen sites at the edge of timberline.

Continuing south on the byway, look east at the Spanish Peaks as you climb 9,941-foot Cucharas Pass. Aspen groves surround meadows bright with columbine, shooting star, cinquefoil, and pussytoes. Look south into the Purgatoire Valley and north into Cuchara Valley. A side trip on Forest Road 415 from the top of Cucharas Pass leads higher yet, over 11,743-foot Cordova Pass and on east to Interstate 25, tunneling through and passing over many of the volcanic dikes. The road is open only in summer. Park at the top of Cordova Pass near the interpretive sign and follow a trail to the summit of West Spanish Peak. The view is absolutely breathtaking.

Descending south from Cucharas Pass, North Lake has good fishing, picnicking, and hiking. The byway parallels the headwaters of the Purgatoire River and goes past the resort and campground at Monument Lake. Purgatoire Campground has twenty-five sites and is situated four miles from the byway.

Stonewall, now a resort community, is named for the steep Dakota Sandstone thrust up vertically by the rising Sangre de Cristo Range. This is part of the same formation you crossed in the Cucharas Valley when driving through the gap. Stonewall, as well as many other communities in the Purgatoire River Valley, is full of interesting history. Adobe churches, community plazas, mines, ghost towns, and ranches dot the landscape of pinyon and juniper type vegetation in this coal mining region. The Cokedale National Historic District is very interesting to walk through, and you can see the old coke oven and waste piles nearby.

Three miles east, Trinidad State Recreation Area has good fishing in the reservoir, summer evening naturalist programs, boating, and hiking trails. Less than a mile long, the Carpios Ridge Trail provides pretty views of the lake and Fishers Peak. Providing a longer walk, Levsa Canyon Trail wanders through the pinyon-juniper vegetation, where wildflowers and cacti may be blooming. The campground has sixty-two sites, and there are electrical hookups, a bathhouse, and a dump station.

The scenic byway ends in Trinidad, a historic city with plenty of activities. The Corazon de Trinidad National Historic District sits like a gem in the middle of museums, shops, and galleries. Visit the Bloom House, Baca House, and Pioneer Museum for a glimpse of the past and save time for at least one more of the several museums. The adobe Spanish-style Baca House was built in 1870 and housed a prosperous sheep-ranching family who contributed a great deal to the region. Nearby, the ornate Victorian Bloom House stands in ostentatious contrast to the simpler Baca House. Both dwellings provide a very interesting look at local lives and history. □

32 GUANELLA PASS SCENIC BYWAY
Arapaho and Pike National Forests · Colorado

General description: A historic and scenic twenty-two mile paved and gravel high mountain route across Guanella Pass.

Special attractions: Outstanding alpine scenery and far-ranging vistas, Mount Evans Wilderness Area, camping, fishing, cross-country skiing, hiking, historic buildings and mines, wildlife, and hunting.

Location: Central Colorado near Georgetown, on the Arapaho and Pike national forests.

Byway route numbers: Clear Creek County Road 381, Park County Road 62, Forest Road 118.

Travel season: Year-round. Not recommended for oversized and towed units. Winter travel necessitates extreme caution.

Camping: Five national forest campgrounds with picnic tables, fire grates, and toilets.

Services: All traveler services in Georgetown.

Nearby attractions: Downhill ski areas, scenic Rocky Mountains, historic districts.

For more information: Arapaho National Forest, 240 W. Prospect Road, Fort Collins, CO 80526-2098, (303) 498-1100. Clear Creek Ranger District, P.O. Box 3307, Idaho Springs, CO 80452, (303) 567-2901. Pike National Forest, 1920 Valley Drive, Pueblo, CO 81008, (303) 545-8737. South Platte Ranger District, 11177 West 8th Avenue, Lakewood, CO 80215, (303) 236-7386.

Description: Guanella Pass is a knock-your-socks-off scenic route. The road travels between 14,000-foot peaks over 11,669-foot Guanella Pass, through alpine vegetation and aspen groves. The two-lane road is paved or oiled for ten miles and gravelled the remaining twelve. There are some turnouts for stopping. Sightseeing and recreation traffic can be fairly constant in summer, depending on weather conditions.

Weather in the high Rockies is unpredictable. Generally, daytime temperatures in summer range from the seventies and eighties down to the forties and fifties at night. Expect afternoon thunderstorms in June and July, which clear up within a few hours. Occasionally it rains for days. The first snows that stick are generally in late October, and snow cover lasts until April or May. Winter days may be sunny with temperatures in the teens and twenties, but the mercury plummets at night. The high lakes remain frozen into May and June.

Scenery on the byway is spectacular when driving from either direction. From north to south, the byway begins in Georgetown, one of the nation's best-kept Victorian towns. There are plenty of attractions here, such as riding the Georgetown Loop Railroad, strolling the historic walking tour, or viewing the Hamill House.

Driving south on the scenic byway, the road immediately climbs via a series of switchbacks. Pull off at one of the scenic overlooks for a wonderful view of Georgetown tucked into the U-shaped glacial valley. The lake sparkles, and the hillsides above have remnants of old silver mines.

At the top of the switchbacks, little remains of Silverdale and Ocean Wave, two mining camps that once had dozens of houses and several stamp mills. Miners in this Guanella Pass region found gold, silver, and copper, and current-day history buffs can see plenty of relics and artifacts.

This byway is one of Colorado's premier sites for spectacular autumn foliage. Deep green hues of lodgepole pine and Engelmann spruce form a backdrop to the stark white bark and shimmering gold leaves of quaking aspen trees. In spring, those same aspen trees leaf out in lime green colors. Up higher, the willow branches turn deep hues of scarlet, russet, and gold.

Take a side trip on Forest Road 748, the Waldorf cutoff road. This road is best for high clearance vehicles, as it follows an old railroad bed to Waldorf. You can hike about two miles farther up to Argentine Pass, on the Continental Divide. Mountain bikes and four-wheel drive vehicles can drive from Waldorf to the top of Mount McClellan, where you get a magnificent 360-degree view of 176 peaks. Look for Pike's Peak, elevation 14,109 feet, as well as Mount of the Holy Cross and Longs Peak.

Continuing south on the byway, Green Lake was formed after a massive avalanche of rocks slid off the valley wall to the west. The byway travels right over the toe of that slide, and you can clearly see the rubble pile and giant

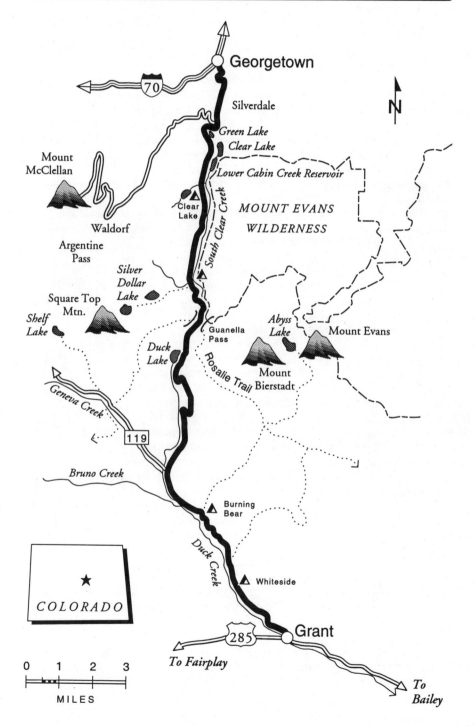

32 GUANELLA PASS SCENIC BYWAY

Georgetown

Silverdale

Green Lake
Clear Lake

Mount
McClellan

Lower Cabin Creek Reservoir

Clear
Lake

MOUNT EVANS
WILDERNESS

Waldorf

Argentine
Pass

Silver
Dollar
Lake

Square Top
Mtn.

Abyss
Lake

Mount Evans

Shelf
Lake

Guanella
Pass

Duck
Lake

Mount
Bierstadt

Geneva Creek

Rosalie Trail

119

Bruno Creek

Burning
Bear

Duck Creek

★

COLORADO

Whiteside

0   1   2   3

285   Grant

MILES

To Fairplay

To
Bailey

boulders. The privately owned Green Lake Lodge was constructed in the 1880s.

Clear Lake was carved out by glaciers. This very deep lake is stocked with rainbow trout, and shoreline fishing access is good. Dams at both Green and Clear lakes are used to generate power.

Power lines descend the mountains throughout this area. The Cabin Creek Hydroelectric Power Plant is one of the highest plants of its type in the world. Water is pumped from Lower Cabin Creek Reservoir to Upper Cabin Creek Reservoir, and power is sent to the Denver area.

Clear Lake Campground has eight sites tucked in an aspen grove. Anglers will find South Clear Creek stocked with rainbows and browns.

The byway follows the creek, and you can see plenty of evidence of beaver activity. Aspens and willows are chewed through, old ponds have silted in and are revegetating naturally, and newer ponds are chock full of fish. You'll have to get your feet wet to take advantage of the great fishing, since the braiding stream channels are diverted across the whole valley in places. This is a wonderful place to learn about habitats and the natural succession of plant communities.

Aspens are very showy through here, and rugged peaks in the Mount Evans Wilderness jut above the thick spruce and fir forests carpeting the steep valley walls. Wildflowers are abundant, including Colorado's state flower, the blue columbine.

Guanella Pass Campground's sixteen sites sit in the forest at 10,800 feet. Views are great in this subalpine environment, and you should expect freezing nighttime temperatures any month of the year. Snow is not unheard of in summer. A nearby foot trail leads to Silver Dollar and other glacial lakes. Watch for bighorn sheep, marmots, and picas.

The byway switchbacks up the final ascent, with several good pullouts for scenic viewing. Up here, the subalpine fir are called krummholtz because they are twisted into fantastic shapes by the winds and extreme weather.

Guanella Pass lies at 11,669 feet. Byron Guanella was the Clear Creek county road supervisor who built the road, which opened in 1952. You can see rugged Mount Bierstadt rising to the east, with its dramatic sawtooth ridge running northeast to Mount Evans. Bierstadt was named for the western artist, and nearby Mount Rosalie honors his wife. Look south into the Duck Creek drainage and west to Square Top and the Continental Divide. You're in an alpine area here, with tundralike conditions and tiny alpine flowers. Above is only rock and ice.

White-tailed ptarmigan winter in the willow thickets on the pass. Theirs is a reverse migration from most birds: they descend to lowlands in the summer and come up to the high country in winter, turning pure white to blend in with the snow. Cross-country skiers are often startled to find the snow beneath their skis explode upward as a ptarmigan flies out suddenly from a hiding place in the snow.

Hikers find several trailheads here. You can take a nearly all-downhill hike beginning at the top of the pass. Walk about four and a half miles on the Rosalie Trail to the Abyss Trail, and return to the highway via that route. The wildflower displays and spectacular scenery are riveting.

The byway now descends, and motorists are advised to slow down by gearing down rather than riding your brakes. Privately owned Duck Lake sits on the west side of the road, with the fire-scarred ruins of the Coors' summer

Guanella Pass Scenic Byway traverses these rugged mountains. This view is from the top of Mount Bierstadt, east of the byway. Pike National Forest photo.

home. Views here extend to the Sangre de Cristo Mountains, nearly one hundred miles south.

About a half mile south of Duck Lake you can see the old ski runs of Geneva Basin Ski Area cut into the side of the mountain. The area is no longer operating.

Cut into the side of the mountain, the road becomes very narrow and steep, with sheer drops to the side. Watch for seeps and ice on the road in cold weather. In winter this route is definitely not for the faint-hearted or poorly prepared.

Descend via big switchbacks, then wind along Duck Creek through big Engelmann spruce and blue spruce. Willows and aspen grow along the creek.

Geneva Park Campground and Duck Creek Picnic Area are situated in a dense lodgepole pine forest near the intersection of the byway and Forest Road 119. The campground has twenty-six sites with drinking water available. Take a walk on very rough Forest Road 119 for a view of Geneva Park, scoured out by glaciers in the last Ice Age. About three miles up 119, hike the Shelf Lake Trail another three miles through wildflower meadows and along the stream, to a high mountain cirque lake. High-clearance vehicles can drive up the road to Geneva City, an abandoned mining complex with old cabins and mines and tailings.

Bruno Creek is home to a state endangered species: the Colorado greenback trout. Introduced trout such as rainbows, browns, and brookies outcompeted and nearly eliminated the species, and today they are protected. No fishing is allowed in Bruno Creek.

Geneva Park is a huge open meadow. Watch for open range cows in the road. All of the parks and forest openings are likely places to spot wildlife, especially in the early mornings and late evenings. Wildlife in this scenic byway region includes Rocky Mountain bighorn sheep, mountain lions, black bears, mule deer, snowshoe hares, marmots, and pikas. A few rare bobcats and wolverines also inhabit the area. Bird watchers may spot ptarmigan, blue grouse, Clark's nutcrackers, and mountain chickadees.

Burning Bear Campground has thirteen sites in the spruce and lodgepole forest, and a nice view of Geneva Park. No drinking water is provided.

Private land in Geneva Park was harvested commercially for the rich peat, and efforts are now under way to reclaim the area. Continuing down the highway, Falls Hill is the top of a heap of terminal moraine, an unconsolidated pile of rock pushed in front of the last glacier. Falls Hill is aptly named— waterfalls cascade down the hillsides to the creek below.

Notice the different shapes of the valleys—above Falls Hill is a classic U-shaped valley carved by glaciers, while below is a sharp V-shaped valley carved by Geneva Creek. The highway descends the steep gradient via a series of switchbacks to the bottom, into lush riparian vegetation along Geneva Creek.

Watch for horseback riders from a nearby dude ranch on this stretch of road. Primitive, dispersed camping is very popular along the creek, and the road is a tunnel of gold aspen leaves in autumn. For a short stretch-your-legs stroll, walk a ways through the spruce and lodgepole on the Threemile Creek trail.

Whiteside Campground provides five sites right on Geneva Creek, under the big Engelmann spruce trees. No drinking water is available there. Watch for bighorn sheep on the hillsides along here, especially in winter.

The byway ends in Grant, named after our former president. A few traveler services are available in Grant, but the closest full-service community is in Bailey. The drive out along the North Fork of the South Platte River is beautiful. □

33 PEAK TO PEAK SCENIC BYWAY
Arapaho and Roosevelt National Forests   Colorado

General description: A fifty-five-mile route through mountain meadows and forests.

Special attractions: Rocky Mountain National Park, Golden Gate Canyon State Park, Indian Peaks Wilderness, hiking, bicycling, hunting, camping, fishing, snowmobiling, and downhill and cross-country skiing.

Location: North-central Colorado on the Arapaho and Roosevelt national forests. The byway travels between Estes Park on the north and Black Hawk on the south.

Byway route numbers: Colorado State Highways 7, 72, and 279.

Travel season: Year-round.

Camping: Six national forest campgrounds, with picnic tables, fire grates, toilets, and drinking water. National park and state park campgrounds near the byway.

Services: Traveler services in Estes Park, Black Hawk, Central City, Lone Pine, Nederland, and Rollinsville.

Nearby attractions: Guanella Pass Scenic Byway, downhill ski areas, Denver city attractions, Mount Evans Wilderness.

For more information: Arapaho and Roosevelt National Forests, 240 West Prospect Road, Fort Collins, CO 80526-2098, (303) 498-1100. Estes-Poudre Ranger District, 148 Remington Street, Fort Collins, CO 80524, (303) 482-3822. Estes Park Visitor Center, (303) 586-3440. Boulder Ranger District, 2995 Baseline Road Rm.110, Boulder, CO 80303, (303) 444-6001.

Description: Peak To Peak Scenic Byway travels through the mountains of Colorado, winding along streams and through historic towns. The two-lane highway is paved and has frequent scenic turnouts. Traffic is moderate and moves between thirty-five and forty-five mph.

Weather in the high Rockies is unpredictable. Summer temperatures range from the forties to the eighties, with frequent afternoon thunderstorms in June and July. Occasionally it will rain for days. Winter days are often sunny, in the teens and twenties, but nighttime temperatures plummet. Snow generally sticks on the ground about mid-October, and the high lakes remain frozen into May and June.

The byway is very scenic driven in either direction. Beginning at the north end, Estes Park provides numerous tourist diversions. The historic Stanley Hotel is a popular gathering place, and the building was used in the film "The Shining."

Drive south on Highway 7, which climbs gradually while winding through the mountains. Views of Rocky Mountain National Park are beautiful: a region of rugged peaks, extensive forests, alpine lakes, waterfalls, and streams. The park has excellent backcountry trails. To the west, Longs Peak soars up to 14,251 feet elevation. The 2,000-foot steep granite face is the headwall of a glacial cirque. Geologists surmise that the rock here corresponds to rock found 22,000 feet lower, in the Denver Basin. That means the mountains have been uplifted about four miles high.

Olive Ridge Campground provides fifty-six sites in the forest of Engelmann spruce and subalpine fir. Take a short side trip west, to Wild Basin in the park. There are picnic tables, hiking trails, a lake, and beautiful views. Stretch your legs on the short trail to Ouzel Falls. Wild Basin is a popular cross-country ski area in winter.

Allenspark has a pleasant downtown with restaurants and shops. About five miles south, the byway leaves Highway 7 and follows Highway 72 south through the forested mountains. Peaceful Valley Campground has fifteen sites, and you can fish for brookies and rainbows in Middle St. Vrain Creek. A mile west, at elevation 8,650, Camp Dick provides barrier-free fishing piers and thirty-four campsites. Walk the easy trail about a mile along the creek. If you feel energetic, continue on up the trail into the wilderness.

Continue south on the byway. A short side trip west on Route 96 brings you into an area burned by forest fires. It's interesting to see how the plants are revegetating the area. Fireweed's magenta-pink blossoms brighten the burn.

Another side trip, west on Brainard Lake Road (Forest Road 112), leads to

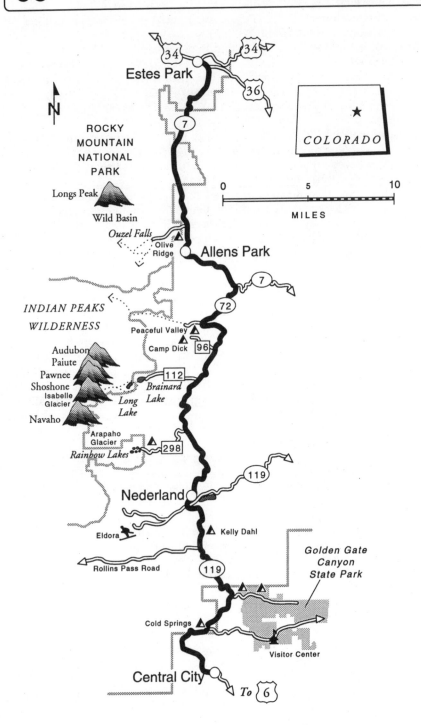

The Indian Peaks Wilderness rises above Brainard Lake, on the Peak to Peak Scenic Byway.
Barbara Lawlor/Mountain-Ear photo.

a spectacular view of the Indian Peaks Wilderness. You can see most of the high peaks, such as Shoshone, Pawnee, and Paiute, as well as Isabelle Glacier and Mount Audubon. This is the most heavily visited portal into the wilderness. It's a short easy walk from Brainard Lake to Long Lake, and you can loop around Long Lake on the Pawnee Pass Trail. You could also hike north a few miles on the Sourdough Trail. There are rainbow trout in Brainard and Red Rock lakes.

Indian Peaks Wilderness protects 73,391 acres of alpine lakes and peaks, mountain meadows, forests, and streams. There are nearly fifty lakes within the wilderness, many cradled in glacial cirques. The high peaks are part of the Continental Divide, which separates waters flowing east to the Gulf of Mexico, or west to the Pacific. Wildlife includes elk, mule deer, black bear, mountain lion, bobcat, coyote, and snowshoe rabbit. Golden eagles can often be seen overhead. This is the most frequently visited wilderness in the Rockies.

Back on the byway, you'll continue rolling up and down through the mountains. West on Forest Road 298, Rainbow Lakes Campground is quite primitive, with eighteen sites in a remote little basin on the wilderness boundary. It's an easy mile hike to the Rainbow Lakes from the campground, or hike the steady, gradual ascent up Glacier Trail to see Arapaho Glacier.

The byway is lined with stands of aspen mixed with evergreens. It's very pretty in autumn when the aspen leaves turn brilliant gold against the deep greens of the conifers. The route passes through Nederland, where you can pass some pleasant time browsing through the little museum and shopping for arts and crafts. A few miles west, Eldora Ski Area is popular with beginning and intermediate skiers who like its gentle slopes. There are good mountain bicycle routes there in summer.

This is the northern end of the "Colorado Mineral Belt," where gold, silver, lead, copper, zinc, molybdenum, uranium, and tungsten have been mined.

Highway 72 turns east, but the scenic byway leaves 72 and now travels south on Highway 119. Along the byway, Kelly Dahl Campground has forty-six sites in the forest of lodgepole pine and quaking aspen. The view of the Continental Divide is nice. About two miles south, the Rollins Pass Road leads west out a dirt road. This was one of the first wagon roads built over the Continental Divide into Middle Park. The railroad follows this route, then tunnels through the mountains via the Moffat Tunnel, bringing Denver skiers to Winter Park.

The scenic byway continues to climb, wind around, and drop through the mountains and ridges. Just east of the byway, Golden Gate Canyon State Park has campgrounds, picnicking, a visitor center, and short walking trails.

Cold Springs Campground has twenty-seven sites in the trees near the creek. The elevation here is 9,200 feet. As you wind south on the byway, you'll see down into various gulches and canyons to the east and west.

Peak to Peak Scenic Byway's southern terminus is in Central City. Central City is a historic and well-preserved mining town with numerous tourist attractions, including the Central City Opera, the Gilpin County Museum, and numerous festivals. In its heyday, notables such as Charles Dickens, Oscar Wilde, and President Ulysses S. Grant visited the opera house. You can stroll the steep, Victorian neighborhoods, and ride a little railroad to Blackhawk, another historic mining town which offers tours of an old gold mine. George Pullman invented the Pullman car while living in Central City. □

34 SILVER THREAD HIGHWAY
Gunnison and Rio Grande National Forests   Colorado

General description: A seventy-five mile route across two beautiful mountain passes, through a historic silver mining region.

Special attractions: Slumgullion Earthflow, ghost towns, Wheeler Geologic Area, fishing, camping, Weminuche and La Garita wilderness areas, panoramic views.

Location: Southwest Colorado on the Gunnison and Rio Grande national forests. The byway travels Highway 149 between South Fork and Lake City.

Byway route number: Colorado State Highway 149.

Travel season: Year-round.

Camping: Six national forest campgrounds, with picnic tables, fire grates, and toilets. Some campgrounds provide drinking water.

Services: Traveler services available in South Fork, Creede, and Lake City.

Nearby attractions: San Juan Skyway National Forest Scenic Byway, downhill ski areas, Curecanti National Recreation Area, Black Canyon of the Gunnison National Monument.

For more information: Gunnison National Forest, 2250 Highway 50, Delta, CO 81416, (303) 874-7691. Cebolla Ranger District, 216 North Colorado, Gunnison, CO 81230, (303) 641-0471. Gunnison Basin BLM Resource Area, 2505 South Townsend, Montrose, CO 82401, (303) 249-7791. Rio Grande National Forest, 1803 West Highway 160, Monte Vista, CO 81144, (719) 852-5941. Creede Ranger District, 3rd and Creede Avenue (P.O. Box 270), Creede, CO 81130, (719) 658-2556.

Description: The Silver Thread Highway winds through the stunning San Juan Mountains, along rivers and streams, and through fascinating historic mining districts. The two-lane road is paved and has frequent turnouts. Traffic is light.

Expect variable mountain weather. Elevations range from about 8,300 feet to more than 11,300 feet, and the temperature differences can be startling. Summer days might be over ninety degrees, or a sudden storm may bring sleet. Snow can fall from October to June. Freezing nights might occur anytime, and afternoon thundershowers are common in the summer.

The byway is spectacular driven from either direction. When driving southeast to northwest the byway begins in South Fork. You can obtain area information and maps at Brown's Store. The byway crosses the Rio Grande River and heads through the foothills along the wide river valley bottomlands. Sentinel Peak juts up to the west. The historic stone enclosure on top was used as a lookout by Native Americans.

The Rio Grande River from South Fork to Wagon Wheel Gap is a designated Gold Medal fishing stretch. Anglers cast for rainbow and brown trout. You'll likely see rafters floating the river: if you have a hankering to float it a commercial outfitter is located in Creede.

The byway passes through Collier State Wildlife Area, which provides winter habitat for elk and deer. Just north, Palisade Campground has thirteen sites on the river, in the forest of ponderosa pine, Engelmann spruce, and Douglas-fir. It's a popular launch point for rafters. The campground is named for the rugged cliff formation seen east of the byway.

The highway climbs to Wagon Wheel Gap, a steep canyon carved through the twenty-five- to thirty-million-year-old volcanic basalt of the mountains. Watch for fallen rocks on the highway. An interpretive sign explains Post Office Rock, and the history of the area. Look on the hillside around Blue Creek for Rocky Mountain bighorn sheep, reintroduced into the area in 1985. Other wildlife inhabiting the byway area includes elk, deer, coyotes, mountain lions, moose, and black bears.

A side trip east on Forest Road 600 leads to Hansons Mill. From there it's about seven miles on foot or by four-wheel drive into the Wheeler Geologic Area. It is a delightful area of pink and white eroded spires and hoodoos.

Continuing along the byway, Creede provides a number of attractions. This historic mining town has an attractive main street, and you can shop, visit the museum and attend a play at the Creede Repertory Theater. Stop by the ranger station for national forest maps and information, and to view the displays about Wheeler Geologic Area.

A self-guided auto loop tour provides an interesting route through the steep canyon and mining relics north of town. This was one of the most productive

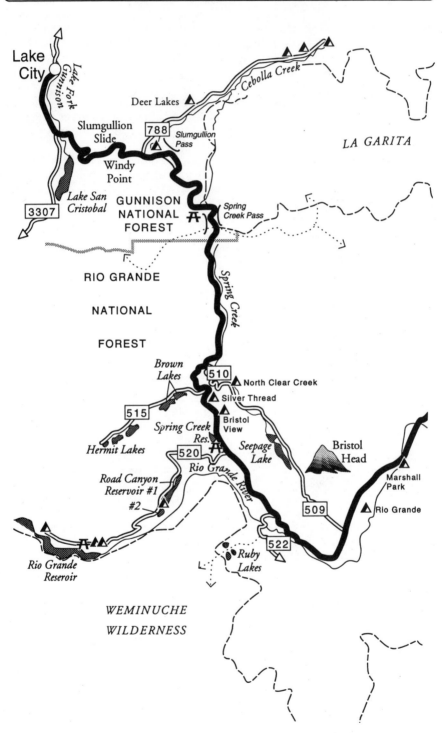

Lake City

Lake Fork Gunnison

Cebolla Creek

Deer Lakes

Slumgullion Slide

788

Slumgullion Pass

LA GARITA

Windy Point

GUNNISON NATIONAL FOREST

Spring Creek Pass

Lake San Cristobal

3307

RIO GRANDE

NATIONAL

FOREST

Spring Creek

Brown Lakes

510

North Clear Creek

Silver Thread

515

Bristol View

Hermit Lakes

Spring Creek Res.

520

Seepage Lake

Bristol Head

Road Canyon Reservoir #1

#2

Rio Grande River

Marshall Park

509

Rio Grande

Rio Grande Reseroir

522

Ruby Lakes

WEMINUCHE

WILDERNESS

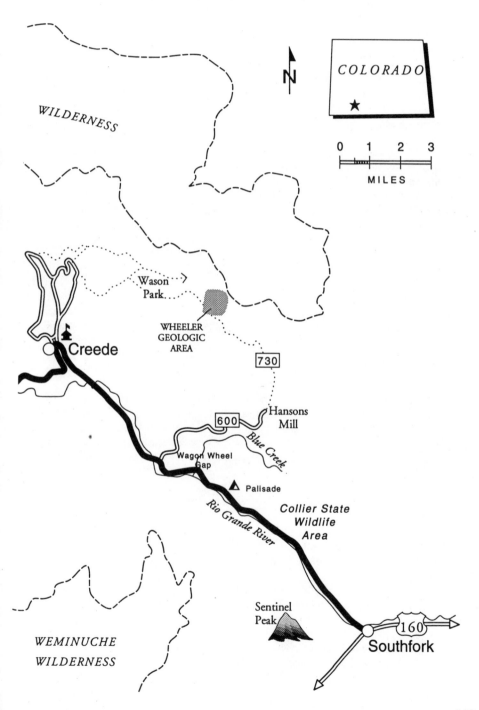

silver mining regions in the United States. Gold, lead, and zinc were also mined here. You could stretch your legs on Trail 787 and hike into Wason Park. There are beautiful wildflowers, stands of evergreens, and views into the La Garita Wilderness. The trail begins near the north end of the Alpine Loop Road.

Continuing along the byway, you'll pass numerous mine structures and old mining camps. Marshall Park Campground provides good fishing access, and sixteen sites along the Rio Grande. A few miles farther along the highway, Rio Grande Campground is less developed, offering four sites down by the river. It's a popular raft launch and fishing spot.

A side trip up Forest Road 509 leads through bighorn sheep country to Seepage Lake. Some record size rainbows, up to eighteen pounds, have been caught in Seepage Lake.

The byway travels through the big, open valley bottomland, with mountains on both sides. A side trip west on Forest Road 522 leads to the Fern Creek Trail, which crosses the valley bottom and ascends to the Ruby Lakes and the Weminuche Wilderness. East of the byway, Bristol Head Mountain juts up prominently, to elevation 12,706 feet.

A side trip west on Forest Road 520 leads through a fairly narrow canyon. Road Canyon Reservoir 1 has good fishing for rainbow and brown trout, and winter ice fishing for pike. A little farther west, Road Canyon Reservoir 2 usually has a lot of ducks and waterfowl. Along this side road, you'll find four campgrounds, picnicking, hiking trails, and the Rio Grande Reservoir.

The byway leaves the Rio Grande River valley and climbs north through intermingled aspen and spruce/fir stands. Spring Creek Reservoir has fishing and picnicking in a very pretty mountain setting. Traveling north, two campgrounds are located within a few miles of each other. Bristol View Campground has sixteen sites along the stream with stunning views of Bristol Head Mountain. An easy trail allows you to stroll 1.5 miles along the creek to a little waterfall. Silver Thread Campground offers a .5-mile loop trail to another waterfall.

A side trip west on Forest Road 515 leads to fishing opportunities in Brown Lakes, and Hermit Lakes.

A few miles farther north on the byway, another side trip, southeast on Forest Road 510, leads to an excellent view of North Clear Creek Falls. North Clear Creek Campground provides twenty-five sites along the creek.

The byway climbs alongside Spring Creek. Look for moose in the willows and riparian areas along the stream. The highway leaves Rio Grande National Forest and enters Gunnison National Forest. Spring Creek Pass lies atop the Continental Divide, elevation 10,898 feet. The Continental Divide separates waters flowing west to the Pacific from waters flowing east into the Gulf of Mexico in the Atlantic.

From the pass, you'll see north across aspen stands and Engelmann spruce into a large, gentle valley. Look east into the La Garita Wilderness. The wilderness protects 103,986 acres of mountains and forest along the Continental Divide.

A kiosk atop the pass displays maps, and information on trails, geology, and recreation. The Continental Divide Trail is a national recreation trail that will eventually go from Mexico to Canada. Here, it follows the path of the Colorado Hiking Trail, which links Denver to Durango. You can hike east five miles along a stock driveway through rolling mountaintops, forests, and meadows, with occasional broad vistas. The stock driveway then connects to the old Skyline Trail #465 and continues on towards Denver. In winter, snowmobiling is very popular from the pass into the West Fork of Cebolla Creek.

The byway now drops down along the headwaters of Cebolla Creek. The creek veers to the east, but the byway climbs to its highest point atop Slumgullion Pass, elevation 11,361 feet. You can see the surrounding forested, rolling mountains, and drainages such as Cebolla Creek.

The byway drops again, and you'll reach Slumgullion Campground. There are twenty-one campsites in the trees, and drinking water is available. This high-elevation camp is generally pretty chilly—bring warm clothing.

A side trip on graveled Forest Road 788 leads along Mill Creek, past Deer Lakes, and into the Cebolla Creek drainage. You can fish, watch the beavers, and camp in developed or undeveloped camp areas. The Danny Carl Memorial Trail is a maintained cross-country ski route, and there are several good snowmobiling opportunities along here.

Continuing along the byway, Windy Point Overlook provides a spectacular view of the San Juan Mountains. Interpretive signs point out peaks higher than 14,000 feet. You can see the crown of the Slumgullion Earthflow from here, as well as Big Blue Wilderness to the west.

The byway crosses a portion of the Slumgullion Slide. The word slumgullion was coined by miners, who thought the multicolored orange and yellow rocks looked like a stew, or slumgullion. An overlook provides an outstanding view of the 800-year-old Slumgullion Earthflow National Landmark. This gigantic rock and mudflow is about four miles long and two thousand feet wide. It dammed the Lake Fork of the Gunnison River and caused Lake San Cristobal

Uncompahgre Peak juts out of the Big Blue Wilderness, seen from Windy Point Overlook on the Silver Thread Highway. Grand Mesa, Uncompahgre, and Gunnison National Forests photo.

to form. You can tell it is still moving by the condition of the highway where it crosses the flow.

Nearby, park at another overlook and walk a very short trail to a clear view of Lake San Cristobal, the second-largest natural lake in Colorado. It covers about three square miles and offers good opportunities for camping, picnicking, and fishing for rainbows. You can drive to the lake on BLM Route 3307.

The highway descends through aspens and lodgepole pines into a deep valley. The byway ends in Lake City, a year-round resort town with plenty to do. The town itself is one of Colorado's largest National Historic Districts, and produced both gold and silver. The historic walking tour is very pleasant, and you can stop at the ranger station to obtain maps, brochures, and other information. □

35 ENCHANTED CIRCLE
Carson National Forest New Mexico

General description: An eighty-four mile paved mountain route encircling Wheeler Peak.

Special attractions: Spectacular scenery, western history and culture, Wheeler Peak Wilderness Area, camping, boating, resorts, fishing, horseback riding, cross-country and downhill skiing, and hunting.

Location: North-central New Mexico on the Carson National Forest. The byway is a loop and follows U.S. Highway 64 between Taos and Eagle Nest, New Mexico Highway 38 between Eagle Nest and Questa, and New Mexico Highway 522 between Questa and Taos.

Byway route numbers: U.S. Highway 64, New Mexico Highways 38 and 522.

Travel season: Year-round.

Camping: Eight national forest campgrounds, with picnic tables, fire grates, and toilets. Some have drinking water.

Services: All traveler services in Taos. All services, with limited availability, in Angel Fire, Eagle Nest, Red River, and Questa.

Nearby attractions: Valle Vidal scenic drive, Latir Peak Wilderness Area, Rio Grande River, resorts, downhill and cross-country skiing.

For more information: Carson National Forest, 208 Cruz Alta Rd, P.O. Box 558, Taos, NM, 87571, (505) 758-6270. Camino Real Ranger District, P.O. Box 68, Penasco, NM 87553, (505) 587-2255. Questa Ranger District, P.O. Box 110, Questa, NM, 87556, (505) 586-0520.

Description: The Enchanted Circle is indeed enchanting. Forested mountains rise a mile above the surrounding mesas and the loop tour encompasses a wide variety of vegetative zones and interesting historic features as it cruises through the cool mountains. Elevations on the loop range from about 7,000 to 9,800 feet.

Plains and mountains mingle along the Enchanted Circle.

The two-lane paved highways have occasional turnouts for scenic viewing. Traffic is generally light to moderate. The highway in Taos Canyon is very narrow with no shoulders, and traffic can bottle up there.

Temperatures may vary as much as twenty degrees between the mesas and the mountains. Summer visitors can expect warm temperatures from the fifties to high eighties, with lightning and thunderstorms most afternoons from late June until the end of August. It can rain up to an inch in an hour. Autumn is cooler and generally dry, with temperatures ranging from the thirties to the sixties. Snow and cold conditions stay throughout the winter. Spring begins about April, and temperatures can warm rapidly.

The byway is a loop that can be entered at several points. Scenery is spectacular and diverse when driven from any direction.

Taos is a popular starting point for the Enchanted Circle. The community is internationally known for visual and performing arts and boasts a full palette of restaurants, galleries, shops, and accommodations. It lies at an elevation just five feet short of 7,000 feet.

Begin your loop tour right in town, where simple adobe structures please the eye. Nine hundred years ago, the Taos Indians built their pueblo near here, and in 1615 the Spanish settled in. A nice walking tour brings you through Taos Plaza, past the Kit Carson Museum and Kit Carson Park, and to many interesting historic structures. Nearby are the Taos Pueblo, the San Francisco de Asis Mission Church, and numerous other attractions.

Driving east from Taos on U.S. Highway 64, the road climbs gradually through residential developments to the national forest boundary. The Rio Fernando de Taos is stocked with rainbow trout, and fishing is generally good. Picnic areas and campgrounds provide easy access to the tiny river.

El Nogal picnic area has five campsites along the river. A one-mile self-guided nature trail from the picnic area is very pleasant. For those with more energy, walk the Devisadero Loop Trail. In three to four hours of hiking you'll travel five miles, climb Devisadero Peak, and get to enjoy its broad vistas. Walking the loop counterclockwise is easiest.

La Vinateria Picnic Area has eight campsites and drinking water. A few miles east, Las Petacas Campground provides nine campsites amongst the sagebrush and pinyon pines. Ascending the canyon, Capulin and La Sombra campgrounds have ten and thirteen campsites, respectively, located in an open forest of Douglas-fir and white fir. Cottonwoods line the river. La Sombra has drinking water available.

Wildlife moves around mostly during the night, early mornings, and late evenings. You may see mule deer and elk in the meadows, and remember to look overhead for golden eagles. Watch for poison ivy when walking in the wet drainages.

The highway winds east along the river through private lands. A side trip on Forest Road 437 leads high-clearance vehicles to Garcia Park, where undeveloped picnicking, camping, and hiking are popular. A passenger car will make it up here, but at times it may be a bit rough. Garcia Park is great for mountain bicycling. In winter people cross-country ski and snowmobile.

The byway climbs steeply up. A side trip on Forest Road 5 leads north up La Jara Canyon from the first major switchback. La Jara is a nice way to get off the beaten track, and the narrow canyon is pretty with grassy meadows, aspens, and mixed conifers. Avoid it in inclement weather, though, as the road gets extremely slick when wet. The canyon is popular with cross-country skiers in winter.

The byway reaches a high point eighteen miles east of Taos, atop 9,101-foot Palo Flechado Pass. The route descends with numerous switchbacks, so drivers will probably have their eyes glued to the road here. To the east, passengers can enjoy big views of Angel Fire Ski Area, high mountain grasslands, and the broad valley below.

A side trip south on New Mexico Highway 434 leads to the resort community of Angel Fire, which features downhill skiing and championship golf. Continuing on the byway, U.S. Highway 64 winds north through open grassland, with views north to the peaks in Colorado and west into the Wheeler Peak Wilderness. The wilderness encompasses almost 20,000 acres of rugged terrain around Wheeler Peak, the highest mountain in New Mexico at 13,161 feet. Numerous hiking opportunities exist in the wilderness.

The DAV Vietnam Veterans National Memorial—an arresting structure north of the highway which beckons travelers—is open daily and commemorates those who died in the Vietnam War.

Eagle Nest Lake, elevation 8,167 feet, provides fine trout fishing, boating, and windsurfing. The community, about thirty miles east of Taos, provides all traveler services on a limited basis.

Leaving U.S. Highway 64, travel north and west on New Mexico Highway 38. About five miles north of Eagle Lake lie the remains of Elizabethtown, the first incorporated town in New Mexico. Elizabethtown was an 1870s gold rush boom town.

Continue north along Moreno Creek, through open grassland. The road climbs up into the spruce and fir forest. At the top a big expansive meadow is bright with wildflowers.

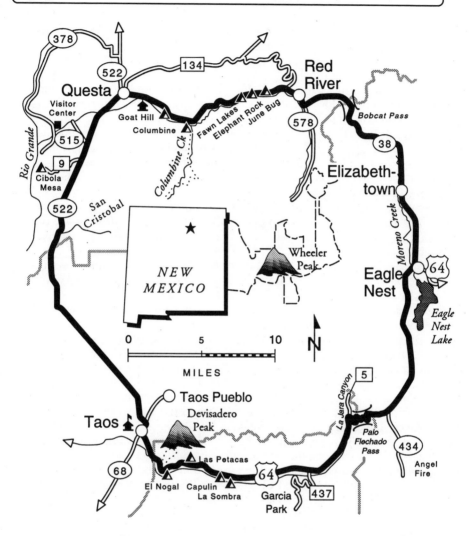

Bobcat Pass is the highest point on the byway. Views from this elevation of 9,820 feet include Baldy Peak, the cone-shaped mountain rising above Eagle Nest Lake.

The route descends and crosses back into the national forest. Enchanted Forest private cross-country ski area provides thirty kilometers of groomed trails. Just east of Red River, New Mexico Highway 578 offers a nice side trip to trailheads leading into Wheeler Peak Wilderness Area. The road offers pretty views as it meanders past summer homes.

Eighteen miles from Eagle Nest, Red River is a pleasant resort town specializing in outdoor activities, as well as providing Old West action such as melodramas, square dancing, and shoot-outs. Winter visitors enjoy downhill and cross-country skiing, and snowmobiling. Other seasons offer opportunities to hunt, fish, hike, camp, ride the scenic chairlift, and ride horses. A self-guided three-mile auto tour originates in Red River and brings you through the historic mining district in Pioneer Canyon. Passenger cars can drive about 2.5 miles of the route.

The highway travels through a narrow canyon with steep hillsides. The tree cover is primarily white fir, Douglas-fir, and Engelmann spruce, much of it devastated by the spruce budworm. The big reddish-orange scars on the hillsides are caused by erosion.

Continuing west on Highway 38, Junebug Campground is popular with anglers interested in the Red River's rainbow trout. The campground has eleven sites and drinking water, and is best suited to self-contained camping units. Elephant Rock Campground has twenty-two sites in the shady ponderosa pines, and drinking water. Across the highway, Fawn Lakes Campground's twenty-two sites are best suited to self-contained camping units. Fawn Lakes are very popular with trout anglers. Many of the campgrounds along the Red River have ranger/naturalist programs.

A few miles west brings motorists to private lands. The Molycorp Corporation mines and mills molybdenum in this area. The big open pit is above the highway, but the mill, tailings piles, and assorted buildings provide evidence of mining activities.

Columbine Campground is probably the prettiest in the canyon. Twenty-seven sites are situated in the cottonwoods, Douglas-firs, and white firs along the Red River, and drinking water is available. A moderately easy 5.7-mile National Recreation Trail up Columbine Creek is a great walk. A few miles west, Goat Hill has just three sites and is quite primitive.

The Questa Ranger Station lies east of town, and interested travelers can stop in for national forest information. Or, the Questa Visitors' Center is located right in town. Questa was originally an agricultural town but now serves tourists. Travelers will find all services here, but in limited quantities. The Valle Vidal Loop Tour, another scenic drive, is accessed here in Questa.

A side trip worth considering brings visitors to the Rio Grande Wild and Scenic River. Turn north on State Highway 522 in Questa, drive a few miles to State Highway 378, and follow the signs. There are campgrounds, an excellent visitor center open during the summer, outstanding vistas, and picnic areas. This hotter, more open area offers a different perspective on the region.

To continue on the Enchanted Circle Scenic Byway, turn south in Questa onto New Mexico Highway 522 and drive up and down the rolling pinyon and juniper-covered hills towards Taos. You'll see several volcanic peaks rise out of the flatlands to the west and north, across the Rio Grande. The river gorge is quite visible, with its dark browns, grays, and blacks. The Sangre de Cristo Range lies to east, the longest continuous range in the Rocky Mountains.

A side trip west on State Highway 515 leads to the Red River Fish Hatchery. There, visitors find an information center, picnic tables, and self-guided tours explaining the process of raising trout.

A mile south of the fish hatchery turnoff, a side trip on Forest Road 9 leads four miles west to Cebolla Mesa Campground, situated with a splendid view of the Rio Grande Gorge. The road is fairly rough and gets slick when wet. Hikers will enjoy the effort expended to reach the river and visitor center.

D.H. Lawrence fans will want to take a side trip off the scenic byway in

San Cristobal. Follow the signs to find the D.H. Lawrence shrine, erected on the ranch where he wrote from 1922 to 1925.

Continue south on State Highway 522, leaving the national forest and traveling past Arroyo Hondo, through sagebrush, pinyon pines, and grazing cattle. The scenic byway loop returns you to the amenities of Taos. □

36 PETER NORBECK SCENIC BYWAY
Black Hills National Forest   South Dakota

General description: A seventy-mile double-loop drive in the heart of South Dakota's Black Hills.

Special attractions: Mount Rushmore National Monument, Custer State Park, lakes, geologic formations, Black Elk Wilderness.

Location: Western South Dakota on the Black Hills National Forest. The byway consists of a loop within a loop. The shorter loop travels on Highway 89 near Custer north to Highway 87, east on 87, and returns west to Custer via Highway 16A. The longer loop follows 89/87 north, turns east on 244 through the national monument, and goes south and then west back to Custer on 16A.

Byway route numbers: South Dakota Highways 89, 87, and 244; U.S. Highway 16A.

Travel season: Year-round on Highways 89 and 244 and on portions of 87. Two sections of the byway are closed from about December through March: Highway 87 between Sylvan Lake and Iron Creek, and Highway 16A between the boundaries of Custer State Park and Mount Rushmore National Monument.

Camping: Two national forest campgrounds, with picnic tables, fire grates, drinking water, and toilets. Eight campgrounds in Custer State Park on or very near the byway. Numerous private campgrounds along or near the byway.

Services: All traveler services in Custer, Keystone, Legion Lake, and nearby Hill City.

Nearby attractions: Wind Cave National Park, Jewel Cave National Monument, National Museum of Woodcarving, Thunderhead Falls, Black Hills Petrified Forest, Spearfish Canyon National Forest Scenic Byway, Badlands National Park.

For more information: Black Hills National Forest, RR 2 Box 200, Custer, SD 57730, (605) 673-2251. Custer Ranger District, 330 Mount Rushmore Road, Custer, SD 57730, (605) 673-4853. Harney Ranger District, HCR 87 Box 51, Hill City, SD 57745, (605) 574-2534. Mount Rushmore National Monument, (605) 574-2523. Custer State Park, HC83 Box 70, Custer, SD 57730, (605) 255-4515.

Description: The Peter Norbeck Scenic Byway traverses a wonderfully diverse region of the Black Hills. The highways are paved; traffic is moderately

36 PETER NORBECK SCENIC BYWAY

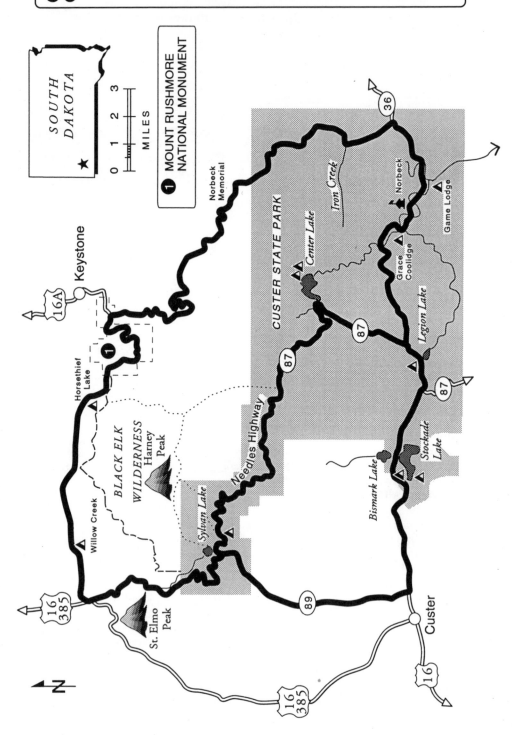

SOUTH DAKOTA

MILES
0 1 2 3

1 MOUNT RUSHMORE NATIONAL MONUMENT

Norbeck Memorial

36

Keystone

16A

Horsethief Lake

Willow Creek

BLACK ELK WILDERNESS

Harney Peak

St. Elmo Peak

16 385

Sylvan Lake

Needles Highway

CUSTER STATE PARK

Center Lake

Iron Creek

Norbeck

Game Lodge

Grace Coolidge

Legion Lake

87

87

87

Bismark Lake

Stockade Lake

89

Custer

16 385

16

N

heavy and moves quite slowly due to the narrow, winding character of the roads.

Summer weather in the Black Hills averages about eighty-five in the daytime, with nights in the sixties. Spring and fall days are often in the seventies, and nights drop to the forties. Winter days reach the forties, while nights are generally below freezing. Snow usually remains on the ground between December and April.

The byway offers scenic views driven in either direction. When starting in Custer, you may wish to stop and visit the Custer County Courthouse 1881 Museum, browse through art galleries, see the National Museum of Wood-carving's animated carvings of animals and people, and go through the Flint-stone's Bedrock City.

The byway begins just east of Custer on Highway 89. Drive north through the ponderosa pine forest into an area of open meadows, pastureland, and working ranches. The steeper terrain and granite outcroppings around Sylvan Lake mark where the Black Hills were uplifted.

To drive the inner, shorter loop on the Needles Highway, turn east on Highway 87 and enter Custer State Park. Sylvan Lake has a mantle of trees and a steep vertical escarpment rimming its basin. A resort and small store provide basic services. The campground has thirty-nine sites, restrooms, and showers.

There are numerous opportunities to hike in this area. Sylvan Lake Shore Trail makes an easy one-mile loop around the lake. Interpretive signs explain the natural and historical aspects of the lake region. The somewhat more strenuous Sunday Gulch National Recreation Trail is well worth the effort. This 3.5-mile loop descends through awesome granite walls, into a spruce and pine forest with unique plants and mosses. Wildflowers are abundant in the meadows. A very rewarding hike ascends a moderate, steady grade three miles to the summit of Harney Peak, the highest point east of the Rocky Mountains. You'll hike into the Black Elk Wilderness, to the fire lookout atop the peak. The lookout appears to have grown out of the rocks. This is truly the heart of this countryside, with views of rugged ridges, vertical cliffs, the Needles, and the forested Black Hills.

The Black Hills are actually a dome-shaped mountain range which has been highly eroded. In alternating periods, huge inland seas deposited sediments, the earth's crust lifted the region, and erosion wore it down until the seas once more covered it. The oldest rocks we see today are over two billion years old and consist primarily of schists, slates, quartzite, granite, and pegmatite.

The highway winds through the Needles, a maze of astounding granite geological formations reminiscent of needles, organ pipes, and cathedral spires. Look for brightly clad rock climbers clambering up some of these sheer formations. Highway builders had to use unconventional engineering techniques such as building pigtail bridges and blasting tunnels through the rock. In 1938 a portion was designated the Blue Star Highway, to commemorate war veterans. The aspens and paper birch provide a pretty contrast against the deep greens of pines and white spruce.

Take a side trip to Center Lake, where you can swim and fish for rainbow trout. The two campgrounds provide seventy-one sites, and naturalists present programs at the amphitheater on summer weekends. Nearby, the Black Hills Playhouse presents musical, comical, and dramatic productions all summer.

The Black Hills was one of the last regions in the West to be settled by

The Needles are an imposing rock formation on the Peter Norbeck Scenic Byway. Custer National Forest photo.

whites. In 1874, the Custer expedition traveled through this area and some of the soldiers found gold, which altered the future of the Black Hills forever. You can still find old mine equipment and exploratory holes in the ground.

Wildflowers are abundant in the Black Hills. Most apparent are the showy blossoms of pasqueflower, coneflower, wild rose, bluebell, fleabane, and common yarrow.

The inner loop of the byway turns west onto Highway 16A and travels through rolling hills to Bismark and Stockade lakes. There you can swim, boat, fish for rainbow trout, and camp. Legion Lake has twenty-five campsites with a view of the lake, and Stockade Lake's two campgrounds provide seventy sites.

The byway leaves the state park and travels through ranchlands and open meadows back to Custer.

The outer loop of the byway also begins in Custer, travels north on Highway

89/87 past Sylvan Lake, and follows a steep sidehill to the junction with Highway 244. Harney Peak juts up to the east, and St. Elmo Peak rises on the west. Turn east on 244 and roll across the forested hills of the national forest. Willow Creek Campground has facilities for horse use and provides nineteen sites in the trees along the creek. This is one of the primary horse-use trailheads into the wilderness. East again, just two miles from Mount Rushmore National Memorial, Horsethief Lake is the most popular campground on the byway. There are thirty-six campsites here and good fishing for rainbow trout. The Horsethief Lake Trail is a moderately difficult route through rugged terrain into the wilderness. It's very scenic and worth the effort.

The byway is carved right into the rock slopes. Road cuts expose feldspar, granite, and veins of quartz. You may see geology classes studying the rocks along the highway. With sharp eyes, you may also spot mountain goats up here. Other inhabitants of the national forest include bald eagles, bobcats, mountain lions, bighorn sheep, coyotes, and mule and white-tailed deer. Watch for shy rattlesnakes on your walks; they don't like to be startled.

The byway enters Mount Rushmore National Monument. The sixty-foot-tall faces of Washington, Jefferson, Lincoln, and Roosevelt are carved into the mountain here. Stop at the visitor center for information. Then take a guided walking tour or attend one of the evening programs.

The byway descends the mountain and provides good views east to the prairie. Keystone, just north of the byway, is a full-service tourist community. Turn south on Highway 16A and travel through the rugged, rolling country up to Norbeck Overlook, at elevation 6,445 feet. This is the highest point on the byway.

Peter Norbeck—politician, engineer, and conservationist—was the driving force behind the development of this area. He devoted many years to preserving the land and wildlife, while providing vehicle access for visitors. He helped engineer the Needles Highway and create the state park. A memorial at the overlook provides a tribute to Norbeck. You can see out over the wild, rugged countryside he loved best: Mount Rushmore, the Norbeck Wildlife Preserve, the Black Hills National Forest, Harney Peak, the Black Elk Wilderness, and Custer State Park.

The byway now drops to Lakota Lake. Three-hundred-year-old pines tower above. An easy trail leads along Iron Creek for a little over a mile, and you and the children can fish as you go. Iron Creek provides a cool, moist respite from the usual dry heat. The lusher vegetation includes edible berries like raspberries, as well as beautiful ferns and thick ground cover.

The byway continues south into Custer State Park, almost into the prairie. Game Lodge Campground has fifty-five sites, as well as swimming, fishing, hiking, and evening naturalist programs. Stay on 16A west, and stop at the Peter Norbeck Visitor Center to view the exhibits and obtain information and maps. Grace Coolidge Campground provides twenty sites, and fishing and hiking opportunities.

The byway follows 16A back to Custer, described already on the inner loop. □

General description: A twenty-eight mile paved route through country rich in wetlands, forests, farms, and lakes.

Special attractions: Blackduck Lookout Tower, wildlife viewing, camping, boating, fishing, and hunting.

Location: North-central Minnesota on the Chippewa National Forest.

Byway route numbers: Beltrami County Road 39 and Cass County Road 10.

Travel season: Year-round.

Camping: Three national forest campgrounds with picnic tables, fire grates, toilets, and drinking water.

Services: All traveler services, with limited availability, in Blackduck, Pennington, and Cass Lake.

Nearby attractions: Avenue of Pines scenic byway, ski areas, resorts, Turtle River canoe route.

For more information: Chippewa National Forest, Route 3, Box 244, Cass Lake, MN, 56633, (218) 335-8600. Blackduck Ranger District, HC3 Box 95, Blackduck, MN 56630, (218) 835-4291. Cass Lake Ranger District, Route 3 Box 219, Cass Lake, MN 56633, (218) 335-2283.

Description: Scenic Highway provides a pleasant route between agricultural lands and forests. The two-lane paved route has narrow shoulders, and traffic is usually light. The traffic picks up a bit in mid-May, at the start of walleye season.

Summer daytime temperatures are generally in the eighties to nineties. Insects can be annoying at times and you may want repellent. Spring and autumn are cooler and often wet, with days in the fifties to sixties, and evenings in the thirties and forties. Winter is nearly always below freezing.

The byway is scenic driven from either direction. When traveling north to south begin in Blackduck, where you may collect additional national forest information at the ranger station. Nearby, Blackduck Lake has camping, picnic areas, great walleye fishing, and a boat ramp.

Drive south on County Road 39, through gently rolling farmland. A barrier-free fishing pier is provided at Gilstad Lake. A few miles south, Benjamin Lake has a nice sand beach for swimming and a pleasant picnic area in the hardwoods. Trees include basswood, birch, and maple.

Nearby, four buildings of historic Camp Rabideau Civilian Conservation Corps (CCC) Camp have been restored and are open for visitation in the summer. The camp was built in 1935, and CCC workers housed there for the next five years planted thousands of trees, built the Blackduck Ranger station and two fire towers, counted deer, and performed numerous other tasks. Today, you can sample history by walking the one-mile interpretive trail through the camp.

Continue driving south on the byway through a beautiful forest of white and red pine intermixed with leafy quaking aspen, paper birch, Burr oak, and sugar and red maple. Autumn colors on this byway are lovely. Creeks

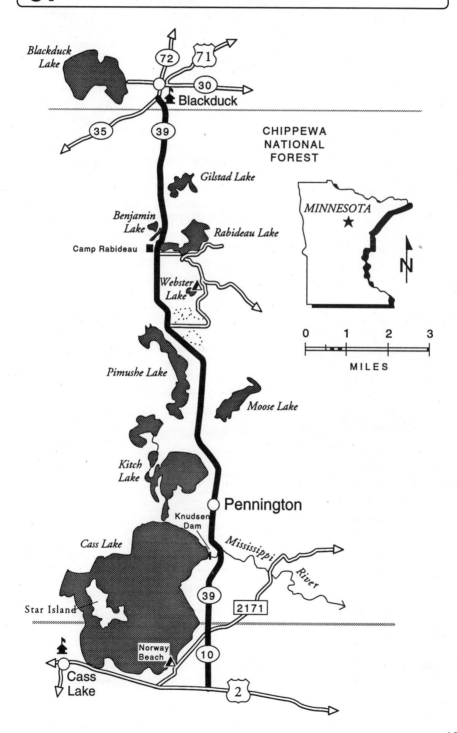

Blackduck Lake

72   71

30

Blackduck

35   39

CHIPPEWA
NATIONAL
FOREST

Gilstad Lake

MINNESOTA

Benjamin Lake

Camp Rabideau

Rabideau Lake

Webster Lake

N

0   1   2   3

MILES

Pimushe Lake

Moose Lake

Kitch Lake

Pennington

Knudsen Dam

Cass Lake

Mississippi River

39

Star Island

2171

Norway Beach

10

Cass Lake

2

and rivers provide openings in the forest, and you can glimpse black spruce bogs and expansive wetlands occupied by great blue herons, loons, a variety of ducks and songbirds. Watch overhead for soaring bald eagles. The Chippewa National Forest has the highest concentration of breeding pairs in the lower 48—one hundred sixty pairs of these endangered creatures. The number of breeding pairs has grown steadily every year, from twenty in 1963, to its present population. Another threatened animal, the gray wolf, is making a gradual comeback, and an estimated one hundred wolves live on the national forest, mostly north of U.S. Highway 2.

Webster Lake is just off the byway to the east. The campground is located on a shady, sandy ridge overlooking the lake. Swimming is pleasant here. The adjacent picnic area is situated in a birch grove and has five tables and some fire rings. A hiking trail with a boardwalk through a bog encircles Webster Lake.

The byway continues through a corridor of trees and passes cabins, homes, and a few resorts. Pennington Bog is a Scientific Natural Area home to rare native orchids. You must have a permit to enter.

South of Pennington, the trees are predominately jack pine, quaking aspen, and paper birch. The byway shares the road with the Great River Road, a nationally designated route following the Mississippi River from its headwaters to the Gulf of Mexico. You'll cross the Mississippi River, which has more species of freshwater fish than any other river on our continent. Stop at Knudson Dam for great fishing (barrier-free access), picnicking, and camping. The area is full of both prehistoric and historic Indian artifacts, including a paleolithic encampment complete with huge bison bones.

A few miles south at the county line, the highway changes numbers, from County Road 39 to County Road 10. Norway Beach has an interpretive center,

A white sand beach invites swimmers to Norway Beach along the Scenic Highway. Chippewa National Forest photo.

ranger-led summer programs, four campgrounds, a lovely white sand beach, and hiking trails. The interpretive center is housed in Norway Beach Lodge, built of red pine logs in the early 1930s by the CCC. You can rent a boat and go to Star Island, unique because it has a little lake of its own —a lake within a lake. Chief Yellowhead and the Ojibwe had villages on Star Island and near the Knutson Dam area. About two-thirds of the Chippewa National Forest is currently located on reservation lands.

The byway ends at the junction of U.S. Highway 2 and County Road 10. Big old white pines lean over the road, their tops misshapen from years of wind. From here you could drive east to Deer River and the Avenue of Pines National Forest Scenic Byway. □

38 AVENUE OF PINES SCENIC BYWAY
Chippewa National Forest   Minnesota

General description: A thirty-nine mile paved highway through extensive forests of red pine; past northern lakes, broad grassy meadows and wetlands, and several historic Indian sites.

Special attractions: Cut Foot Sioux, Turtle Mound, experimental forest, Laurentian Divide, lakes, resorts, fishing, hiking, mountain biking, horseback riding, camping, snowmobiling, and cross-country skiing.

Location: North-central Minnesota on the Chippewa National Forest. The byway travels Minnesota State Highway 46 on national forest lands between Deer River and Northome.

Byway route number: Minnesota State Highway 46.

Travel season: Year-round.

Camping: Seven national forest campgrounds, with picnic tables, fire grates, drinking water, and toilets.

Services: Groceries, gas, and lodgings with limited availability at Squaw Lake and Deer River. All travelers services in nearby Grand Rapids.

Nearby attractions: Scenic Highway and Northwoods national forest scenic byways, state parks, downhill ski areas.

For more information: Chippewa National Forest, Route 3, Box 244, Cass Lake, MN 56633, (218) 335-8600. Deer River Ranger District, P.O. Box 308, Deer River, MN 56636, (218) 246-2123.

Description: Avenue of Pines Scenic Byway travels through low rolling hills covered in pine forests and lakes. The two-lane highway is paved and has narrow shoulders and frequent pullouts. Traffic is generally light. There are numerous private campgrounds, with full hookups.

Summer daytime temperatures in northern Minnesota are generally in the eighties to nineties. Insects can be annoying at times and you may want repellent. Spring and autumn are cooler and often wet, with days in the fifties to sixties, and evenings in the thirties and forties. Winter is nearly always below freezing.

When driving the byway from south to north, you may wish to visit the Deer River Ranger District office to collect additional national forest information and maps or during the summer visit the Cut Foot Sioux Visitor Information Center in the middle of the scenic byway.

From Deer River, drive a mile west on U.S. Highway 2, then turn north on Minnesota State Highway 46. The scenic byway begins at the national forest boundary about six miles from Deer River and travels through relatively flat countryside, where agricultural fields are intermixed with forest. In the uplands, stands of red pine, aspen, birch, and fir dominate, while black spruce, tamarack, and cedar grow in the lowlands.

The Winnie Dam Corps of Engineers campground is located right below the dam, where the Mississippi River pours out of Lake Winnibigoshish. Winnie Dam was built in 1884. The campsites are located in a cool forest of red and white pines, and some sites have electric hookups. A trailer dumping station is provided. Boaters can launch into the Mississippi River and on into Little Winnibigoshish Lake.

Nearby, Plug Hat Point Campground (open only in springtime) sits in a grove of mature pines, oaks, and aspen on a small bluff above the lake. Several of the twelve sites overlook the lake, and a boat launch provides access to Lake Winnibigoshish.

North of Winnie Dam, the scenic byway enters the corridor of red pines, also known as Norway pines. Many of these trees were planted in the 1930s by the Civilian Conservation Corps (CCC). The corridor, or avenue of pines, becomes increasingly dense as you drive north.

Williams Narrows Campground's seventeen sites sit in a shady stand of mature red and white pine, with a few Burr and red oak, and red maple. Some of the campsites overlook the lake. O-Ne-Gum-e Campground is in a similar woodland setting, with forty-six sites. Some sites are barrier-free, and a few overlook Little Cut Foot Sioux Lake. There are additional campgrounds on the west side of Cut Foot Sioux Lake.

The Cut Foot Sioux area is a focal point for this scenic byway. Cut Foot Sioux is named for a warrior slain in 1748 in a battle between the Chippewa and the Sioux. A summer visitor information center has displays, a bookstore, and evening naturalist programs. A historic ranger station, listed in the National Register of Historic Places, is the oldest remaining station building in the Forest Service's eastern region. You may arrange a tour at the visitor center.

The fish hatchery operates in April and May and provides guided and self-guided tours. Walleye eggs are gathered nearby at the narrows, and by June the new fingerlings are shipped out to various lakes around the state.

Good hiking trails are scattered throughout this area. Simpson Creek Trail has some shorter loops in its thirteen-mile length. Twenty-two-mile-long Cut Foot Sioux Trail is a National Recreation Trail which meanders through this beautiful lakes and forests country and traverses the Laurentian Divide, the geographical high ground separating waters north to Hudson Bay or south to the Gulf of Mexico.

Just east of the byway, Turtle Mound is situated on the banks of Little Cut Foot Sioux Lake. A self-guided walk leads .5 mile through the site. The turtle shape was pressed into the mound and is still a sacred place for Indians practicing the traditional religion.

A few miles north of the visitor's center, motorists can take a twenty-mile-

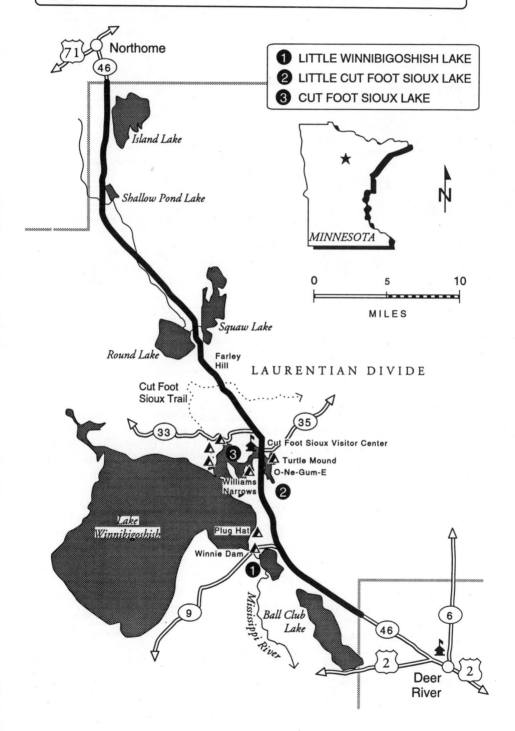

38 AVENUE OF PINES SCENIC BYWAY

1 LITTLE WINNIBIGOSHISH LAKE
2 LITTLE CUT FOOT SIOUX LAKE
3 CUT FOOT SIOUX LAKE

71
Northome
46

Island Lake

Shallow Pond Lake

MINNESOTA

N

0   5   10
MILES

Squaw Lake

Round Lake   Farley Hill

LAURENTIAN DIVIDE

Cut Foot
Sioux Trail

33   35

Cut Foot Sioux Visitor Center

3   Turtle Mound
            O-Ne-Gum-E

Williams
Narrows   **2**

Lake
Winnibigoshish

Plug Hat

Winnie Dam

1

Mississippi River

Ball Club
Lake

9   6

46

2   2

Deer
River

Avenue of Pines cuts a straight swath through the beautiful forest of big red pines. Chippewa National Forest photo.

loop side trip on paved and gravel roads. The Cut Foot Sioux Scenic Drive leads through the forest to campgrounds, beautiful lake views, and wildlife observation points. A brochure is available at the visitor center.

Continuing north on the byway, Farley Hill Lookout is in the heart of the Cutfoot Experimental Forest. This old fire tower is built on an esker, a high point in the otherwise flat region. An esker is a geologic formation left by receding glaciers. You can't climb the old tower, but take a hike on a portion of the Cut Foot Sioux National Recreation Trail. If you choose to hike west, you'll hike through the forest past several beautiful little lakes. In fall you can enjoy munching on wild blueberries or gathering wild hazelnuts from the bushes.

Typical wildlife seen in this region includes bald eagles, white-tailed deer, black bears, and beavers. Bird-watchers find over 230 species of birds on the Chippewa National Forest. Look for crossbills, ruffled grouse, woodcock, broad-winged hawk, red-eyed vireo, and white-throated sparrow. The Chippewa National Forest has the highest concentration of breeding eagles in the lower 48, one hundred forty-four pairs. Look for them on the Mississippi River and around Winnie and Cass lakes.

This stretch of highway gives the scenic byway its name, Avenue of Pines. The big red pines stretch in all directions and give a feeling of expansiveness to the forest. Pull off the road and walk through the shady understory of this beautiful, open forest.

The Indian community of Squaw Lake has a long history. Native Americans came here for hundreds of years to harvest the wild rice that nearly covers nearby Squaw Lake. The village has all traveler services, available on a limited basis. Round and Squaw lakes both have excellent walleye fisheries.

North of Round Lake, the scenery opens up more and the route travels over low rolling hills and wetlands. Aspen, birch, and balsam fir mix with farms and fields of hay. You may be lucky enough to spot a shy timber wolf some evening.

Island Lake offers good fishing, and the Elmwood Island Trail System provides a nice place to stretch your legs after riding in a boat.

The byway ends at the national forest boundary, and the road continues to Northome, a small community that provides all traveler services—available on a limited basis. □

39 NORTHWOODS SCENIC BYWAY
Chippewa National Forest   Minnesota

General description: A twenty-two-mile paved road through hardwood forests and along numerous lakes.

Special attractions: Suomi Hills and Trout Lake semiprimitive areas, Rice River Canoe Route, autumn colors, lakes, boating, fishing, camping, hiking, cross-country skiing, snowmobiling, historic sites.

Location: North-central Minnesota on the Chippewa National Forest. The byway is located within national forest boundaries on Minnesota State Highway 38, between Grand Rapids and Bigfork.

Byway route number: Minnesota State Highway 38.

Travel season: Year-round.

Camping: One national forest campground, with picnic tables, fire grates, toilets, drinking water.

Services: All traveler services in Grand Rapids. Limited services in Marcell, Effie, and Bigfork.

Nearby attractions: Avenue of Pines Scenic Byway, Big Fork River, numerous lakes, Scenic State Park, historic Iron Range, Iron World.

For more information: Chippewa National Forest, Route 3 Box 244, Cass Lake, MN 56633, (218) 335-8600. Marcell Ranger District, Marcell, MN 56657, (218) 832-3161.

Description: Set in a region of hardwood forests and freshwater lakes, Northwoods Scenic Byway travels twenty-two miles along the edge of two beautiful semiprimitive areas. The two-lane highway is paved, with narrow shoulders and limited pullouts. A good portion has no passing lanes and traffic is light and generally slow because of the rolling, winding route.

Summer daytime temperatures are generally in the eighties to nineties. Insects can be annoying at times and you may want repellent. Spring and autumn are cooler and often wet, with days in the fifties to sixties and evenings in the thirties and forties. Winter is nearly always below freezing and this byway gets a lot of snow.

Driving north to south, begin in Bigfork. To the west, the Bigfork River is

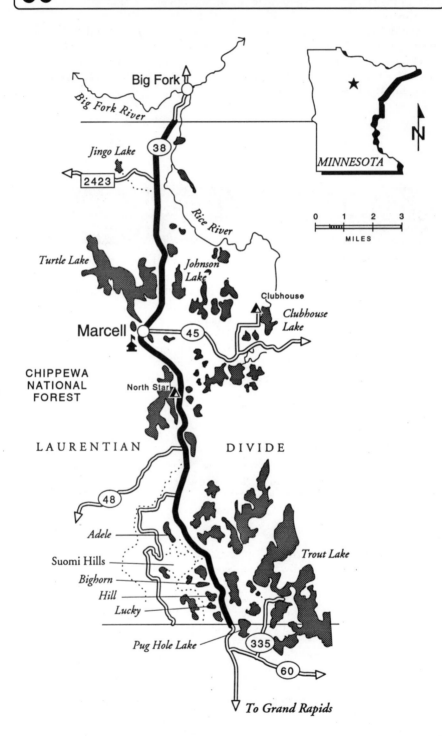

very scenic, with excellent canoeing, fishing, and boating opportunities. The Rice River Canoe Route begins in Marcel and travels nineteen miles of river and lakes between Bigfork and Marcel.

The byway parallels much of the old "Gut and Liver" railroad route between Bigfork and the national forest boundary north of Grand Rapids. Now the railroad bed is a groomed snowmobile trail with many optional loops and sidetrips along the route.

The byway travels south on Minnesota State Highway 38, through gently rolling terrrain. White spruce, red pine, jack pine, paper birch, and tamarack surround lowland wetlands and meadows. This is a hilly region, where lakes are cradled by glacial moraine from the last Ice Age. The Chippewa National Forest has over 700 lakes, 920 miles of streams, and 150,000 acres of wetlands. The Jingo Lake walking trail leads five miles through this pretty, rolling area. You could also take a short side trip east for good fishing in Johnson Lake.

Clubhouse Campground is about seven miles east of Marcel, situated on the lake in a stand of 200-year-old red pine trees. There are forty-eight sites, a nice sandy swim beach, and a boat launch.

Marcel has a small store, motel, restaurants, and gas, and area events. Activities are posted on the township's park kiosk. The Marcell Ranger District office has additional national forest information, such as brochures for The Chippewa Adventure, a 17.5-mile self-guided auto tour that loops east out of Marcell and travels the lakes and resort country; or the Fall Color Tour, thirty-six miles of brilliant autumn colors. With a Chippewa National Forest map, you can also design your own off-the-beaten-path loop on the many side roads along the byway. It's wise to check road conditions with the ranger first.

Watchable wildlife includes white-tailed deer, black bears, ruffed grouse, nesting bald eagles, and numerous species of geese and ducks. The first stop on The Chippewa Adventure points out an osprey nest built on top of a dead tree. Another stop shows you super canopy white pine, which are virgin 200-year-old trees which stand well above the rest of the forest. These huge trees are used frequently by bald eagles, for nesting and perching.

The Forest Service has ongoing projects to enhance trumpeter swan habitat. In the mid-1980s one pair established themselves on the Chippewa National Forest on their own, and they are one of just a few breeding pairs in Minnesota.

South of Marcel is very pretty. You'll get glimpses of lakes, surrounded by tree-covered hills. Hardwoods begin to dominate the forest south of Marcel. The white bark of quaking aspens and paper birch attract your eye, and sugar maples and red oaks add variety. Autumn colors can be breathtaking.

North Star Campground overlooks the lake and has some barrier-free sites. Aspens and other hardwoods are beginning to revegetate the area, which has a swimming beach and thirty-eight campsites.

A few miles south, the byway crosses the Laurentian Divide. An interpretive sign on the highway explains that this geographic high point determines whether streams and rivers run north to Hudson Bay, or south into the Gulf of Mexico.

Continuing south on the byway, the Suomi Hills Semiprimitive Nonmotor-ized Area lies nine miles south of Marcell, west of the scenic byway. For nonmotorized travel only, these 6,000 acres provide twenty-one miles of trails among the hills and lakes. Visitors come to camp, hike, mountain bicycle, canoe, cross-country ski, and bird watch. Try fishing for bass and panfish in Hill, Big Horn, Spruce Island, and Adele lakes. Lucky and Kremer lakes are

The Northwoods Highway meanders through gently rolling, forested terrain. Chippewa National Forest photo.

stocked with trout. Just south of Day Lake, you can choose from several loop trails west of the highway. These hikes meander through the forest and bring you to beautiful backcountry lakes, including Spruce Island and Adele.

East of the byway, Trout Lake Semiprimitive Nonmotorized Area protects 4,500 acres of forest and lakes. Watch for loons, great blue herons, and occasional bald eagles. Gray wolves and coyotes also move through here. You can hike about three miles to Trout Lake, which is beautiful and very cold, with good fishing. The historic Joyce estate was built on the southwest corner of the lake, and provides a look at life in another era. Timber baron David Joyce built thirty buildings for his private hunting camp/summer home and included a golf course and shooting range. Today you can walk through the big log lodge and stroll the grounds. The Forest Service plans to restore the main lodge and two of the guest cabins. There are opportunities for dispersed primitive camping around the lake. To reach the trailhead, turn east on Highway 60, then north on 335. Park at the locked gate and walk in.

The scenic byway ends at the national forest boundary, in the birch and aspens along Pug Hole Lake. This is a pretty place for a picnic. The highway continues south to Grand Rapids. □

General description: A fifty-eight-mile route between the shores of Lake Superior and the rocky inland hills.

Special attractions: Lake Superior, camping, fishing, hiking, bicycling, historic sites, autumn colors, resorts, wildlife, downhill and cross-country skiing, snowmobiling.

Location: Northeast Minnesota on the Superior National Forest. The byway travels Minnesota State Highway 61 between Schroeder and the national forest boundary eleven miles southwest of Grand Portage.

Byway route number: Minnesota State Highway 61.

Travel season: Year-round.

Camping: Two state park campgrounds. Seven national forest campgrounds within fifteen miles of the byway.

Services: All traveler services in Grand Marais. All services, with limited availability, in Schroeder, Tofte, and Lutsen.

Nearby attractions: Boundary Waters Wilderness Canoe Area, Grand Portage National Monument, Quetico Provincial Park in Canada.

For more information: Superior National Forest, P.O. Box 338, Duluth, MN 55801, (218) 720-5324. Tofte Ranger District, Tofte, MN 55615, (218) 663-7981. Gunflint Ranger District, P.O. Box 308, Grand Marais, MN 55604, (218) 387-1750.

Description: Lake Superior provides an ever-changing variety of moods to travelers on the North Shore Drive. Pounding storms alternate with peaceful sunsets and white-capped waves. To the west, rocky hillsides rise up to 1,500 feet above the lake, and waterfalls pour over ledges in a rush to the lake. The two-lane road is paved and very busy—the busiest highway in Minnesota. Shoulder widths vary, but there are numerous pullouts for scenic viewing. This byway is part of the well-known Lake Superior Circle Tour, crossing three states and Canada. It is a popular resort region, and you may encounter joggers and bicyclers on the route.

Weather along the North Shore is moderated by Lake Superior, which keeps the shoreline lagging behind seasonal changes inland. Spring and summer are cooler, and fall and winter are warmer than the rest of the state. In summer, daytime temperatures vary according to wind direction. When winds blow from the east, temperatures can hover in the forties and fifties. West winds bring warmer temperatures up to eighty-five degrees. The rainiest times, generally accompanied by dense fog, are from about mid-May to early July. Driest months are August and September. Expect temperatures in the thirties and forties along the shore in autumn, while the interior is ten or twenty degrees colder. Winter is generally sunny, with temperatures dropping below zero, and snow covering the ground from about mid-November to late March.

The byway is very scenic when driven from either direction. West to east provides bigger vistas over Lake Superior, while east to west allows more views of the big ships heading into harbor at Duluth. The microclimate along the shore here supports trees unable to withstand the cold at the top of the adjacent ridges. Red maples, sugar maples, quaking aspen, and white birch along the byway enliven autumn with their bright colors.

If traveling west to east, the byway begins at the Cross River in Schroeder. Stop to admire sheets of river water glistening down the granite faces, then walk onto the tiny peninsula to see the memorial to Father Baraga. He was sent to Duluth in 1843 to start a mission but was shipwrecked right here and decided this was where he should set up the mission. And so he did. Along with the cross, weatherbeaten redcedar and a few hardy black and red spruce adorn the rocky peninsula. There is a good view of rounded boulders on the rocky shoreline and bays on either side.

Temperance River State Park is off the highway a bit. Water cascades off the adjacent mountains into Lake Superior, while the deep river gorge funnels numerous waterfalls through its volcanic stone walls. Brook, brown, and rainbow trout are stocked in both the Temperance and the Cross rivers, and hikers can walk on eight miles of trails. One trail leads to the Superior Hiking Trail, which offers 125 miles of maintained trail along the ridge of the Sawtooth Mountains.

Stop at the district ranger station in Tofte for national forest information and permits for the Boundary Waters Canoe Area. Tofte has interesting little arts and crafts shops. Nearby, you can take a short side trip north on State Highway 2 to the Carlton Peak trailhead at the top of the first big ridge. This very short, very steep trail climbs up to 1,600-foot Carlton Peak in just .25 mile. It's worth it. The views sweep east over Lake Superior, and west into the Sawtooth Mountains. The Sawtooths rise abruptly from the lake along the

The North Shore Drive travels along the shoreline of Lake Superior. Superior National Forest photo.

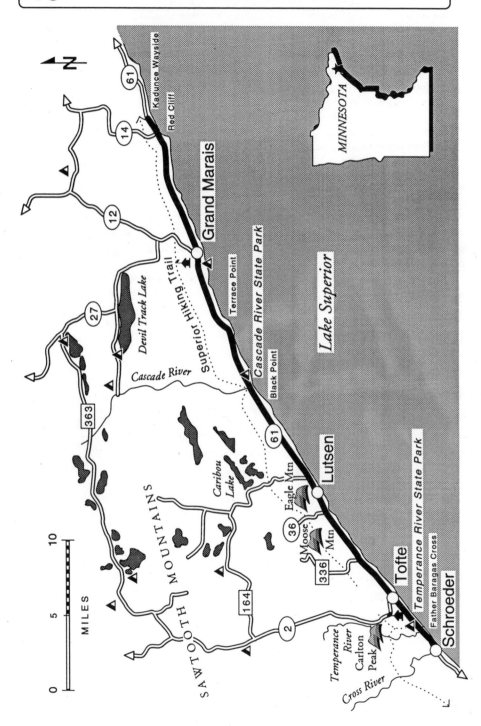

scenic byway then stretch west into a broad plateau. They include the highest point in Minnesota—2,301-foot Eagle Mountain.

A good place to hike a portion of the Superior Trail is at Moose Mountain. Drive north a few miles on State Highway 36 then climb to the rocky bluffs at the top of the mountain. A 360-degree view is your reward.

Lutsen is one of the oldest resorts in the state. Downhill and cross-country skiing, golf, and other activities are offered.

A side trip north on State Highway 4 leads past Caribou Lake to the turnoffs to two national forest campgrounds. The soils at the top of the ridge are thin and rocky from repeated glaciation. The vegetation is known as a boreal forest, characterized by upland black spruce swamps and mixed stands of balsam fir, ponderosa pine, white birch, and quaking aspen. You may be lucky enough to spot a moose, black bear, or timber wolf. Easier to spot are deer, beavers, otters, eagles, osprey, peregrine falcons, loons, and ruffled grouse.

Fishing is a popular activity on the Superior National Forest. Anglers fish the small lakes for walleye, northern pike, bass, lake trout, and various panfish. The salmon run in autumn, and smelt run in springtime. For competitive anglers, Lake Superior offers trophy-size fish.

The byway crests a rise and Black Point offers a sweeping view of the glistening waters of Lake Superior. On a clear day you can see the lighthouse at Grand Marais and the profile of the Sawtooth Mountains rising from the lake.

Cascade River State Park has ten streams within its boundaries. Waterfalls and gorges, deer and chipmunks add allure to the park. You can walk along the river to Cascade Falls on one of the fifteen miles of hiking trails.

The byway continues east to Terrace Point, which has a nice sand beach for swimming. You may emerge blue, though—the water in Lake Superior stays about fifty-two degrees year round.

Grand Marais is a center for arts and crafts festivals and regional celebrations. The ranger station has national forest information, and it's nice to sit on the shore and watch the boats sail in and out. The municipal park allows camping, and the lighthouse juts out from Circular Harbor. Visitors may want to tour St. Francis Xavier church and the Colvill Homestead. For a different perspective, drive north on State Highway 12 to a scenic overlook of the city and harbor. Grand Marais has plenty of winter activities, from the famous John Beargrease Sled Dog Marathon, to cross-country skiing and snowmobiling.

Continuing east on the byway, Red Cliff provides another view of the lake and mountains. The scenic byway ends at the national forest boundary at Kadunce Wayside Rest Area. □

41 HERITAGE DRIVE
Nicolet National Forest   Wisconsin

General description: A scenic drive through a hardwood forest in a region rich in history.

Special attractions: Hiking, picnicking, boating, swimming, Blackjack Springs and Headwaters wilderness areas, historical buildings, autumn foliage.

Location: Northeast Wisconsin on the Nicolet National Forest. The byway travels two roads that form a "Y"—the Military Road between Wisconsin State Highways 32 and 70, just east of the communities of Three Lakes and Eagle River; and east from Military Road onto Butternut Road, ending at Franklin Lake Campground.

Byway route numbers: Forest Road 2178, and Forest Road 2181.

Travel season: Year-round.

Camping: Four national forest campgrounds within two miles of the byway, with picnic tables, fire grates, toilets, and drinking water.

Services: No traveler services available on the byway. All services in nearby Eagle River.

Nearby attractions: Resorts, Eagle River Chain of Lakes, Nicolet Scenic Rail, Three Lakes museum, winter sports.

For more information: Nicolet National Forest, 68 South Stevens Street, Rhinelander, WI 54501, (715) 362-3415. Eagle River Ranger District, P.O. Box 1809, Eagle River, WI 54521, (715) 479-2827.

Description: Heritage Drive consists of two connecting roads that form a "Y" shape. Freshwater lakes and forests of northern hardwoods and pines characterize this area. The two-lane roads are paved and mostly narrow. Traffic is moderately heavy in the summer and fall, and light the rest of the year.

Daytime summer temperatures vary from the mid-seventies to the low nineties, with occasional thunderstorms. Fall and spring daytime temperatures range from the forties to the seventies. Winter is usually below freezing, dipping down below zero on occasion. Snow generally covers the ground between December and March.

The byway is scenic driven from either direction. When driven south to north, begin at the junction of Wisconsin State Highway 32 and the Military Road (Forest Road 2178). The terrain is flat or gently rolling, and the highway travels through national forest interspersed with private property. Pockets of huge, old-growth white and red pines can be seen from the road, as well as northern hardwoods such as red maples, sugar maples, white birch, and yellow birch. Autumn colors are lovely.

Take a side trip east on Forest Road 2182, into Headwaters Wilderness. The 20,000 acres of wetlands and dry uplands provide opportunities to explore bogs and black spruce swamps. Orchids are one of the many wildflowers to adorn this wilderness. Beavers are abundant, as well as eastern white-tailed deer. Deer hunting is popular here in autumn. An occasional timber wolf moves through the area, and in spring you can see great blue herons nesting in their rookery.

The Pine River usually has enough water for canoeing, or you may wish to walk through Giant Pine Grove. To get to this mile-long, lovely hike through virgin white pines, travel east on Forest Road 2182, then southwest on Forest Road 2414. The trail is clearly marked and easy to follow.

A few miles west of the byway, Laurel Lake Campground has twelve sites in a grove of big white pines. Anglers fish for musky, walleye, bass, and northern pike, and boaters find access to the fifty-mile-long Three Lakes/Eagle River Chain of Lakes.

The byway follows an ancient, well-worn Indian route originating from Green Bay on Lake Michigan and ending along Lake Superior's Keweenaw Peninsula. Artifacts of Indian encampments of 4,000 years ago can be found. Early white settlers used the trail as a mail route. In the late 1860s it was developed as a military transportation road and provided access to the rich timberlands of northern Wisconsin.

The byway meanders north through a beautiful forest. Conifers include red pine, jack pine, eastern white pine, hemlock, tamarack, cedar, spruce, and balsam fir, providing a deep green contrast to the various northern hardwoods. In autumn blazing reds, yellows, and oranges adorn sugar maples, red maples, paper birches, yellow birches, basswoods, and quaking aspens. Wildflowers along the byway include trillium, Dutchman's breeches, orchids, wild iris, and daisies.

A side trip northwest on Forest Road 2207 (Old Military Road) leads to Four Mile Lake and the Sam Campbell Memorial Trail. This 1.25-mile self-guided footpath encounters a wide variety of native vegetation, including a white cedar swamp, old growth red pines, bogs, black spruce, and upland hardwoods. The trail is very pretty, with lots of gentle ups and downs along its winding course.

Continuing north on the byway, you'll see big stands of jack pines, planted in the 1930s by the Civilian Conservation Corps. Openings in this corridor of trees provide glimpses of wetlands and bogs. Turn off the byway on Forest Road 2435 to Sevenmile Lake Campground, which has twenty-seven sites perched on a hill above the lake. There is a nice sandy swimming beach and a good hiking trail. The trail leads from the campground southeast to several small lakes, passing under big red pines and crossing a boardwalk over a cedar swamp.

Wildlife you may spot on the Nicolet National Forest includes white-tailed deer, pine martens, fishers, black bears, beavers, and racoons. Bird watchers will delight in seeing bald eagles, osprey, great blue herons, loons, and many species of owls, hawks, and ducks. Songbirds are abundant and include warblers, vireos, wrens, thrushes, and finches.

Near its northern terminus, the byway offers two choices for travel. Turn east onto Butternut Road (Forest Road 2181), or continue north on the Military Road. A trip up Butternut is very pleasant, winding through stands of old, large hemlocks and northern hardwoods. The road provides access to excellent cross-country ski trails, then travels past Butternut Lake to end at Franklin Lake Campground and Picnic Area. The campground provides eighty-one sites, a swimming beach, and a boat launch. Summer evening ranger-led interpretive programs are offered. Topics include naturalist programs on loons, eagles, osprey, and archaeology.

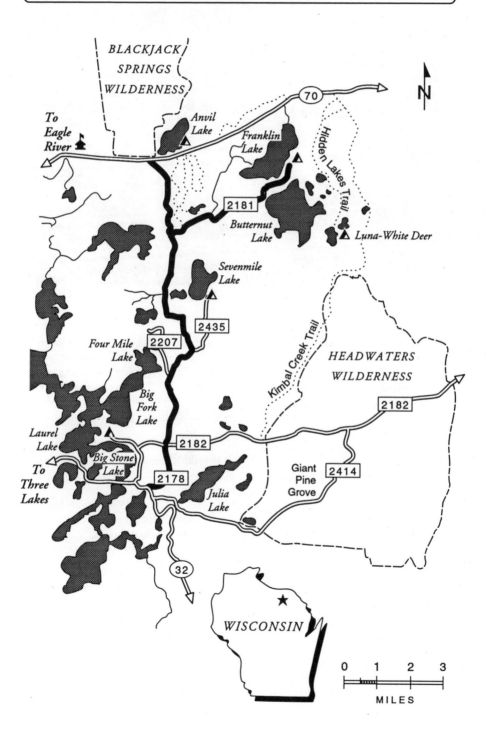

A tiny pond nestles in an opening in the forest along Heritage Drive. Nicolet National Forest photo.

A one-mile interpretive nature trail offers an easy walk along the eskers and potholes of this glacially carved region. Old-growth white pines tower overhead and an unspoiled shoreline beckons swimmers. You can enhance the hike by following four-mile-long Hidden Lakes Trail, which ends at the Luna-White Deer Campground. Listen for the distinctive call of a loon on the lakes you stroll by. Many other hiking trails allow you to fully explore this region.

To complete driving the scenic byway, return to the Military Road and turn north. A few miles ahead, the Anvil Lake National Recreation Trail provides twelve miles of summer hiking and winter groomed cross-country skiing. Maps of the trail system are available at various trailheads.

The scenic byway ends at the junction of Military Road and Wisconsin State Highway 70. A mile east on 70, Anvil Lake Campground has eighteen sites in the hardwoods. Some sites overlook the lake. The swimming beach is very popular, and the 380-acre lake offers good fishing opportunities. Hikers can stretch out on a six-mile walk to Franklin Lake Campground. □

General description: A seventy-mile route through the historic and scenic features of the Shawnee Hills and the Ohio River.

Special attractions: Cave-In-Rock, Trail of Tears National Historic Trail, Garden of the Gods, hiking, Tower Rock, historic buildings, locks and dam.

Location: Southeastern Illinois on the Shawnee National Forest. The byway travels between Smithland Locks and Dams on the south and Mitchellsville on the north.

Byway route numbers: Illinois State Highway 34 between Mitchellsville and a few miles south of Herod; Karbers Ridge Road (Gallatin County Road 13 and Hardin County Road 9) along Karbers Ridge between Highway 34 and Highway 1; Illinois State Highway 1 from the junction of Karbers Ridge Road to Cave-In-Rock; Illinois State Highway 146 between State Highway 1 near Cave-In-Rock and Golconda; County Road 1 between Golconda and Smithland Locks & Dam.

Travel season: Year-round.

Camping: Six national forest campgrounds on or near the byway, with picnic tables, fire grates, toilets, and drinking water.

Services: Traveler services in Cave-In-Rock, Elizabethtown, Rosiclare, and Golconda, with limited availability.

Nearby attractions: Lake Glendale Recreation Area, Dixon Springs State Park, Glen O. Jones Lake, The Old Slave House, Lake of Egypt Recreation Area.

For more information: Shawnee National Forest, 901 South Commercial Street, Harrisburg, IL 62946, (618) 253-7114. Elizabethtown Ranger District, Route 2 Box 4, Elizabethtown, IL 62931, (618) 287-2201. Vienna Ranger District, Route 1 Box 288B, Vienna, IL 62995, (618) 658-2111.

Description: Shawnee Hills on the Ohio Scenic Byway tours through hills and ridgetops before dropping down to follow the Ohio River. The road is two-lane and paved, with occasional turnouts. Traffic is generally heavy and moves at forty to fifty-five miles per hour. Karbers Ridge is especially busy in spring and fall. South of Golconda tends to receive moderate use.

Summer temperatures range from seventy to ninety, with high humidity. Spring and fall are between sixty-five and eighty, with less humidity and frequent rain. Winter temperatures average in the thirties and forties, and snow generally melts off fairly quickly.

The byway is diverse and scenic driven in either direction. Beginning in Mitchellsville (about six miles south of Harrisburg), you'll drive through open pasturelands and get a preview of the forested Shawnee Hills ahead. The byway follows Highway 34 southeast, and enters the Shawnee National Forest. The route rolls up and down the hills, climbing through pretty pastoral scenes and woodlands.

The byway turns east and climbs up Karbers Ridge. The forest is composed of oaks and hickories, along with tulip poplars, elms, maples, cedars,

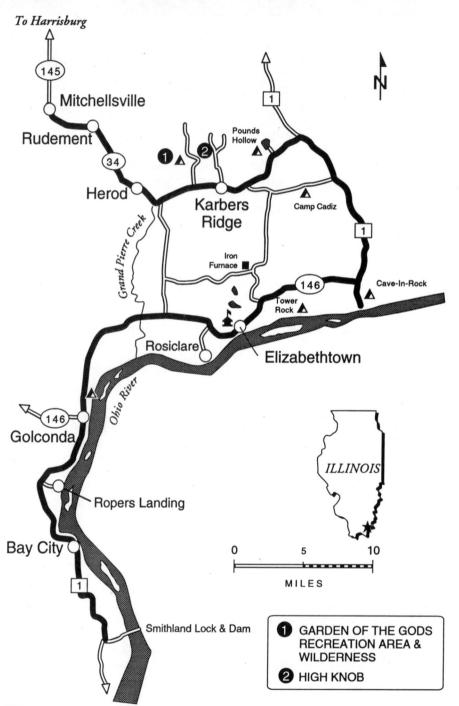

42 SHAWNEE HILLS ON THE OHIO SCENIC BYWAY

To Harrisburg

145

Mitchellsville

Rudement

34

Herod

1

Pounds Hollow

Karbers Ridge

Camp Cadiz

1

Iron Furnace

146

Cave-In-Rock

Tower Rock

Rosiclare

Elizabethtown

Grand Pierre Creek

Ohio River

146

Golconda

Ropers Landing

Bay City

1

Smithland Lock & Dam

ILLINOIS

```
0        5        10
|_____|_____|
        MILES
```

1 GARDEN OF THE GODS RECREATION AREA & WILDERNESS

2 HIGH KNOB

dogwoods, redbuds, sumacs, and sassafras. Spring-flowering shrubs and autumn leaves are absolutely breathtaking.

Take a side trip north to Garden of the Gods, an area of fascinating sandstone rock formations. There is picnicking, the campground has twelve sites, and interconnecting footpaths and horse trails allow you to explore easily. A quarter-mile long barrier-free path (completed in 1992) leads to a viewpoint above the cliffs, where you'll see the Shawnee Hills and Garden of the Gods Wilderness. Look for unique rocks such as Anvil, Mushroom, and Camel.

The sandstone outcrops and bluffs visible at Garden of the Gods were deposited as sand and mud in a 300-million-year-old marine and river environment. Wind, annual freeze/thaw cycles, and melting glaciers eroded the soft rock into valleys and the weird shapes we see today. The reddish streaks and bands you see on exposed rocks are caused by oxidizing iron.

Back on the byway, the route traverses Karbers Ridge. A side trip north to High Knob provides extensive views of the Shawnee National Forest, including the east side of Garden of the Gods.

The national forest shelters a wide variety of wildlife: 237 species of resident or migrating birds; seventy-nine species of amphibians and reptiles; forty-eight species of mammals; and 109 species of fish.

Continue east on the byway then take another side trip north. Pounds Hollow Recreation Area provides opportunities to picnic, hike, camp, swim, boat, and fish. The campground has seventy-six sites, a play area, and drinking water. Boats can be rented, and anglers fish for largemouth bass, channel catfish, and sunfish. Campfire interpretive programs are presented on holiday weekends in the summer.

The Rim Rock National Recreation Trail wanders less than a mile through hardwoods and cedar, goes near the Ox-Lot Cave and through Fat Man Squeeze, encircles the Rim Rock Escarpment and provides a pretty view of Pounds Hollow Lake. You can continue on to the Beaver Trail and walk around the lake.

Back on the byway, travel east to Highway 1, then turn south on 1. Another side trip leads about three miles west to Camp Cadiz, which has eleven sites, drinking water, a horse corral, and remnants of the old Civilian Conservation Corps camp structures. This is the eastern trailhead for the River-to-River Trail, popular with horseback riders and backpackers.

Cave-In-Rock State Park lies at the southern end of Highway 1, right on the Ohio River. A high limestone bluff faces the river, and a fifty-five-foot-wide entrance arch leads into Cave-In-Rock, which extends about 160 feet back into the cliff. The cave sheltered numerous river bandits and other unsavory characters in the 1800s. Today you can look down into the cave from above. The cave was used in filming the movie "How The West Was Won."

The park also offers boating, fishing, hiking, camping, picnicking, and a resort facility. The restaurant features fresh Ohio River catfish dinners.

The byway goes back north on Highway 1 a few miles, then turns west on 146. Tower Rock is the highest point on the Ohio River. The campground has thirty-five sites in the sycamores and cottonwoods along the banks of the Ohio. A quarter-mile trail goes near the top of Tower Rock and provides a splendid view of the river and islands and the surrounding hills of Illinois and Kentucky. A boat ramp provides access to the Ohio River.

Elizabethtown has several historic structures, such as the Rose Hotel, the First Baptist Church, and the Hardin County Courthouse. A ranger station

Camel Rock juts out among the rock outcrops in Garden of the Gods, along the Shawnee Hills Scenic Byway. Shawnee National Forest photo.

has national forest information, maps, and permits. Take a side trip north to Iron Furnace Recreation Area. Interpretive signs explain the workings of this furnace, which produced pig iron in the 1800s. The furnace was rebuilt to its present form in 1967. A pleasant .5-mile interpretive trail follows Big Creek and points out natural and historic features.

Canoeists can enjoy floating Big Grand Pierre Creek. A popular float begins on Highway 146 and goes about four miles to the Ohio River then continues on down the river to Golconda.

Rosiclare hosts the oldest mining company in the U.S., mining for lead and fluorspar. The byway continues through low rolling hills, cultivated fields, pasturelands, and small settlements. The forested Shawnee Hills lie to the north.

Many of Golconda's buildings are listed on the National Register of Historic Places. Visit the museum and pick up a guide for the walking tour, which meanders through "silk stocking row" and the estates on the bluff. Nearby, the new marina caters to boaters and anglers. Fishing is excellent, for bass, bluegill, crappie, and catfish.

The Cherokee Indian Trail of Tears passes through this area. In 1938, 15,000 Cherokees were forced to leave their homes, and were marched nearly 1,000 miles away. At least 4,000 Cherokee died along the way, from malnutrition, cholera, and exposure. Monuments along their route mark this shameful event in our nation's history.

The byway continues south, now on County Road 1. Boat launches are provided at Roper's Landing and Bay City. The byway ends at Smithland Lock and Dam. You can watch the boats pass through the locks, and tour the visitor center to learn about this interesting process. □

General description: A forty-four mile highway that winds through scenic hills and past numerous covered bridges.

Special attractions: Little Muskingum River, historic tours, Marietta riverfront and attractions, covered bridges, autumn foliage, wildflowers, wildlife.

Location: Southeast Ohio on the Wayne National Forest. The byway travels Ohio Route 26 between Woodsfield and Marietta.

Byway route number: Ohio State Highway 26.

Travel season: Year-round.

Camping: Five national forest campgrounds, with picnic tables, fire grates, and toilets.

Services: All traveler services in Marietta and Woodsfield. Limited services available at various communities along the byway.

Nearby attractions: Ohio River, Ohio River Museum, Campus Maritius Museum, mound cemetery, Middleton Doll Company tours, Blenner Hassett Island.

For more information: Wayne-Hoosier National Forest, 811 Constitution Avenue, Bedford, IN 47421, (812) 275-5987. Athens Ranger District - Marietta Unit, Route 1, Marietta, OH 45750, (614) 373-9055.

Description: Covered Bridge Scenic Byway winds through the hilly, picturesque region of southeastern Ohio. The narrow two-lane road has a few pullouts, and traffic moves about thirty-five to forty-five mph along the twisting route. Traffic is generally light.

Summertime temperatures reach a humid ninety degrees, with thunderstorms and occasional flash flooding along the river. Fall and spring temperatures range from about the thirties to the sixties. Spring tends to be wet, and autumn is mostly sunny. Winter days reach the forties and fifties and nighttime temperatures are below thirty.

The byway is very scenic driven in either direction. When driving south to north, begin in Marietta—the first non-native settlement in the Northwest Territory. Marietta was established in 1788 and has retained a rich historical flavor. Riverboat trade was a major part of Marietta's economy, and today you can tour the maritime museum to revisit the past. An attractive riverfront has a walking mall, red brick streets, shops, paddle wheel boat, and restaurants. The town cemetery is located around two large Indian burial mounds.

There are several historic tours around Marietta, including trolley car tours through town. During the summer months a ferry shuttles people to Blennerhassett Island in the Ohio River. The mansion built here in the 1700s has been restored, and there are tours, buggy rides, picnicking, and shopping opportunities on the island.

Other area tours include the Fenton Glass Factory and Rossi Pasta factory; historic Parkersburg, West Virginia; and the Middleton Doll Factory at nearby Belpre. The doll factory produces porcelain dolls. The factory itself looks like a giant dollhouse and is especially beautiful when lit with Christmas lights.

The byway follows Highway 26 along the Little Muskingum River. This river corridor winds through some of the most picturesque rural farmland in the Midwest. Small farms and crossroad communities are interspersed with forested land. Weathered barns painted as Mail Pouch Tobacco billboards are found here, and covered bridges, over a century old, are still in use. There are a variety of recreation opportunities along the scenic byway.

Canoeing is excellent from fall through spring, and there are some nice swimming holes. The river appears muddy, and in fact, the Indian word Muskingum translates to mean muddy river. Fifty-two species of fish inhabit the river, including the native stream muskellunge and endangered Ohio brook lamprey. Anglers fish for smallmouth, spotted, and largemouth bass; crappie; sauger; bluegill; and catfish, among others. Chiggers, ticks, and poison ivy can all be a nuisance to the unwary.

The byway winds through a region of farms and rolling hills, and you'll travel either along the river valley or up to ridgetops for extended views. American beech; sugar maple; black, white, and swamp oak; and shagbark and pignut hickory vegetate the steep slopes. Dogwood and redbud blossoms brighten the forest understory each spring.

The first covered bridge along this byway appears near the community of Hills. Nearby, Lane Farm is a small recreation area in the trees that provides opportunities to picnic, fish, and camp. There are three campsites available. Walk across the covered bridge to hike a portion of the North Country Trail. This moderate trail winds east and north from here as far as Woodsfield. The North Country Trail is a National Scenic Trail that will eventually wind through the country, linking New York and North Dakota.

Hikers are likely to see beavers, white-tailed deer, and turkeys. Other forest inhabitants include rabbits, squirrels, muskrats, red and gray foxes, minks, racoons, skunks, and opossums. The endangered river otter and bobcat also reside in this region. Bird watchers can look for endangered king rails, as well as great blue herons, Canada geese, bluebirds, warblers, vireos, and red-tailed and sharp-shinned hawks.

The byway leaves the river near Moss Run, and climbs up to a good view of the ridges and drainages lying to the east and south. Continue north on the highway, and take a side trip east from Dart. Park at the North Country Trailhead and hike south about a mile to Archers Fork, to see a natural stone bridge. There are many scenic rock outcrops and rock formations in the area, but the most impressive is the massive rock bridge that you can actually walk across.

This is a region rich in oil and gas, with some of the oldest wells in the country. Occasionally you may see cables crossing the road, from antiquated wells connected to a pumphouse down by the river. If the flags are moving, the oil well is pumping. Most of the wells, however, are well hidden by vegetation.

Back on the byway, travel north past Steel Run to the Hune Bridge Recreation Area. You can drive right over this picturesque covered bridge into the camping and picnic area. There are two campsites and good access for launching a canoe on the Little Muskingum River. You can hike another portion of the North Country Trail, here called the Covered Bridge Trail, which runs from Hune north 4.5 miles to the Rinard Covered Bridge just past Wingett

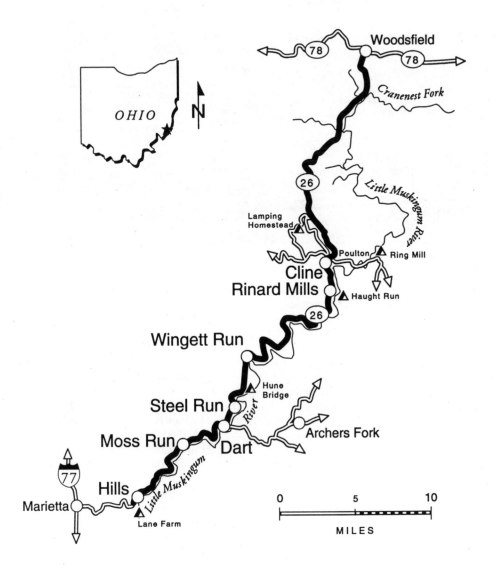

43 COVERED BRIDGE SCENIC BYWAY

OHIO

N

Woodsfield
78
78

Cranenest Fork

26

Little Muskingum River

Lamping
Homestead

Poulton Ring Mill

Cline
Rinard Mills Haught Run

26

Wingett Run

Hune
Bridge

Steel Run River

Moss Run Dart Archers Fork

77

Hills

Marietta Little Muskingum

Lane Farm

0   5   10

MILES

A typical scene along the Covered Bridge Scenic Byway. Wayne-Hoosier National Forest photo.

Run. Another recreation area at Rinard, called Haught Run, provides three campsites and good river access.

The byway continues north, through pastoral, rural countryside. The Knowlton Covered Bridge is near Cline, and a small county park provides picnic facilities.

A side trip east from Cline leads about three miles to Ring Mill, a historic mill site. En route, the road goes right between a house and barn, so watch for chickens and cows on the road. Ring Mill is the northernmost launch point for canoeing the Little Muskingum River. There are three campsites and a picnic area. An interpretive sign explains about the Walter Ring House, which housed four generations of millers from 1846 until 1921.

Continuing north on the byway, the Lamping Homestead has picnic sites and a five-mile loop trail. This tranquil site includes a five-acre pond stocked with bluegill, bass, and catfish.

The byway leaves the river and follows smaller streams, climbs ridges to expansive vistas, then drops back into the valley to end at Woodsfield. This small community has a quaint rural atmosphere and some antique shops. □

LONGHOUSE SCENIC BYWAY
Allegheny National Forest   Pennsylvania

General description: A twenty-nine-mile loop through beautiful hardwood forests and around Kinzua Bay on the Allegheny Reservoir.

Special attractions: Allegheny National Recreation Area, autumn colors, lake recreation, wildlife watching, bicycling, hunting, cross-country skiing, snowmobiling, camping.

Location: Northwest Pennsylvania on the Allegheny National Forest. The byway travels a triangle—Highway 321 from Bradford Ranger Station south eleven miles to the junction with Forest Road 262; Forest Road 262 from its junction with Highway 321 northwest to its junction with Highway 59 near Morrison Bridge; and Highway 59 from Morrison Bridge east to Bradford Ranger Station.

Byway route numbers: Pennsylvania State Highway 321, Forest Road 262, Pennsylvania State Highway 59.

Travel season: State Highways 321 and 59 open year round. Forest Road 262 closed by snow from about mid-December through March.

Camping: Three national forest campgrounds along the byway, with picnic tables, fire grates, flush toilets, showers, drinking water, playground, and dumping stations. Numerous public and private campgrounds within thirty miles of the byway.

Services: Traveler services in Bradford, Kane, and nearby Warren and Sheffield. Gas, boats, bait, snacks, some lodging, and meals available at various places along or near the byway.

Nearby attractions: Allegheny State Park; National Seneca Iroquois National Museum; Kinzua Bridge State Park; Hickory Creek Wilderness; Lake Chautauqua State Park and Institute; Knox, Kane, Kinzua Railroad.

For more information: Allegheny National Forest, 222 Liberty Street (P.O. Box 847), Warren, PA 16365, (814) 723-5150. Bradford Ranger District, Star Route 1 Box 88, Bradford, PA 16701, (814) 362-4613.

Description: The Longhouse Scenic Byway winds through hardwood forests atop a large plateau and along an arm of Allegheny Reservoir. The two-lane route is paved and has frequent scenic turnouts. Traffic moves slowly and is moderate from spring through fall, tapering off in winter.

Summer daytime temperatures average about eighty degrees; spring and fall range from about forty to seventy degrees. Rainfall is moderate throughout. Winter sees plenty of snow, with average temperatures ranging from about ten to forty degrees.

The byway is very scenic driven in either direction. Begin at the Bradford Ranger Station, where you can obtain national forest information and maps.

The Allegheny Mountains are part of the Appalachian Mountain chain. This region was once under an ocean, but movements of the earth's crust pushed up the mountain chain. The limestone from the ocean was compressed into shale, which trapped rich pockets of oil and natural gas.

The mountains are generally flat-topped, and covered with a lush growth

Longhouse Scenic Byway encircles part of the Allegheny Reservoir, seen here from Rimrock Scenic Overlook. Allegheny National Forest photo.

of hardwoods. Rivers and streams have cut steep channels into the mountains and exposed interesting rock outcrops. The dense forest is predominately black cherry, maple, northern red oak, beech, aspen, and white oak.

About a half mile south of the ranger station you can see a working oil well at the Pennzoil Powerhouse. The highway follows North Fork Creek, then Chappel Creek. Chappel has a nice fishery of native and stocked rainbow trout.

The North Country National Scenic Trail crosses the byway about five miles from the ranger station. This eighty-five mile trail crosses the entire national forest from north to south. Stretch your legs and sample a few miles of the trail: hike north up a small mountain for the reward of several nice views over Allegheny Reservoir. A good half-day hike takes you about seven miles north to the Highway 59 portion of the scenic byway.

The Allegheny National Forest has a variety of wildlife, including at least forty-nine mammal species. Most abundant are rabbits, squirrels, turkeys, grouse, white-tailed deer, and black bears. Raptors such as hawks, osprey, and eagles soar overhead, while great blue herons can often be seen fishing along the banks of streams and the reservoir.

The byway travels along Chappel Bay, providing several nice views of the reservoir through the screen of trees. Allegheny Reservoir encompasses 7,634 acres on the upper Allegheny River. In addition to generating power, the reservoir offers numerous recreation opportunities to camp, fish, boat, watch wildlife, and swim.

Red Bridge Campground has fifty-five sites nestled in a large grove of maple and white pines. Many of the sites are right near the water.

44 LONGHOUSE SCENIC BYWAY

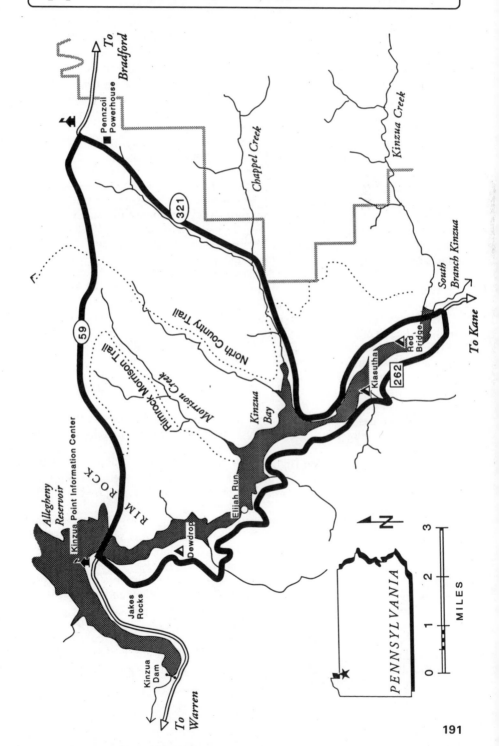

Boating is very popular on Allegheny Reservoir and you'll likely see people fishing, water-skiing, and sightseeing from the water. Boats can be rented at various marinas along the byway.

Turn northwest onto Longhouse Scenic Drive (Forest Road 262) at the National Forest Scenic Byway sign about eleven miles from the Bradford Ranger Station. This section of the byway twists and turns and rolls up and down the hills and valleys. The speed limit is 35 mph. In places the road travels right along the edge of the reservoir; other times it climbs as much as a thousand feet above the water. There are several boat ramps along the route and numerous places to park off the road and walk down to the reservoir for bank fishing.

Kiasutha Campground provides ninety sites in the forest. Look for delicious blackberries around the campground in August. There is a picnic area, boat launch, and beach. Evening naturalist programs are presented in summer at the amphitheater. Hikers can walk on an easy mile-long interpretive trail and learn about natural resources, trees, and wildlife.

Elijah Run boat ramp has a great view across the water to Morrison Campground, which is accessible only by boat. Just past Elijah Run, another scenic view looks down the whole southern stretch of Kinzua Arm.

Dewdrop Campground has seventy-four sites in the dense forest. Some sites are next to the water. Nearby, follow the short paths at Jake's Rocks Scenic Overlook to look down more than a thousand feet to the reservoir. This is the highest point along the scenic byway.

About .5 mile past Jake's Rocks another spectacular view is presented. Morrison Bridge and the reservoir to the north are framed by the large oak trees at the overlook. It's a photographer's delight.

The byway continues north to its junction with Highway 59. The Kinzua Point Information Center has interpretive displays explaining area history and uses of the national forest and Allegheny Reservoir. You can talk to staff about the area and obtain maps, brochures, and interpretive materials.

A side trip west on 59 goes to the community of Warren, which has traveler services. Cross the river and go back east if you would like a self-guided tour of the Allegheny Fish Hatchery.

Kinzua Dam has two viewing places: one atop the dam and one at the bottom. An information center at Big Bend presents videos and explains the workings of the dam.

The byway travels east on Highway 59, crossing Morrison Bridge across the upper arm of Kinzua Bay to a marina, boat ramp, and picnic area. The Rimrock Scenic Overlook provides yet another great view from atop a big rock outcrop, across the reservoir.

The byway rolls through the hardwoods atop the plateau. The abundant white pines and hemlock trees of this region were heavily logged and nearly wiped out in the latter 1800s. They left the hardwoods, and today the Allegheny National Forest has dense, mature forests of fine hardwoods such as black cherry, maple, ash, and oak. Autumn foliage is absolutely breathtaking, and in June the mountain laurel blossoms are beautiful. Other understory plants include striped maple, blackberries, and blueberries.

Rimrock Morrison Trail winds 9.5 miles from the byway through the forest, to Morrison Boat Camp. You could choose a shorter three-mile cutoff loop to enjoy strolling through this beautiful forest. About two miles farther east, North Country Trail crosses Highway 59. The byway reaches its eastern terminus at Bradford Ranger Station. □

General description: A seventeen-mile Y-shaped route along a landscaped parkway, to a pretty lake.

Special attractions: Davis Lake, Indian Mounds, historic features, camping, hunting, fishing.

Location: Northeast Mississippi on the Tombigbee National Forest. The byway travels the Natchez Trace Parkway between the national forest boundaries east of Houston and south of Tupelo. The spur on County Road 903 leads between the parkway and Davis Lake.

Byway route number: Natchez Trace Parkway and Chickasaw County Road 903.

Travel season: Year-round.

Camping: One national forest campground at Davis Lake, with picnic tables, fire grates, showers, toilets, RV hookups, trailer dump station, and drinking water.

Services: No traveler services on the byway. All services in Houston and nearby Tupelo.

Nearby attractions: Tupelo National Battlefield, Trace State Park, Brices Cross Roads National Battlefield Site, Tupelo State Park, Chickasaw Village.

For more information: National Forests in Mississippi, 100 W. Capitol Street, Suite 1141-Federal Bldg., Jackson, MS 39269, (601) 960-4391. Tombigbee Ranger District, Route 1 Box 98A, Ackerman, MS 39735, (601) 285-3264.

Description: Natchez Trace Scenic Byway travels a Y-shaped route along a portion of the Natchez Trace, with a spur road west to Davis Lake. The two-lane roads are paved. The parkway has wide shoulders and frequent scenic turnouts and is a popular bicycle route. Traffic is generally light to moderate. The spur road to Davis Lake is narrow, and traffic moves slowly.

Summers are long and hot, with frequent heavy thunderstorms. Daytime highs can reach 100 degrees with sixty to seventy percent humidity. Nights don't offer much relief. Spring and fall are more pleasant, with temperatures ranging from the sixties to the eighties. Winter temperatures can drop to the teens at times.

The byway is very scenic driven in either direction. Driving on the Natchez Trace Parkway from north to south, the byway begins at the national forest boundary and winds through a closed canopy of trees. Tree species here include loblolly pines; southern and northern red oaks; white oaks; shagbark, mockernut, and pignut hickories; Eastern redcedars; shortleaf pines; dogwoods; red maples; and sweetgums. The state tree is the southern magnolia, commonly found in the wetter, streamside areas along the byway.

Spring and autumn tours here are spectacular. Dogwoods and redbud provide a beautiful display of spring blossoms, usually beginning in early April. About the middle of October, the hardwoods begin turning brilliant reds, golds, and yellows.

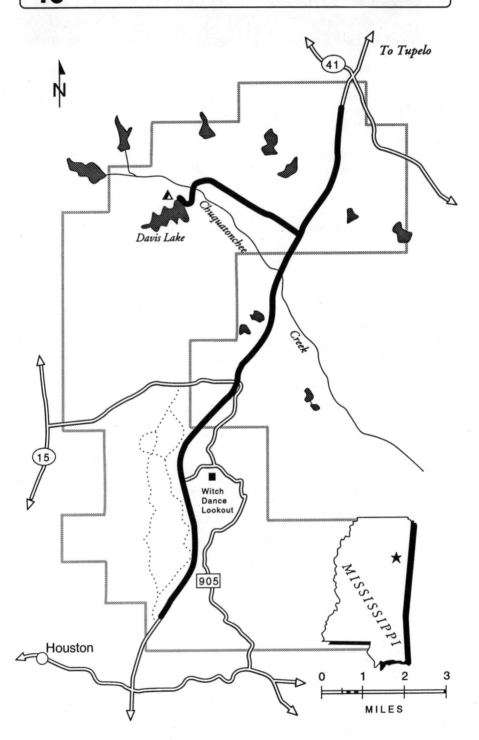

Wildflower enthusiasts will find plenty of blossoms. Look for agave, jack-in-the-pulpit, golden club, spiderwort, iris, star grass, wild hyacinth, fairy wand, and fawn lily, among many others.

This region was once under a great inland salt sea. In places you can still see a white, chalky soil from the limestone and eroded and weathered seashells. Stop at a roadside exhibit to see fossils of marine organisms.

Hunting is a popular activity on the national forest. Hunters look for white-tailed deer, turkeys, quail, squirrels, and ducks.

The byway turns west on a spur road and travels through rural farms and pastures toward Davis Lake. The Owl Creek Indian Mounds are listed on the National Register of Historic Places. This is a series of five mounds built around a central plaza. Two of the mounds were built by Native Americans sometime between 1000 and 1300 A.D., and used for burials and religious ceremonies. It is very interesting to stop here.

Two-hundred-acre Davis Lake provides multiple recreation opportunities. There is a fine grassy swimming beach and good fishing for largemouth bass, hybrid striped bass, crappie, catfish, and bream. The campground has twenty-four sites on the lake. You can pull your boat right up to many of the camp-sites. A two-mile fishing trail wanders along the north edge of the lake to several earthen fishing piers.

Bird watchers can look for Canada geese, snow geese, and a variety of ducks including mallards, pintails, canvasbacks, wood ducks, and black ducks. Songbirds and raptors are plentiful and include meadowlarks, tanagers, bluebirds, chickadees, and thrashers. Look overhead for soaring red-tailed and sparrow hawks, and watch herons fish along streambanks. The distinctive coo of mourning doves is a pretty sound. You may spot a shy fox or even a bobcat in the forest.

Natchez Trace winds through a beautiful forest of southern hardwoods and pines. Tombigbee National Forest photo.

Return to the parkway and turn south again. The landscape varies from timberlands to farmlands. Primary crops in this region are soybeans, cotton, and corn. Stop for a hike along Witch Dance Horse Trail, a nine- or fifteen-mile riding trail. You can hike this loop through the forest. Note the vegetation changes from the higher lands at the beginning of the loop, to the lower bottomlands. Witch Dance is named for an old superstition claiming that when witches met here to dance, the grass died each place their feet touched the ground.

The byway continues south on the parkway and ends at the national forest boundary near Houston. □

46 HIGHLANDS SCENIC TOUR
George Washington National Forest   Virginia

General description: A twenty-mile loop tour through stream valleys and along a ridgetop overlooking the Allegheny Highlands and Blue Ridge Mountains.

Special attractions: Rich Hole Wilderness, historic mines, spring blossoms, autumn foliage, far-ranging vistas, fishing, hiking.

Location: West-central Virginia on the George Washington National Forest. The byway travels Highway 850 north from Longdale Furnace (Interstate 64-Exit 10) to its junction with Route 447 (Interstate 64-Exit 11); 447 south to its junction with Highway 770; and 770 west to Longdale Furnace.

Byway route numbers: Virginia State Highway 850 (formerly U.S. Highway 60), Forest Road 447, and Virginia State Highway 770.

Travel season: Year-round on State Route 850. Routes 770 and 447 occasionally closed by winter ice and snows, usually between December and early March.

Camping: No national forest campgrounds on the byway.

Services: All traveler services in nearby Clifton Forge and Lexington.

Nearby attractions: Rough Mountain Wilderness, Longdale Recreation Area, Lake Moomaw, Appalachian Trail, Blue Ridge Parkway, downhill ski areas, Douthat State Park, Natural Bridge and Caverns, Virginia Horse Center, Highland National Forest Scenic Byway (West Virginia).

For more information: George Washington National Forest, Harrison Plaza, 101 North Main Street (P.O. Box 233), Harrisonburg, VA 22801, (703) 433-2491. James River Ranger District, 313 South Monroe Avenue, Covington, VA 24426, (703) 962-2214.

Description: The Highlands Scenic Tour travels through diverse vegetation and historic mining country, providing beautiful views and access into a wilderness area. Highway 850 is a paved two-lane road. Routes 447 and 770 are narrower, two-lane gravel roads. Route 770 is steep with hairpin turns, not recommended for large RVs or towed units. Traffic is usually light to moderate on the byway.

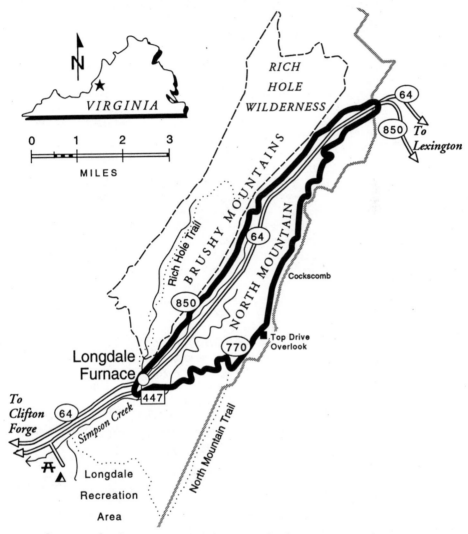

Summer daytime temperatures average in the seventies to low eighties and nights cool down to the fifties or sixties. Winter days usually climb to the fifties, and may drop to freezing at night. Most of the region's thirty-eight inches of annual precipitation comes in spring and summer thundershowers.

Beginning your tour in Longdale Furnace, evidence of the 19th Century pig iron industry remains. The two tall chimneys still standing are remnants of the Lucy Selina Furnace, now registered under Virginia Historic Landmarks.

A few miles west, Longdale Recreation Area was the site of a busy Civilian Conservation Corps camp in the 1930s. It has a small lake with a swimming beach, bathhouse, picnic sites, and an easy walking trail.

The byway follows two nearly parallel routes in its loop. Highway 850 is the paved "low road" along Simpson's Creek and Bratton's run. This narrow valley is steep and has lush vegetation. Brushy Mountain, containing the Rich Hole Wilderness, fills the western horizon. This wilderness protects 6,450 acres of streams and hardwoods on Brushy Mountain. The forest is composed primarily of red, white, and scarlet oaks; tulip poplars; white pines; dogwoods; hemlocks; and sugar, red, and silver maples.

Down along the creek, pockets of rhododendrons brighten the streambanks with their spectacular springtime blossoming. Blossoming dogwood, redbud, sourwood, and mountain laurel usually peak in mid- to late-April along this low road, and peak in early- to mid-May along the high road.

Take a side trip north on Forest Road 108 to the Rich Hole Wilderness trailhead. This 5.9-mile moderately strenuous footpath traverses the wilderness and ends back out on the highway. Have one person shuttle the car and pick you up at the other end. The trail follows the cascading waters of North Fork Simpson Creek through stands of big poplars, oaks, and hickories. A unique feature for this region is a large stand of old hemlock. The creek has native brook and rainbow trout. There are occasional views east to the Shenandoah Valley. From the ridgetop, you'll see west into Rough Mountain Wilderness, before descending back to the byway.

Wildlife in this region includes black bears, whitetail deer, wild turkeys, ruffed grouse, and squirrels. Look for beaver dams along Simpson Creek. Bird enthusiasts may hear the songs and calls of mockingbirds, robins, cardinals, warblers, wrens, nuthatches, flycatchers, and kingfishers. Red-tailed hawks and buzzards soar overhead.

Simpson Creek valley has abundant reminders of the mining industry. The Allegheny Highlands were an important source of pig iron in the late 1700s and throughout the 1800s. Iron for Confederate Army ammunition came from this region during the Civil War. Remnants of building foundations, bridge abutments, and mine entrances remain. A narrow gauge, or "dinky," railroad ran from the Longdale iron mine to furnaces in the valleys, and you can still make out the terrace for railroad tracks, carved into the sidehill. Streams still run red from the iron oxidizing at abandoned mines, but the charcoal hearths and brick foundations are now covered in vegetation. The forest was clearcut to make charcoal and has now regenerated. Some of this can be viewed from the road but is more likely to be seen by taking short walks through the valley.

The byway continues northeast, passing the northern trailhead for the Rich Hole Trail. George Washington National Forest covers 1,055,000 acres and extends 140 miles along the Appalachian Mountains, in Virginia and West Virginia. There are over 800 miles of hiking trails.

The byway descends along Bratton's Run (which has good fishing for native brook trout), leaves Highway 850, crosses under the interstate, and follows Forest Road 447 south. You'll climb North Mountain via a series of hairpin turns. Occasional vistas open up to the west, into Rich Hole Wilderness and beyond to the Allegheny Highlands. The road crosses the ridge and follows the eastern side of North Mountain, providing great views over the Shenandoah Valley.

The forest here is primarily oaks, walnuts, and tulip poplars. Rhododendrons and mountain laurels adorn the ridgetop. Spring blossoms and fall foliage are stunning. The bright yellows, oranges, and reds of autumn foliage usually peak in mid- to late-October.

After traveling about 4.5 miles on Route 447, you can get out of your car

The Highlands Scenic Tour winds through the hickory/oak forest atop North Mountain, providing views of the Shenandoah Valley and Blue Ridge Mountains. George Washington National Forest photo.

for a short, ten-minute hike up to a vertical rock outcrop called Cockscomb. This is a .3-mile, fairly steep trail leading to a terrific view. It's worth the effort. About 1.5 miles farther south on the byway, Top Drive Overlook provides another spectacular panoramic view of the area.

Highlands Scenic Byway traverses the ridge and valley physiographic region characteristic of the Appalachian Mountain Range. Steep-sloped, parallel ridges run southwest-northeast, with long, narrow valleys between. Here, the Blue Ridge Mountains are to the east, the Allegheny Highlands to the west.

To extend your appreciation of the big vistas here, hike the North Mountain Trail. It follows the crest of North Mountain about four miles, then drops down another 4.6 miles to Longdale Recreation Area. It's an excellent hike, well worth your time.

The scenic byway completes the loop by returning to Longdale Furnace on Highway 770. A large turnaround area at Top Drive Overlook permits RVs and cars towing trailers to return via Route 447 to avoid the steep, switchbacking hairpin turns on 770.

State Route 770 is a charming road, lined with stone retaining walls built over 150 years ago by prisoners and slaves. It was constructed to transport charcoal, from Collierstown on the east side of North Mountain to the furnaces on the west side of the mountain. Charcoal was necessary to process the iron ore. Route 77 is one of the oldest roads in use in the Commonwealth of Virginia, and the quality of craftsmanship is outstanding. □

47 TALLADEGA SCENIC DRIVE
Talladega National Forest   Alabama

General description: A twenty-three-mile highway along the crest of Horseblock Mountain into Cheaha State Park.

Special attractions: Extensive vistas, Cheaha Wilderness, Lake Chinnabee Recreation Area, Pinhoti Trail, Cheaha State Park, Cheaha Peak, autumn foliage, hiking, camping, fishing.

Location: East-central Alabama on the Talladega National Forest. The byway travels Highway 281 from its junction with U.S. Highway 78 three miles west of Heflin, south through Cheaha State Park to Turnipseed Hunter Camp, just outside the state park.

Byway route number: Alabama State Highway 281.

Travel season: Year-round.

Camping: Four state park campgrounds. Two provide only drinking water, and are within walking distance of bathhouse facilities. Two campgrounds are fully developed, with power, sewer, and water hookups; fire grates; picnic tables; bathhouses.

Services: Food, lodging, and small store in Cheaha State Park. All traveler services in nearby Anniston, Oxford, Talladega, Munford, and Heflin.

Nearby attractions: Pine Glen and Coleman Lake recreation areas, Clay County Public Lake, DeSoto Caverns.

For more information: National Forests of Alabama, 1765 Highland Avenue, Montgomery, AL 36107, (205) 832-4470. Talladega Ranger District, 1001 North Street (Highway 21 North), Talladega, AL 35160, (205) 362-2909. Shoal Creek Ranger District, 450 Highway 46, Heflin, AL 36264, (205) 463-2272. Cheaha State Park, Route 1 Box 77H, Delta, AL 36258, (205) 488-5115 or 1-800-252-7275.

Description: The Talladega Scenic Drive takes you up a long ridge with a splendid, far-ranging view, to popular Cheaha State Park. The two-lane highway is paved and has frequent turnouts. Traffic is moderately light, but increases during the fall color season, between about late October until the end of November.

Summer daytime temperatures average in the mid-eighties to the low nineties, and humidity is very high. Expect frequent late afternoon thundershowers. Summer nights may cool to the sixties. Spring and fall temperatures range from the mid-sixties to seventies, dropping to forty or fifty at night. Winter days in February and March are usually in the forties and fifties but may drop to the high thirties, with a rare freeze. Most rain falls in winter and spring.

The route is pleasant driven in either direction. When traveling northeast to southwest, the scenic byway begins three miles west of Heflin on U.S. Highway 78 and follows Highway 281 southwest along a ridge overlooking wooded valleys and farmland communities. Numerous scenic overlooks allow a leisurely view of the surrounding area, including Cheaha Mountain, Dugger Mountain, and Horseblock Lookout.

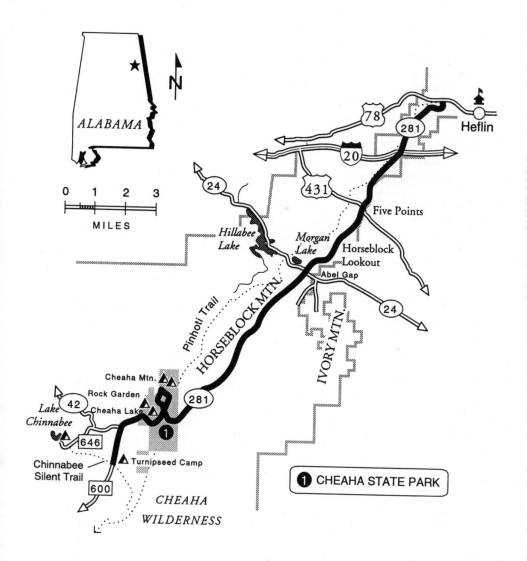

47 TALLADEGA SCENIC DRIVE

ALABAMA

0 1 2 3
MILES

78
281 Heflin
20
24
431
Five Points
Hillabee Lake
Morgan Lake
Horseblock Lookout
Abel Gap
Pinhoti Trail
HORSEBLOCK MTN.
IVORY MTN.
24
Cheaha Mtn.
Rock Garden
Lake Chinnabee
42
Cheaha Lake
281
646
Chinnabee Silent Trail
Turnipseed Camp
600
CHEAHA WILDERNESS

❶ CHEAHA STATE PARK

While driving the byway, you'll pass numerous access points to the Pinhoti Trail. The Pinhoti Trail is a popular horseback and backpack trail, stretching over eighty miles across the Talladega National Forest and Cheaha State Park.

The byway crosses over the interstate, winds through Five Points, and climbs the ridge of Horseblock Mountain. This is a very steep ridge that falls away on both sides and provides extensive views in both directions. You can look west to the Coosa River Valley and the town of Oxford. The national forest dominates the foreground.

You could hike up the old road to the base of Horseblock Lookout, for another view of the area. A mile or so farther north, take a side trip west to Morgan Lake on graveled County Road 24. There you can picnic, fish for smallmouth bass and crappie, and take a walk along the lake on a portion of the Pinhoti Trail. East on County Road 24 takes you to Abel Gap's pretty little white church that looks especially picturesque at sunrise.

The Talladega Scenic Drive continues along Horseblock Mountain, with views of Ivory Mountain to the east. In the 1940s, prospectors found some gold in Ivory Mountain's streams. Just north of the county line, a jeep road runs northwest. You could walk a few miles on it to see the handlaid rockwork done by the Civilian Conservation Corps (CCC) in the 1930s. There are stone culverts and reinforcing walls, and the stone bridge over Hillabee Creek is quite beautiful.

The byway now enters Cheaha State Park, which charges a small fee for day use. Cheaha is taken from the Choctaw Indian word chaha, which means high. There are abundant recreation opportunities in the park. Take a side trip north to the top of Cheaha Mountain, the highest point in Alabama at 2,407 feet. The view is splendid, and on a clear day you may see sixty miles. The surrounding tree-covered mountains are beautiful, and you can see the towns of Anniston to the north, and Talladega to the west.

The primary tree species here are shortleaf pine, mixed with hardwoods such as red oak and hickory. Wild azalea blossoms provide a stunning display each spring, and rival the autumn foliage for beauty.

This area is the southern end of the Appalachian Mountain Range, a northeast-southwest trending series of parallel ridges. The dominant rock type is granite and quartz. You'll see lots of scenic white-colored quartz rock outcrops and cliff faces in the park.

The summit observation tower was built by the CCC who worked here in the 1920s and '30s. The CCC also built the cabins, bathhouses, and dam. Here at the top of Cheaha Mountain there is a restaurant, store, motel, group lodge, two campgrounds, a picnic area, and various short walking paths. The summit is a popular place for rapelling, hang-gliding, and cliff-climbing.

Wildflowers throughout the park include goldenrod, rosinweed, pokeberry, blazing star, wild indigo, horseweed, golden aster, bluebell, and flowering spurge.

Wildlife watchers can look for white-tailed deer, red fox, and wild turkeys, as well as skunks, racoons, squirrels, and possums. The rare red-cockaded woodpecker inhabits the surrounding Talladega National Forest.

Another good viewpoint in the park is from the Rock Garden, a scenic rock outcrop. A very short footpath leads to a view of the sheer cliffs, and Cheaha Lake below.

You may see turkey vultures or red-tailed hawks soaring overhead. Other birds in the park include cardinals, wrens, and finches. You'll likely see lots

Talladega Scenic Drive.

of eastern bluebirds, too. The park has an active bluebird recovery program, and there are lots of nesting boxes throughout the park.

Stretch your legs on the Odom Scout Trail, which begins in the park on Highway 281. You can make a day of the whole eleven-mile trail, or walk out a few miles and return. There are lots of lookout points as you wind through the trees along the top of the ridge.

The road drops about 1,200 vertical feet from the top of Cheaha Mountain to Cheaha Lake. At the lake you'll find two more campgrounds, one primitive and one developed, as well as a swim beach, and good fishing possibilities for bluegill, catfish, and bass.

The scenic byway leaves the state park and reenters the Talladega National Forest. The route is very pretty, rambling along ridges and through the forest, with occasional views out to the west.

A side trip west on Forest Road 646 brings you to Lake Chinnabee Recreation Area. The lake is picturesque, situated in a little mountain valley. The campground has thirteen sites right on the lakeshore. Anglers cast for bass and bream and hikers have several good trails to walk. The Lakeshore Trail encircles the lake in an easy two-mile hike. Chinnabee Silent Trail is moderately strenuous, and follows Cheaha Creek about three miles from the lake up to Forest Road 600. The views along the trail are very nice.

Just east of the byway, the Cheaha Wilderness protects 7,490 acres of rugged terrain. The forest on the lower slopes is composed of white, scarlet, and chestnut oaks; hickories; and longleaf and shortleaf pines. On the higher ridges chestnut oak and Virginia pine dominate.

The byway ends near Turnipseed Camp, a historic hunting camp. The campground is primitive, and will provide drinking water and toilets by late 1992. The road continues on as Forest Road 600. This gravel route is best suited for high-clearance vehicles. □

48 RIDGE AND VALLEY SCENIC BYWAY
Chattahoochee National Forest   Georgia

General description: A forty-seven-mile loop drive along scenic ridges and through lush valleys.

Special attractions: John's Mountain, wildflowers, autumn colors, hunting, picnicking, camping.

Location: Northwest Georgia on the Chattahoochee National Forest. The byway travels an oblong loop out of Villanow, east on Highway 136; south on Furnace Creek Road, Pocket Road, John's Creek Road, and Floyd Springs Road; southwest on Highway 156; northwest on Highway 27; and back north on Thomas Ballenger Road and East Armuchee Road.

Byway route numbers and names: Georgia State Highway 136, Furnace Creek Road, Pocket Road, Johns Creek Road, Floyd Springs Road, Georgia State Highway 156, U.S. Highway 27, Thomas Ballenger Road, East Armuchee Road.

Travel season: Year-round.

Camping: One national forest campground, with picnic tables, fire grates, toilets, drinking water.

Services: Traveler services in Villanow, as well as in nearby Summerville, LaFayette, Dalton, Calhoun, Ringold, and Rome.

Nearby attractions: Chickamauga and Chattanooga National Military Park, Cloudland Canyon and James H. "Sloppy" Floyd state parks, Chattanooga urban attractions.

For more information: Chattahooche National Forest, 508 Oak Street, Gainesville, GA 30501, (404) 536-0541. Armuchee Ranger District, 806 East Villanow, P.O. Box 465, LaFayette, GA 30728, (404) 638-1085.

Description: Ridge and Valley Scenic Byway traverses an eye-catching region of long, narrow ridges and wide, fertile valleys. The two-lane roads are paved; some have narrow shoulders and some provide numerous scenic turnouts. Traffic on Highway 27 is constant; the other roads are moderately busy.

Summer days are hot and somewhat humid, with temperatures in the seventies to low nineties. Nights are cooler, in the fifties to seventies. Spring and fall temperatures generally range from the fifties to the seventies. Expect some snow in winter, with daytime temperatures in the forties and fifties and nights dropping to freezing.

The byway is very scenic driven in either direction. Beginning in Villanow and driving in a clockwise direction, go east on Highway 136, then follow Furnace Creek Road and Pocket Road south through the forest. A side trip west on Forest Road 208 leads to a good overlook on Johns Mountain. You

Lake Marvin offers a serene place to relax along the Ridge and Valley Scenic Byway. Chattahoochee National Forest photo.

can see Georgia, Alabama, and Tennessee from this 1,800-foot elevation.

The ridge and valley physiographic region of the Appalachian Mountain Range is easy to see here. Long, narrow ridges have a characteristic southwest-northeast trend, and between the rocky ridges lie fertile valley bottoms with farms and creeks.

The turnoff to Keown Falls Scenic Area is west on Forest Road 702. This 218-acre recreation area has picnic tables, and a 1.8-mile loop trail through the forest to an observation deck overlooking a set of two waterfalls. It's an easy walk and a good opportunity to stroll through a lovely region.

The forest is primarily southern hardwoods such as white, northern red, and black oaks; yellow poplars; beech; sourwood; and shagbark hickory. Some shortleaf and Virginia pines are found along the highway. Azaleas and dogwoods usually bloom in April, and late October is the best time to view the brilliant colors of autumn leaves.

Johns Mountain has a variety of wildlife, including white-tailed deer, turkeys, racoons, skunks, chipmunks, gray squirrels, and fox squirrels. Look overhead to see soaring red-tailed hawks.

Continuing south on the byway, The Pocket Recreation Area has twenty-seven campsites along a pretty little spring-fed stream that runs between the steep ridges of Horn Mountain. An easy 2.5-mile loop trail winds through the woods and offers a pleasant way to enjoy the area.

The byway follows Johns Creek, a fast-flowing, rocky stream stocked with rainbow trout. The road winds through the dense forest, with steep mountainsides on both sides. At Everett Springs, turn west and follow Floyd Springs Road south through a rural setting. There are hayfields, cattle, farms, and

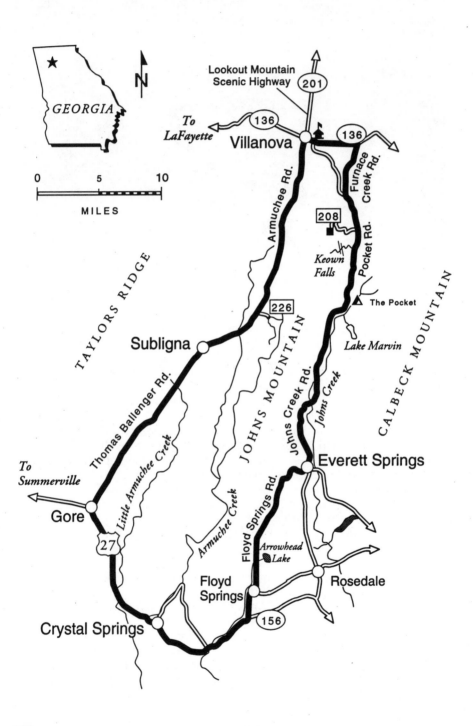

GEORGIA

N

0   5   10

MILES

Lookout Mountain
Scenic Highway 201

136
To
LaFayette
Villanova
136

Armuchee Rd.

Furnace Creek Rd.

208

Keown
Falls

Pocket Rd.

The Pocket

226

Lake Marvin

TAYLORS RIDGE

Subligna

JOHNS MOUNTAIN

CALBECK MOUNTAIN

Thomas Ballenger Rd.

Johns Creek Rd.

Johns Creek

To
Summerville

Everett Springs

Gore

27

Little Armuchee Creek

Armuchee Creek

Floyd Springs Rd.

Arrowhead
Lake

Floyd
Springs

Rosedale

156

Crystal Springs

residences in the valley. Johns Mountain rises to the west; Calbeck Mountain is to the east. There are a few picnic tables at Arrowhead Lake, and you can fish for bass, bluegill, and catfish.

The byway leaves the mountains in Floyd Springs and travels southwest on Highway 156, then northwest on Highway 27 to Gore. You'll then drive north on Thomas Ballenger Road, paralleling Taylors Ridge on the west. Old barns are picturesque, and the pastoral valley is quite pretty.

At Subligna, bear northeast on Armuchee Road. A side trip east on Forest Road 226 leads to dispersed, primitive campsites and good redeye bass fishing in Armuchee Creek. Back on the byway heading north, you'll get some of the best views of Taylors Ridge and Johns Mountain. Armuchee is an Indian word meaning "land of wildflowers." Wildflowers you may see along the byway include pink ladyslipper, goldenrod, Queen Anne's lace, daisies, Solomon's seal, gaylax, trillium, and fire pinks.

The byway completes the loop in Villanow. The quaint general store there has been operated continuously since 1847. ☐